LIFE MOVES PRETTY FAST

THE LESSONS WE LEARNED FROM 80s MOVIES

(AND WHY WE DON'T LEARN THEM FROM MOVIES ANY MORE)

4th ESTATE · *London*

4th Estate
An imprint of HarperCollins*Publishers*
1 London Bridge Street
London
SE1 9GF
www.4thestate.co.uk

First published in Great Britain in 2015 by 4th Estate
This 4th Estate paperback edition first published 2016

A catalogue record for this book is available from the British Library

ISBN 978-0-00-758561-8

Typeset in Minion Pro by Palimpsest Book Production Ltd,
Falkirk, Stirlingshire

Printed and bound in Great Britain by Clays Ltd, St Ives plc

MIX
Paper from
responsible sources
FSC
www.fsc.org FSC™ C007454

For Andy, who is even better than Andrew McCarthy,
Michael J. Fox, Matthew Broderick, Eddie Murphy,
Bill Murray and Dan Aykroyd.
Combined.

Contents

Introduction

'Whatever happened to chivalry? Does it only happen in eighties movies? I want John Cusack holding a boombox outside my window. I wanna ride off on a lawnmower with Patrick Dempsey. I want Jake from *Sixteen Candles* waiting outside the church for me. I want Judd Nelson thrusting his fist into the air because he knows he just got me. Just once, I want my life to be like an eighties movie, preferably one with a really awesome musical number for no apparent reason. But no, no, John Hughes did not direct my life.'

I am not actually quoting myself here, though heaven knows I could be (except for the part about wanting the moronic Jake from *Sixteen Candles* for reasons that shall be explained soon enough). That monologue comes from the film *Easy A*, which was released in 2010, and is spoken by Olive, played by Emma Stone, an actress who was born years after most of the movies her character mentions came out. Two years after *Easy A* was released, *Pitch Perfect* arrived and, once again, a film made thirty years earlier was the inspiration and crucial plot point for a twenty-first-century teen film: '*The Breakfast Club*, 1985, the greatest ending to any movie ever. [The Simple Minds'] song perfectly sums up the movie in that it's equally beautiful and sad,' Jesse (Skyler Astin) tells a sceptical Beca (Anna Kendrick). But, of course, Beca's scepticism is as misplaced as the assistant principal's mistrust in Molly Ringwald, Judd Nelson and the rest of the kids in the 1985 film, because it is only when she watches John Hughes's *The Breakfast Club* that Beca learns to open up emotionally (moviespeak for 'stop being such a frigid cow and snog some dude') and, more importantly, win the a cappella competition. (Winning an a cappella competition. That is what teens have to live for today. To quote one of the greatest of all eighties teen films,[1] 'I weep for the future.') Every week, it seems, it's announced that another eighties film is being remade, sequelised or turned into a stage musical, from *Top Gun* to *The Goonies* to *Dirty Dancing*, invariably starring actors who weren't even born when the originals came out. In 2013 the pop band The 1975 said of their newly released eponymous debut album, 'We're massive fans of John Hughes. We wanted to make a record [that] was almost a soundtrack to our teenage years. If he made a movie about us, this would be the soundtrack.' Their lead singer was born in the nineties.

I was born in New York City in 1978 meaning that, while I did exist in the eighties as more than a zygote, I wasn't yet a teenager either. Instead, actual teenagehood for myself felt as distant and desirable as the moon. I was a typical older child from a middle-class Jewish family: well-behaved, anxious, bookish, and therefore especially curious

---

[1] *Ferris Bueller's Day Off*, of course.

about the vaguely imagined freedoms I fancied being a teenager would bring. My little sister and I weren't allowed to watch television stations that showed commercials – yes, I come from one of those families – meaning that our viewing options were limited to *Sesame Street* and whatever our mother allowed us to rent from East 86th Street Video. When I was nine years old, she, for the first time, allowed me to rent something that featured neither animation nor starred Gene Kelly: *Ferris Bueller's Day Off*. I couldn't believe it. How on earth could she – the dorkiest mother EVER, who only ever gave us FRUIT for dessert, I mean I ask you – let me watch such a film? This movie featured BOYS, actual real life BOYS! Kissing girls – with their tongues! Within the extremely limited framework of my life experience on the Upper East Side in Manhattan, my mother had basically allowed me to rent hardcore porn (tongues!).

Ferris proved to be a mere gateway drug, and I became such a heavy user of East 86th Street Video that for my tenth birthday my parents gave me my own membership card. I was soon mainlining the classics: *Mannequin, Romancing the Stone, Good Morning Vietnam, The Breakfast Club, Short Circuit, Indiana Jones, E.T., Spaceballs, Coming to America, Three Amigos!, Planes, Trains and Automobiles*, anything produced by Touchstone Pictures and absolutely everything featuring the two actors who I assured my little sister were the real talents of our era: Steve Guttenberg and Rick Moranis. My highbrow taste, which has lasted all my life, was forged then.

These movies, which were largely seen as junk when they came out, were deeply formative, and everyone I know in my generation feels exactly the same way. They provided the lifelong template for my perceptions of funniness (Eddie Murphy), coolness (Bill Murray) and sexiness (Kathleen Turner). They also taught me more about life than any library or teacher ever would. My parents could have saved literally thousands of dollars, jacked in the schools and kept the membership to East 86th Street Video and I'd still be essentially the same person today.

But for a long time, these films had a terrible reputation, critically speaking. They were – and largely still are – dismissed as being as drecky as Ray, Egon, Winston and Peter at the beginning of the *Ghostbusters* sequel. Sold out and bloated, something faintly embarrassing from the past that has left an ugly legacy of franchises and superheroes. Eighties Hollywood, goes the popular critical thought, is when movies started to go wrong: they became obsessed with money and sequels and explosions and cheap gags as opposed to Art. Whereas the far more respected 1970s was the era of the auteur, when Hollywood directors like Robert Altman and Michael Cimino were allowed to pursue their creativity unhindered by studio meddling, the 1980s was the era of the producer, when entertainment took precedence and cartoonish figures like creepy Don Simpson and Jon Peters – who started his career as Barbra Streisand's hairdresser – were the ones with the power.

Many have bemoaned this shift in power from the seventies to the eighties, aghast that the man who once permed Yentl's hair commanded the kind of industry respect once accorded to Altman. But my personal feeling is, when working in the entertainment business, an emphasis on actual entertainment is not necessarily a bad thing, especially if it means producing something like *Top Gun* instead of *Heaven's Gate*. After all, pretty much everyone, if they're honest, is happy to watch some eighties Cruise on a Friday night, but only a very special few would kick off the weekend by cracking open a Cimino DVD.

Yet snooty critics aside, eighties movies have maintained an astonishing level of popularity among actual audiences, now, it feels, more than ever. It is taken as a given that mainstream American films from the 1980s have a kind of ironic appeal – everyone wants to watch *Trading Places*, *Scrooged* and *Die Hard* at Christmas – to the point that to use a photo from an eighties movie as your Facebook avatar is pretty much a hopeless cliché. Partly this veneration comes from what I call the thirty-year rule. This is when movies – and fashions, and TV shows, and pop music – that were dismissed as trash in their day are given their overdue status when their original fans grow up and insist that the culture of their youth was ACTUALLY really important and ACTUALLY nothing's been as good since. But adults today who saw those eighties movies as kids still adore them in a way that those who came of age in, say, the sixties most definitely do not of the *Beach Party* franchise, the teen movies of their youth. If anything, I love these eighties movies even more than when I first saw them, which is not something I'd say about anything else that I considered cool in the eighties (sorry, Milli Vanilli. Although if it's any consolation, you're still on my iPod and I'm not ashamed of that). More strikingly, teenagers today who were born long after the decade itself love eighties movies in a way I certainly never did of the movies my parents grew up with.

'Some of the people who come up to me were teenagers when the movies originally came out, but the vast majority of the approaches I get on a daily basis come from eleven- to fifteen-year-old kids,' says Alex Winter, who appeared in two of the most fun eighties teen films, *The Lost Boys* and, of course, *Bill and Ted's Excellent Adventure*. 'They come up to me and are like, "Hey, you're Bill!" It's amazing.'

I should probably pause here and explain what, precisely, I mean by 'eighties movies'. When I started to think about writing this book, I spoke to a few film critics for their thoughts on eighties movies, including Peter Biskind, whose excellent book, *Easy Riders, Raging Bulls*, is probably the best known example of the kind of dichotomy I just described: 1970s Hollywood good, 1980s Hollywood tacky hell. To his enormous credit, he didn't slam the phone down on me when I told him my idea.

'It's true, I haven't been very kind about eighties films, but they are ripe for revisionism,' Biskind said.

I took a deep breath, gearing up to explain my deeply involved critical theory about *Three Men and a Baby*.

But Biskind spoke first: 'Take *Salvador*, for example,' he said, referring to Oliver Stone's 1986 movie about leftist guerrillas in the Salvadoran Civil War. 'That's a fascinating film. You should really write about *Salvador*.'

Dear reader, I have not written about *Salvador*. As you might have gathered by now, my tastes lie in a different direction: an unabashedly, unremittingly mainstream direction. I'm sure there are plenty of eighties film aficionados out there who, when they think of the eighties, think of James Woods being terrorised by death squads in Central America. But when I think of the eighties, I think of the Giant Stay Puft Marshmallow man crushing New York cabs underfoot. I'm not saying one take is better than the other,[1] but I am saying, when was the last time you fancied watching *Salvador*? At ten past never, probably. And when did you last want to watch *Ghostbusters*? Two seconds ago, when I mentioned Mr Stay Puft, right? Popularity is never a guarantee of quality (just look at *Two and a Half Men*), but it is a sign of something when a movie made over thirty years ago is still regarded as one of the best comedies of all time (something, I guarantee, will not happen to *Two and a Half Men*). Anyway, no one needs telling that *Salvador* – or *Blade Runner*, or *Aliens*, or *Scarface*, or *Full Metal Jacket* – are Good Eighties Movies. Everyone knows that. I wanted to write about why the Fun Eighties Movies – like *Die Hard*, *Steel Magnolias*, *Pretty in Pink* and *Adventures in Babysitting* – are also Good Eighties Movies.

The eighties movies I watched as a kid are still the eighties movies I love today, and, yes, there is, inevitably, some sentimentality going on here. But there is something else, too, that lies behind my love of them and that of everyone else's love of them: these movies offer something that equivalent movies today don't.

Obviously, good movies get made today. Classics, even. Hell, I can name loads of movies[2] that I love that were made after 1990, so I'm certainly not saying that only in the eighties were good films forged, or that all films made in the eighties were stone-cold classics. (*Mannequin*, for a start, is absolute dross.) There were loads of things that were completely rubbish about eighties movies, but not the

---

[1] Mine is better.
[2] Well, maybe seven.

things that people generally talk about when they complain about eighties movies.

For a start, the social attitudes occasionally leave more than something to be desired. There was a weird tendency in some eighties films to treat rape as a comedic plot device. Tedious Jake in *Sixteen Candles* hoots about how his girlfriend Caroline is so drunk he 'could violate her ten ways if I wanted to'. Did I mention this is the film's romantic lead, the one we're supposed to cheer on? I don't think so, John Hughes. And then, just to prove Jake's theory, the school geek (played by Anthony Michael Hall) has sex with Caroline when she's pretty much comatose. There's a similarly gruesome moment in *Revenge of the Nerds*, when one of the nerds tricks a girl into having sex with him by pretending he's someone else. Finally in *Overboard* – a movie I enjoy way more than I know I should – a handyman (Kurt Russell) convinces a rich lady with amnesia (Goldie Hawn) that she's his wife and has sex with her accordingly. In all these films, the women end up happily partnered with their rapists, which is just what happens in all rape scenarios, right?

Then there are the casual racist epithets, homophobic slurs (it is deeply depressing to see actors as lovely as Michael J. Fox and Molly Ringwald using words like 'faggot' with gleeful abandon) and the forays into faintly deranged American patriotism. But in the main, I'll defend eighties movies with the ferocity of Crocodile Dundee protecting his mullet-haired woman. THIS is a knife.

'I still get stopped in the street by people who ask, "Why don't they make movies like they did in the eighties?" And

I don't really know the answer,' muses my thespian eighties icon, Rick Moranis.

The reason it feels as if they just don't make fun movies today like they did in the 1980s is because they don't, and this is down to three specific factors: economics, shifting social attitudes and (the following should be said in your deepest James Earl Jones voice, either as Darth Vader or as the angry author in *Field of Dreams*) the changing world order. When people talk about eighties movies, by which I mean the eighties movies I love, they tend to focus on the kitschiness of them: the outfits, the anachronistic jokes, the endlessly quotable quotes. And I do, too (I've tried to limit myself to just one quote in each chapter as otherwise this book would have become a massive quote-a-thon). I love the silliness of eighties movies, their sweetness, the stirring music (the theme music for *Back to the Future*, *Top Gun*, *Beverly Hills Cop* and *Indiana Jones* would all definitely be on my *Desert Island Discs* list), the power ballads, the formulae. But there is more to these movies than kitsch. Kitsch is fine but it tends not to have much longevity. These movies have certain qualities and feature particular lessons that you simply don't see in films made today. That, for me at least, is a large part of what makes them feel so special.

To divide up anything by decade is, by nature, totally spurious – best nineties dance music! Best seventies hair-styles! – but in the case of eighties movies there is a point because movies made in Hollywood in the 1980s marked the beginning of a new era (the Producer Era) and, by 1989, the start of another (the corporate buyouts of the studios). As anyone who has ever watched an eighties film knows, or even is (gasp!) old enough to remember the eighties, life has changed a lot in the past thirty years: mobile phones aren't the size of cars and men don't tend to sport eighties Michael Douglas-style bouffant hair, more's the pity. Movie-making in Hollywood has changed a lot in those years, too. The big studios are now owned by international conglomerates: Columbia has been owned by the Sony Corporation since 1989; Warner Brothers merged with Time Inc. and became Time Warner, also in 1989; 20th Century Fox has been owned by Rupert Murdoch's News Corporation since the mid-1980s; Universal has gone through a series of owners in the past twenty years, including a French water and media company and General Electric and is now owned by cable provider Comcast; Paramount is owned by Viacom. Whereas once movie-making was the sole business of the studios, now it is a relatively tiny part of a big company.[*1]

'There are a million reasons why movie-making is different now, but a big one is the conglomerates,' says John Landis, who in the eighties alone directed *An American Werewolf in London*, *The Blues Brothers*, *Trading Places*, *Three Amigos!* and *Coming to America*. 'Between Disney and Rupert Murdoch, only four or five companies own the media now, and they own everything. This means that management has become much more corporate. I had final cut on my movies for twenty years – now they never give you final cut. Of course we had arguments [with studios in the eighties], but not like it is now. Now if you make a studio picture it's like – uh oh . . .'

'The studios had been individually held entities that were focused on making movies. But when they were sold off and bought by multinational corporations, they became

---

[*1] *The Big Picture: Money and Power in Hollywood*, Edward Jay Epstein. A very good primer if you're interested in this wonky sort of stuff.

cogs in the wheels of these big corporations and the priority is never about making movies – the priority is about making money,' says film writer Melissa Silverstein. 'So those pressures took over and the people who were executives were more focused on the financial bottom line, not the artistic bottom line.'

'The eighties,' adds Landis, 'is the last era of the studio system.'

The world has changed, too. Back in the mid-eighties, the international market would make up about 20 per cent of a film's revenue. Now it's 80 per cent because, while US audiences have gently fallen (although box office takings have generally remained steady due to rising ticket prices), the international market has grown exponentially, led by China. On the one hand it's great that America – or Hollywood, at least – is acknowledging the importance of audiences outside its borders. But it's less brilliant if that means it just makes more films like 2014's mind-numbing *Transformers: Age of Extinction*, a film that was expressly made with the Chinese market in mind. If you wondered why there are so many big dumb franchises and mind-numbing blockbusters around these days, the answer is, simply, because they make an absolute tonne of money overseas, even when they lose money in the US, as they increasingly do.'[1] Conversely, it has never been harder for smaller, original movies with good storylines to get made in today's Hollywood studios.

'I doubt very much I could get a studio to make

---

*1 In 1993, twenty-two blockbusters opened on US screens in the summer. In 2013, it was thirty-one, all costing over $100 million to make and most of them flopped ('Hollywood's Tanking Business Model', Catherine Rampell, *New York Times*, 3 September 2013).

Cocoon today – it would be seen too much as an oddity and too eccentric,' says the not exactly clout-less Ron Howard. 'I could probably get it made as an independent, but then it wouldn't get the kind of distribution that made it a top ten box office hit [back in the eighties]. I think in a lot of ways, the system is less flexible and less open today.'

'Half of my movies wouldn't have been made today. Not in a million years would a studio make *The Blues Brothers*,' says John Landis.

Instead, studios focus almost solely on big movies – or 'tentpoles', so called because they are intended to act as financial support for a whole studio – like *Twilight*, *Transformers*, *X-Men*, *Hunger Games* and superheroes that will work around the world (it's easy to translate explosions for foreign markets; long dialogue about old people travelling to other planets? Not so much). Obviously big movies and blockbusters existed in the eighties – the seventies and eighties damn near invented them – but they were seen as annual one-offs by studios rather than the only interest. The ridiculous irony now is that the very filmmakers who coined the seventies and eighties blockbuster, Steven Spielberg and George Lucas, can't get studios to back their films. In June 2013 the directors gave a talk at the University of Southern California School of Cinematic Arts and discussed how studios 'would rather spend $250m on a single film [rather] than make several, personal quirky projects': 'The studios are going for the gold,' said Lucas. 'But that isn't going to work forever. And as a result they're getting narrower and narrower in their focus. People are going to get tired of it. They're not going to know how to do anything else . . . [Spielberg's] *Lincoln* and [Lucas's] *Red Tails* barely got into theatres. You're talking about Steven Spielberg and George Lucas can't get their movies into theatres.'

The movie business itself is in what one producer describes as 'chaos', flummoxed by how to compete with the internet and on-demand TV, and how to make the most money possible from streaming. 'It's very much like when television started and the studios went reeling. We're seeing that seismic shift again,' says John Landis.

Also, movies and the marketing of movies have become insanely expensive (in 2012 the MPAA stopped revealing how much they spend on marketing movies but one studio chief told *Variety* that '$150–175m for global marketing costs' is pretty standard). So now studios will only back films that are easy to sell and will work around the world because this then guarantees they will make their money back. This also means that they want movies that appeal to as many demographics as possible, or 'quadrants', as film marketing staff refer to people: men, women, old people and young people. This in turn has led to the demise of traditional women's movies, because they wouldn't appeal to enough quadrants (according to a Hollywood theory, that has only been around for the past thirty years, women will see movies starring men and women, but men will only see movies starring men). It also means that films become less interesting because whenever anyone says they want to make something appeal to everybody, they inevitably blandify it to such a degree that it is loved by nobody.

What studios don't want any more is the kind of mid-budget movies that were made alongside the blockbusters and blockbuster franchises in the eighties, which is what John Hughes's films were. *The Breakfast Club*, let alone *Ferris Bueller's Day Off*, would simply not get made today by a studio. The eighties invented the film franchise, and now it's film franchises that are killing the best sort of movies that were made in the eighties. Teen actors who would have made for perfect sensitive teen stars – Elijah Wood, Tobey Maguire, Shia Laboeuf – instead get shuffled into blockbuster action McFranchises.

'Without a film that can work on thousands of screens and draw in big audiences based upon a pre-sold property, i.e. a remake, sequel, bestseller, major star vehicle, no one will commit the money to marketing the film. So we're getting a certain kind of film, the McMovie, and there's a growing sameness to what works in these big mainstream releases. Thirty years ago in 1984 films like *Amadeus* and *The Natural* were all top hits. Would they get greenlights today? I doubt it,' says Steven Gaydos, editor of *Variety*.

'*Field of Dreams*? *The Big Chill*? *Moonstruck*? No way, not today,' says film producer Lynda Obst.

Comedy, too, has suffered because of this. But wait! you cry. Surely this is the golden age of comedy! *Hangover*! *Bridesmaids*! APATOW. Ah, but those are gross-out comedies, and raunch is funny in all languages. What is less easy to translate is Nora Ephron-style comedy, the kind of comedy you quote for ever and live and die by. No one will ever live and die by anything that is said or happens in *The Hangover*. But I know people who have changed their entire lives because of a line of dialogue from *When Harry Met Sally* . . ., and when I say 'people' I obviously mean 'me'.

But this is not just about studio system shenanigans. It's also about how western culture and politics have changed. American culture has become increasingly conservative since the 1980s. This might seem counterintuitive, considering the legalisation of gay marriage and the election of a two-term mixed-race President. But the fightback from these and other

developments has been vicious and this and the growth of
pressure groups have impacted on what studios feel able to
show now in movies, especially when it comes to young
women's stories, sexuality and abortion. 'What happens in
movies always reflects what's happening in the culture and
what we're seeing onscreen is an American culture trying to
put women back in their place,' says Melissa Silverstein.

Then there are the increasingly screwy ideas about beauty,
desirability and maturity that come from western pop
culture. It is impossible to imagine a young woman playing
the romantic lead in a movie today without perfectly blow-
dried hair, a size 0 body and body-clinging clothes – or if
she did go without any of those, it would be some kind of
statement about her (and she'd certainly remedy her over-
sight by the end of the film). But this was simply not the
case back in the 1980s. Molly Ringwald, Jennifer Grey, Ally
Sheedy, Jennifer Jason Leigh, Elisabeth Shue, Annie Potts,
Susan Ursitti: the reason young women loved those actresses
so much is because they felt recognisable to them. They still
do. The sight of Melanie Griffith's gorgeously curvaceous
and pale body in *Working Girl* when she's dolled up in her
lingerie feels downright subversive compared with nowadays
when actresses' bodies are tanned and toned to an occasionally painful fault. That movies from the eighties – the
eighties! – look so much more innocent and politically
engaged and female-friendly and even moral than many of
today's mainstream films says quite a lot about how things
have changed since, and without many of us really noticing
because these changes happen incrementally.

Now, a word of warning: there is an excellent chance
that your favourite eighties movies are not discussed in this
book. That is because this book features my favourite

eighties films and, as such, is faintly autobiographical and deeply subjective. To spare you the shock and disappointment, here are some of the eighties movies that are pretty much ignored in this book:

The Empire Strikes Back
The Return of the Jedi (fine, I admit it: I never got into
    Star Wars)
Star Trek (ditto)
Most films starring Arnold Schwarzenegger
Ditto Sylvester Stallone
Friday the 13th and *Nightmare on Elm Street* (I find the
    opening scene of *Ghostbusters* terrifying enough, thanks)
Anything horror, in fact
Iron Eagle (apparently guys really love this movie)
Salvador (sorry, Peter Biskind)
Many, many more that I love but just couldn't fit in
    (*St Elmo's Fire* is an especially regretted omission here)

This is not an encyclopedia of eighties movies. If you want that, buy an encyclopedia (although probably the last time you saw an encyclopedia was in the eighties). But I think even if your favourite movie of all time is *The Return of the Jedi* (weirdo), you'll find things here that will go some way to explaining why the *Star Wars* films in the seventies and eighties were great and why the new ones are absolute cack.

Another word of warning: I tried to talk to the main people from each of the movies I look at in this book, and that has been one of the real joys of writing it. It took thirty years but I finally found a (vaguely) legitimate excuse to make Molly Ringwald and Ivan Reitman speak to me. But in some cases I was just too late. Three of my favourite filmmakers from the eighties died in the past decade and it is a source of real regret that I didn't get my act together sooner in time to talk to John Hughes, Nora Ephron and Harold Ramis. They feel like big omissions from this book because they have all been such a huge presence in my life.[*1]

I love these movies because they're hilarious and sweet and smart – because they're fun. They're Good, capital G, and it might sound odd to say this of a film behemoth like *Ghostbusters*, but they're also underrated. These films didn't just make us all happy, they teach you more than you learn from movies today. Yes, 'the force is in you, Lone Star – it's in you,' to quote one particular eighties film[*2] I loved so much as a kid that I watched the video cassette to ribbons. But that force is in me because of these movies. Thanks to them, the true eighties force will always be strong with us.

[*1] I also made the decision in the chapter about *Batman* to use an interview I did with Tim Burton for the *Guardian* a few years ago along with my favourite book about the director instead of bother the poor man again. When I met up with him before, I was so excited I burbled to him for about ten minutes about how much I loved his artwork. 'Wow, you really . . . like my drawings,' he eventually replied. When Tim Burton pretty much tells you that you're an obsessive nerd, you know you've crossed a line.

[*2] The mighty, mighty *Spaceballs*.

Dirty Dancing:
Abortions Happen
and That's Just Fine

Few movies have been as underrated and misunderstood as 1987's *Dirty Dancing*. I first saw it when I was ten and I'm afraid that far from appreciating that I was bearing witness to one of the great feminist films of all time, I was so excited to be watching a movie that had the word 'Dirty' in the title that I spent the whole film waiting for it to finish so I could call my friend Lauren to brag about this achievement.

'Well, I just saw *Can't Buy Me Love*, twice,' said Lauren balefully, referring to the Patrick Dempsey teen romcom, 'and two viewings of *Can't Buy Me Love* is worth one *Dirty Dancing*.'

Out of politeness, I agreed, but we both knew that was totally not true (*Can't Buy Me Love* doesn't have a single sex scene so, like, come on). But just to make sure, I then watched *Dirty Dancing* two more times in a row so that Lauren would definitely not be able to catch up with my coolness. And just to prove how cool I was, I then called Lauren again to tell her that, too.

Adult critics and audiences at the time were just as blind as ten-year-old me when it came to seeing the feminism in *Dirty Dancing* (although presumably most of them didn't immediately brag to their frenemies about having just seen the movie). Partly this comes down to sexism. Partly it's a reflection of how times have changed in the past thirty years. And mainly it's because the film's writer, Eleanor Bergstein, rightly thought the best way to deliver a social message was 'to present in a pleasurable way so that the moral lessons would sneak up on people'. But for a long time I was so distracted by the pleasure – specifically, the soundtrack, the sex, the Swayze – that the moral lessons didn't sneak up at all. For years I didn't realise I was watching one of the great feminist tracts of the 1980s, easily up there with Susan Faludi's feminist study of the eighties, *Backlash*. But then, Faludi's book doesn't come with a half-naked Patrick Swayze, so it is easier to recognise it as a contribution to the fight against misogyny.

By the mid-eighties, both *Flashdance* and *Footloose* had been released and studios were desperate for another teen movie that featured dancing and came with a great commercial soundtrack. But one movie they definitely did not want was *Dirty Dancing*.

'I cannot be clear enough about this: everybody thought *Dirty Dancing* was just a piece of teenage junk,' says the charmingly chatty Bergstein. 'Nobody wanted to make it. Nobody. I would send out the script to studios along with a tape of the soundtrack that I'd made to go with it, that was just recordings of my old 45s from the 1960s, and executives would call me and say, "Oh yeah, Eleanor, we're not going to make the movie, but could you send me another cassette? I wore out the last one." But not even that convinced them of the movie's potential.'

MGM briefly took on the script at the encouragement of several female executives (the men there all hated it), but then dropped it. Not a single other studio would consider it. Eventually a small independent production company looked at it, saw it as an easy quick buck and offered to make it for $4 million, about a fifth of the average cost of a movie at the time. Bergstein and her producer, Linda Gottlieb, accepted.

Bergstein had already had one screenplay produced, the undeservedly forgotten 1980 film *It's My Turn* in which Jill Clayburgh plays a mathematics professor who has an affair with an athlete played by Michael Douglas. The inspiration for that came from Bergstein's observations of female mathematics students at Princeton, where her husband was and still is a professor, and the condescension they had to endure from men, including accusations that their boyfriends did all their work for them ('It made me so mad!' she wails, still just as infuriated today as she was three decades ago). During the making of that film, Bergstein included a dance sequence inspired by the kind of dancing she used to do with her friends when growing up in Brooklyn, but it was ultimately cut. This was fortunate for two reasons: one, just the thought of Michael Douglas dirty dancing is faintly traumatising; and, two, this then made her determined to write a movie that foregrounded the dancing. After a few years, she wrote the story of a young woman known as Baby (Jennifer Grey) who goes to a holiday camp in the Catskills with her parents and sister in the summer of 1963 and falls in love with the dance instructor, Johnny (Patrick Swayze).

After having endured so much studio scepticism about the film, Bergstein has become pretty hardened to critics misunderstanding and dismissing her film. Proving author William Goldman's adage that no one knows anything in the film business, one producer said before the film was released that it was so bad they should just burn the negatives and collect the insurance money, and, hundreds of millions of pounds later, Bergstein laughs at the memory. But there are two comments she frequently hears that drive her crazy: 'I hate it when people describe Baby as an Ugly Duckling, because Jennifer [Grey]'s beautiful, obviously. I also can't stand it when people describe it as a Cinderella story, because all Cinderella ever did was sit on her rump!'

Baby definitely does a lot more with her rump than just sit on it. When the film opens she is reading a book about economic development because she's going to major in the economics of underdeveloped countries – not English literature, she impatiently corrects a condescending suitor – and join the Peace Corps. 'Our Baby's going to save the world!' her proud father, Dr Houseman (the delightfully eyebrowed Jerry Orbach), boasts to the folk at Kellerman's, the (not very subtly Jewish) holiday camp (*Dirty Dancing* is easily the most Jewish eighties teen film, which is probably another reason it is so close to my own Jewish heart. As Bergstein says, 'You just have to know how to spot the clues').

But until she can save the world, Baby sets about saving everyone she meets. Grey is perfect as a naïve and idealistic but likeable teenager, one who is determined to help the poor and downtrodden, and yet has no concept of what life is like for anyone who is anything other than

Jewish[1] and middle class (another probable reason why I found it so easy to relate to this film so much). She is repulsed by the disdainful manner with which the holiday camp's bosses treat the (Catholic) working-class entertainment staff, and she is horrified when she realises her father is just as big a snob. When she learns that the dance instructor Penny (Cynthia Rhodes[2]) is pregnant with the waiter Robbie's (Max Cantor[3]) baby, she tells Robbie to pay for Penny's abortion. When he refuses, she gets the money herself. When Johnny needs someone to stand in for Penny for the dance routine, Baby offers herself. When Penny's abortion is botched, she gets her father to step in.

Baby doesn't understand the lower-middle-class world in which Johnny and Penny live, a world in which one can easily lose one's dreams in a snap, but she doesn't judge. Baby is a great film heroine. As Johnny says, Baby looks at the world and thinks she can make it better, and at first he finds this irritating and dismisses her as a 'Little Miss Fix-It'. But it's also what makes him fall for her:

---

[1] Winona Ryder was originally considered for the role, and she would have been good at conveying Baby's nerviness – and Jewishness – but it would have been much harder to accept her as a wide-eyed sixties teenager. Ryder, even back in the eighties, has always been just that bit too ironic and cool. Grey, on the other hand, was all wide-eyed sweetness.

[2] Rather thrillingly, in real life Rhodes was married to eighties pop star Richard Marx. Hard to get more eighties than that.

[3] Max Cantor had probably the creepiest post-eighties teen movie career of anyone. After a privileged New York upbringing and a very brief acting career he became an investigative journalist. He came across a story about a cannibalistic cult in downtown New York and, in order to gain their trust and get the story, he started taking drugs. He soon became addicted and was eventually found dead. Some alleged he was killed by the cannibal, Daniel Rakowitz, but others said he simply overdosed. Whatever the truth, it's hard not to think poor old Robbie should have stuck with Ayn Rand and stayed away from the cannibals.

when she messes up the dance and misses the lift, she improvises and they get away with it. 'That is when Johnny falls in love with her,' says Bergstein. 'Because he sees how she always wants to make it better, and she shows him that she can.'

She is just as determined when it comes to getting what she wants in her own life, and what she wants in *Dirty Dancing* is to have sex with Johnny, and the film is very, very clear about that. It's no surprise that at MGM none of the men liked the script, or that it was ultimately produced by a woman, because *Dirty Dancing* is very much a film about female sexuality. In particular, the physicality of female sexuality, and all the excitement and messiness that entails. It's Baby who makes all the moves on Johnny when she turns up at his cabin at night and then, as he stands stock-still in helpless befuddlement, she takes the lead again by asking him to dance. As they dance, her hands pour over his half-naked body, taking real pleasure in his skin, and the camera zooms in on her hand sliding down to feel his bottom. The whole film is told from Baby's point of view, which is why there are so many adoring shots of Johnny with his top off and barely any similarly lustful ones of her. There are occasional close-up shots of her pelvis in what is arguably the greatest 1980s montage scene of all, when Johnny is teaching her how to dance while 'Hungry Eyes' plays on the soundtrack, but these feel more like a visual nudge about Baby's sexual excitement than the film panting over Grey's slim hips. Instead, it's the man who is objectified by the camera and the woman who gets turned on, in a manner not seen again until Brad Pitt frolicked with a hairdryer for Geena Davis in 1991's *Thelma & Louise*, and hardly seen at all now.

'The whole film is told through the female gaze, if I can use that jargon, because I wanted to make a movie about what it's like, as a young woman, moving into the physical world, which means the sexual world,' says Bergstein. 'So you get those shots of Jennifer looking up with her big eyes and then about a hundred shots of Patrick. I remember when we were in the editing suite and people were saying, "Why do you have all those shots of Patrick?" I'd say, "It's because that's what she sees. The film is through the female gaze and most movies are not."'

Johnny is no cipher – and no one other than Swayze, the son of a cowboy and ballet dancer, could have captured Johnny's feminised masculinity – but other eighties teen films such as *Pretty in Pink* and *Say Anything* at least offered male characters who young straight male audiences might empathise with. Johnny, however, is a character for the girls. *Dirty Dancing* is wholly a film for female audiences, and, lo, male critics gave it terrible reviews. Roger Ebert dismissed it as 'relentlessly predictable' and *Time* magazine's Richard Schickel was similarly dismissive. The *New Yorker*'s Pauline Kael, on the other hand, wrote that the film left her 'giggling happily'. The *Philly Inquirer*'s film critic Carrie Rickey wrote decades later: '[The *New York Times*'s then film critic] Vincent Canby agreed with me that, as with *Desperately Seeking Susan*, the critical resistance to *Dirty Dancing* might have been because it was a female-centered story.' It is nothing new for a woman's movie – or book, or TV show – to be dismissed by male film critics as frothy nothingness.[*1] What is more striking is that so many aspects of the film

---

[*1] *Sex and the City*, starring Jennifer Grey lookalike Sarah Jessica Parker, would suffer a similar fate two decades later, even though, in its heyday, it was at least as smart and sharp as any critically lauded male TV drama.

that seem extraordinary now were so overlooked at the time.

Not only does Baby want sex with Johnny, but she loves having sex with Johnny, and the film emphasises this with the not exactly subtle analogy the film draws between dancing and sex. Her face shines with happiness on the mornings after, her dancing improving as she gains in sexual confidence. Baby's rejection of her father for the sexy staff at Kellerman's Hotel is as symbolic as that of Rose's abandonment of her wealthy life for the Irish jigging working classes in 1997's *Titanic* (the poor: there to provide a buttoned-up wealthy girl's sexual awakening. And such good dancers, too!). It's only by losing her virginity that Baby sees the fallibility of her parents and sheds her Baby-ness to become Frances, and the film applauds this. (As did audiences: Baby and Johnny's sex scenes were the formative erotic experience for an entire generation; there is still a large part of me that believes I haven't actually had sex yet because none of my sexual encounters has started by a lip-synching 'Love is Strange', although God knows not through lack of trying on my part.)

'Baby risks everything for integrity and love, and she doesn't pay the price,' says Bergstein. 'Most movies make girls pay the price.'

Girls in eighties teen movies love sex, and suffer few consequences for it. In the now deservedly little seen *Valley Girl* (only worth seeing, really, for Nicolas Cage's waistcoat and to hear Modern English's 'I Melt With You' on the soundtrack), the teenage girls discuss sex lustfully with one another. In *Mystic Pizza*, Jojo (Lili Taylor) sneaks into bathrooms every spare minute with her fiancé (Vincent D'Onofrio) and they end up happily married, while Daisy

(Julia Roberts) seduces her wealthy boyfriend and the two apparently end up contentedly, if improbably, together. (Of the *Mystic Pizza* trio, only Kat – Annabeth Gish – has a bad sexual experience in that she realises afterwards that her lover will never leave his wife. But this plot twist strikes me as more of a comment on the man specifically rather than on sex in general, as Kat seems far more upset by the former than the latter.) In *Say Anything*, Diane (Ione Skye) seems completely unbothered after losing her virginity to Lloyd (John Cusack) in his car. Lloyd, by contrast, is utterly shattered by the encounter and can only pull himself together by listening to a Peter Gabriel ballad, poor sod.[*1]

This fairly basic truism – teenage girls enjoy sex – is a lesson gleaned far more rarely from films today. Today, a girl in a teen film who has sex – or even just wants to have sex – risks being ravaged by her boyfriend and eaten from within by a vampire baby (Bella in *Twilight*). At the very least, a girl who has sex is certainly emotionally damaged (*The Perks of Being a Wallflower*) and will be universally shamed (*Easy A*). Good, smart, sane girls don't have sex, or

---

[*1] Boys, too, enjoy their sexual maturity in eighties teen films. In *Risky Business*, Joel (Tom Cruise) enjoys aerobic if somewhat improbable sex with Lana (Rebecca De Mornay) when he loses his virginity. In *Teen Wolf*, as the film's title emphasises, the old trope about werewolfishness as a symbol for male puberty is employed to its most delightfully ridiculous extent, and in a far sillier way than it was in 1957's *I Was a Teenage Werewolf*. It is almost certainly the best movie ever made about male puberty; what Judy Blume's *Are You There God? It's Me, Margaret* is to girls, *Teen Wolf* should be to boys. When Scott (Michael J. Fox) changes into a wolf, he becomes irresistible to girls in high school, and he enjoys sex with them with a howl. Similarly, the teen vampires in the presciently emo *The Lost Boys* take enormous pleasure in their vampirism. Compared to both these films, the vampire and the werewolf in *Twilight* make sexuality and maturation look a lot less fun.

at least are extremely reluctant to do so and only submit under sufferance because the boys want it so badly (Dionne in *Clueless*, Vicky in *American Pie*). It's a weird harking back to one of the biggest teen films of the seventies, *Halloween*, in which any teenage girl who has sex is promptly dispatched by a dungaree-wearing psycho. Now, instead, they are destroyed from within. A teen film today can show teens having sex – as long as it's in a raunchy comedy and the sex is presented as extreme or slapstick, such as 1999's *American Pie*, 2007's *Superbad*, 2012's *Project X* or 2013's *The To Do List* and, from the UK, *The Inbetweeners*, and is pretty much invariably from the boy's point of view. What you don't see any more are tender depictions of teen sexuality, or realistic ones. Instead, teen sex comes with warnings or in the nervily ironic coating of raunch.

'You can have a movie with a wild party and lots of sexual comedy, but you can't have a movie in which a fifteen-year-old girl is teaching her friends about sex,' says *Fast Times at Ridgemont High*'s director Amy Heckerling. 'Like in *Borat*, you can have naked men with their dicks swinging around for ten minutes as long as they're not sexual. But you don't see any more young people realistically exploring their sexuality together.'

Film producer and director Jon Avnet agrees that one of the biggest differences between today's teen films and those of the eighties is the depiction of sexuality, and, as the producer of *Risky Business*, one of the sexiest and most influential[1] eighties teen films, he should know.

---

[1] John Hughes's teen films were clearly and heavily influenced by *Risky Business*, minus the plot about prostitutes (thank God).

'The subway scene in *Risky Business* between Rebecca [De Mornay] and Tom [Cruise] is really pretty hot, and I don't think you could have something that hot in a teen film now. Sex as a form of intimacy is tantamount to death in teen films today,' he says. Instead, he suggests, sex in teen films is now either non-existent or 'like something out of *Porky's*'.

One woman in *Dirty Dancing* very nearly does get punished for having sex: Penny, who almost dies after undergoing an illegal abortion. I'm not sure what I thought was going on with Penny when I was a kid; maybe I thought she'd fallen down some steps and hurt herself, maybe I was so baffled by it that I simply ignored it. But when I came back to the film as a teenager, expecting to spend a happy ninety minutes wallowing in sexy dance sequences, familiar one-liners ('I carried a watermelon') and Jennifer Grey's magnificent original nose (since tragically mutilated), it was something of a shock to realise that what *Dirty Dancing* is really about, at its heart, is the importance of legal abortion. The film is astonishingly open about the brutality of illegal abortions. Penny, we are told, went to 'some butcher' who had 'a folding table and a dirty knife'. This was, we are repeatedly told, 'illegal', which is why she can't go to a doctor when it goes wrong and she nearly bleeds to death.

'When I wrote the film, abortion – like feminism – was one of those issues that people thought just wasn't relevant any more. A lot of young women thought those battles were won, and talking about it was tiresome,' says Bergstein. 'But I thought Roe vs Wade was precarious, and that's why I put in all that purple language about the "dirty knife" and everything. The film is set in 1963 but came out in 1987 and I wanted young women seeing the film to understand that it wasn't just that she went to Planned Parenthood and it went wrong.'

No one – not the studio, not the critics – complained at the time that the movie's entire plot is put into motion by an illegal abortion: 'They didn't even notice that it was there,' says Bergstein. 'The studio thought the script was stupid and bad for so many reasons they scarcely noticed that. Certainly no one suggested that it might be controversial. They thought it was just a stupid teenage dance movie.' The first objection raised came from an acne cream company who wanted to sponsor the film – and get their tube of cream on every poster – but they backed away when they saw the film. The studio suggested that the film be reshot but Bergstein pointed out that the abortion is integral to the movie, as it's how Johnny and Baby meet and, most interestingly, prompts them into having sex for the first time, and so the studio backed down.

'I knew that if I put in a social message it had to be carefully plotted in. A lot of movies have social messages but they end up on the cutting room floor. It's true that not many people talked about the abortion plot when it came out, but it meant that I was getting the message to people who wouldn't go see a documentary about abortions, and we were also getting big feminist audiences,' says Bergstein.

Just as eighties teen movies didn't shy away from showing how much teenage girls like sex, nor did they avoid discussing one possible result of the activity: getting an abortion. In 1980's *Fame*, wealthy Hilary (Antonia Franceschi) has an abortion after accidentally becoming pregnant. The only question anyone raises about her decision is from the nurse, who asks which credit card she is going to use to pay for the operation. In 1982's *Fast Times at Ridgemont High*, Stacy (Jennifer Jason Leigh), who, at fifteen, is underage, loses her virginity and becomes pregnant after a hurried encounter with nineteen-year-old Damone (Robert Romanus). He then fails to help her pay for the abortion and doesn't even turn up to give her the promised lift to the clinic so she has to turn to her dopey brother (Judge Reinhold). The film never judges her, nor does it turn into some terrible morality tale about what happens to loose girls. The only person who is damned by the movie is the feckless Damone for failing to help her. In fact, Stacy ends up completely fine, utterly unaffected by her abortion and dating Rat (Brian Backer), the boy she should have been with all along and who appears similarly untroubled by Stacy's abortion.

'The studio had no problem at all with a fifteen-year-old female character having an abortion. The whole thing was realistic: teenagers were having sex [offscreen], some teenagers were having abortions, and the film reflected that,' says Heckerling. 'When [Damone] doesn't give her the cheque for the abortion, we're saying that these kids aren't ready for kids. He can't even get a cheque, how's he going to be a father?'

As in *Fast Times*, the woman in need of the abortion in *Dirty Dancing* is not criticised by the film, only the idiot who got her pregnant and then refuses to help. But *Dirty Dancing* is far more vehement in its criticism of feckless men than *Fast Times*, possibly because, unlike *Fast Times*, it was written by a woman. 'Some people count and some people don't,' sneers the evil impregnator and Ayn Rand fan Robbie, who then heartlessly accuses Penny of sleeping around.

Perhaps the most extraordinary onscreen discussion about abortion comes in *Fatal Attraction*, the ultimate example of the eighties backlash against feminism that Faludi writes about. Yet despite the film's hilarious scaremongering about the risks of feminism, it is strangely, even crazedly, if not strictly speaking pro-choice then certainly pro-abortion. When Alex (Glenn Close) tells Dan (Michael Douglas) that she is pregnant after their affair, he – the good guy – desperately wants her to have an abortion but she – the bad woman – refuses, and this, the film suggests, is proof of his responsible nature and her selfish one. As this is *Fatal Attraction*, and an Adrian Lyne film, there are, inevitably, misogynistic impulses underpinning the film's pro-choice message: namely, that it is unfair that women hold the control when it comes to abortion (I know: ha ha ha) and that the most important thing is that Dan preserves the sanctity of the nuclear family he has at home by making his mistress have an abortion. Still, it's quite something now to see a movie in which a man is good for demanding a woman have an abortion and a woman is bad for refusing to have it.

Obviously, this being the Reaganite 1980s, not all films were jumping up and down and cheering 'Yay! Abortion!'. Going back to *Backlash*, Faludi details at length the movies that came out in that decade that she feels were explicitly anti-choice, some of which are singled out fairly (Woody Allen's *Another Woman*, in which a woman realises, too late, that her biggest mistake in life was having an abortion), some less so (Ron Howard's sparkling comedy *Parenthood*, in which an eighteen-year-old, to my mind, credibly decides to have a baby with her deadbeat boyfriend because she is gooey in love). But these predictable voices against abortion make the contemporary movies that endorsed it look all the more extraordinary.

'It's not like movies hadn't talked about abortion before *Fast Times*,' says Heckerling. 'You can look back to that Steve McQueen film [1963's *Love with the Proper Stranger*] which is all about him trying to find money for an abortion. *Fast Times* was born out of [the film's screenwriter] Cameron Crowe's investigations into modern high schools, and this is what high schools were like. Women were having abortions and the movies then talked about this.'

Women still have abortions, but you wouldn't know it from today's mainstream movies, teen or otherwise. Even smart films that are forced to confront the issue dodge it awkwardly. In 2007's *Knocked Up*, which focuses on a couple who conceive after an awkward one-night stand, the only two people who mention the word – her mother, his flatmate – are derided as heartless. Whereas *Fame*'s Hilary has an abortion to pursue her dreams as a ballet dancer, twenty-two-year-old Alison in *Knocked Up* recoils in disgust at the thought of putting her burgeoning career ahead of an unexpected, unwanted pregnancy. In the 2007 film *Juno*, the eponymous teenager is dissuaded from having an abortion after an anti-choice protester tells her that her baby will have fingernails, and she then goes into a clinic that appears to have been dreamed up by the Westboro Baptist Church's press office. In 2012's *Bachelorette*, a character reveals that she had an abortion as a teenager and this, the film intimates, is why she's such a promiscuous druggy mess as an adult.

What makes the movie industry's increasing conservatism especially bizarre is that roughly the same percentage of Americans support the legalisation of abortion as they did in the 1980s. In fact, today's audiences actively like seeing honest depictions of abortion onscreen, in the very few movies that show them. The indie film *Obvious Child*, about a woman who decides to get an abortion, was released only in 202 theatres in the States, and yet it made a very impressive $25,772 per theatre in its opening weekend. By contrast, the unpleasantly misogynistic 2014 comedy *The Other Woman*, in which the female characters are two-dimensional jealous, sexualised harpies, was released in over 3,000 theatres and made only $7,727 per theatre in its opening weekend. So much for audiences not liking complex female themes.

Teen abortion rates in the US are at a historic low, having declined by 64 per cent between 1990 and 2010 thanks to the commendable work by sex education workers who have so effectively taught young people about the importance of contraception. Therefore why movies should be so fearful of discussing them seems bizarre. Whereas in the eighties there were movies that were both pro- and anti-choice, Hollywood speaks with one voice on the issue today.

'The entertainment industry has elected to silence the discussion on abortion,' said Robert Thompson, director of the Bleier Center for Television and Popular Culture at Syracuse University in New York. 'It's an issue fraught with moral and ethical challenges and Hollywood has been almost silent on it for the past 20 years. It has been the one controversial subject matter that has not only not progressed, but has totally retreated from popular culture. If you'd watch TV or films in this country, you'd never guess that abortion is such a big issue.'

Bergstein says:

I used to say, oh maybe *Dirty Dancing* was ahead of its time and that's why I had to do talk about abortion in this covert way. But if you look what's happened since, that's not really true. I would have thought all these movies like *Juno* and *Knocked Up* and *Waitress* would take its place, but in those movies the girls don't have the abortion: at the last minute they take what looks to be the moral choice and they don't do it, and they end up with the guy all happy. So it's presented now as a moral decision not to have the abortion and you have a cute little baby and it's fine. I don't know, maybe that's what you can get financed from studios these days.

When I ask Judd Apatow why there was no discussion of abortion in *Knocked Up*, he replies that there was, originally, but it ended up on the cutting floor. 'Anyway, I'm as pro-choice as you can get, but the movie would have been ten minutes long if she'd had an abortion.'

Diablo Cody, the writer of *Juno*, is even more dismissive of objections to the depiction of abortion in her movie: 'Any feminist out there who doesn't support me gets a big boo because you've got one person out there who is advocating for women in Hollywood and you're going to slag that person? If you're a feminist, you should be up my butt.'

But *Juno*'s star, the very thoughtful and engaged Ellen Page, is a little more open to the issue, and less concerned with anyone being in her butt. At first she uses Apatow's argument, saying that if Juno 'had the abortion it would be a short movie', which is a fair point, but it does provoke the response that the screenwriters should either have written a less improbable scenario in which that particular woman would keep the baby, or they should have been more deft at dealing with the woman's reason for not having the abortion. Page's voice rises a little when she adds: 'And at least we say the word abortion,' suggesting she knows that's a pretty weak argument.

But the problem isn't that Juno had the baby, I say. It is that she decides not to have the abortion because of something a pro-life protester said.

'Ohhhh, I see, that's a good point,' Page says, sitting back in her chair.

So how does she feel about the film in light of that perspective?

'Well, I feel like we –' she begins gamely, before giving up. 'No, that's a good point. But it's funny, I never thought that she responds to the protester but of course you're right.'

It would initially seem to make no sense that eighties teen films were so relaxed about sex, especially compared to teen films today. In 1980s America, Aids was ravaging the country, the anti-abortion movement was emerging and Republicans were in the White House. If there was ever a time when pop culture might have tried to scare teenage girls off sex, then the eighties was surely it. Yet instead, eighties teen movies generally make sex look, well, great, even (gasp) for women, while teen movies today make sex look absolutely terrifying, especially for women.

It would be easy to see this shift as a reflection of the rise of the Christian right and growing conservatism of America, but there is another way of looking at it. Yes, girls in eighties movies joyfully jump into the sack with everyone from Patrick Swayze to Andrew McCarthy, but this looks less cheering when one considers that, offscreen, teenage pregnancy rates were, for the first time in decades, rocketing in the US. The *LA Times* described the eighties as a 'greenhouse' for teenage pregnancies due to a combination of the fraying of unions leading to many teenagers' parents losing their jobs, budget cuts on afterschool programmes and rising school drop-out rates. Worse, the Reagan administration cut budgets for abortions, health clinics, sex education and birth control programmes. While rates of teen sex were just as high in Europe, rates of teen pregnancy in England were half as high as they were in America because, as the *LA Times* put it, 'contraception is far more common [there]', by which they mean it was easier for teenagers to have access to free contraception thanks to the NHS and health clinics. By 1989, one out of every ten American girls was pregnant before her twentieth birthday.

So one could argue that teenagers in today's US teen films aren't more scared of sex than they were in the 1980s; they're just being more responsible about it. This attitude shift is reflected in their offscreen behaviour: from 1991 to 2000 the number of teenage pregnancies fell by 50 per cent across the United States, across all demographics. But despite the strenuous efforts of the Christian right and Republican Party, while American teenagers are having sex slightly later than they were in 1988, they are not, in the vast main, abstinent (all politicians would be very depressed if they knew how little what they say affects teenagers' behaviour). Instead, increased use of contraception accounts for as much as 86 per cent of the decline in teenage pregnancies since 1990. The rise in condom use also means that boys and men are taking more responsibility when having sex. So one could even look at a film such as *Twilight* and see – beneath the scaremongering and weirdness about sex – a sliver of modern relevance in that Edward, in his own vampiric way, tries to be responsible with Bella and protect her from his death juice (or something).

This argument works less well, though, if one looks at the wider culture alongside the facts as well as at the specifics of the films. For a start, and most obviously, if teenagers are, as the figures strongly suggest, leading more responsible sex lives, then it makes no sense for movies to be so hysterical about the subject, suggesting either that all teens are having orgies or telling teenagers that sex will kill them. Fine, films shouldn't show teenagers shagging in every car on every street corner because, first, the gear stick digging into one's back is a major turn-off, but also because that's not how teenagers live today, and they never did. But teenagers also don't live lives in which if they have sex they are then emotionally damaged, publicly shamed and turned into zombies.

'American movies have become much more conservative since they were in the 1980s, and this is partly because of the international market,' says film producer Lynda Obst. Profits from China, for example, have grown by over 400 per cent in the past half decade. This then affects what studios feel they can and can't show onscreen, and one issue they are especially conscious of showing to the increasingly important foreign markets is teenagers having sex and abortions.

But the morality of American movies isn't just being determined by the morals of other countries: it also comes from within.

'Teen movies are much more conservative today than they were in the eighties because we've gone backwards domestically in terms of cultural attitudes, and studios have reacted to that,' says Obst. 'Pressure groups from the right have become much stronger over the past few decades, and this very much affects studios.'

'We're like lobsters in a tank and don't notice how the temperature has been changing over the decades because we're in the pot. Hollywood has followed America in its move to the right and we're a much more conservative country now than we were then,' says the editor of *Variety*, Steven Gaydos.

This growing conservatism has been very much reflected in America's attitudes towards teen sex: as part of the 1996 federal welfare reform legislation in the US, Congress authorised $50 million annually to fund abstinence-only education. By 2008, the US government had spent over $1.5 billion on abstinence-only sex education and federal guidance forbade any discussion of contraception except to emphasise its failure rates. Between 2006 and 2008 one in four teenagers in America received abstinence-only sex education with no instruction about birth control; in 1988 only 8 per cent had done so. The Obama administration and Congress have since eliminated two abstinence-only sex education programmes yet thirty-seven states still require sex education that includes abstinence, twenty-six of which stress abstinence is the best method, even though states that teach abstinence-only sex education, such as Mississippi, notoriously have the highest rate of teenage pregnancies. As of 2011, more than half of all women of reproductive age in the US lived in a state hostile to abortion rights, an increase of 31 per cent in just one decade.

The big teen films today are characterised by brutal and graphic violence in a way they never were in the eighties. In *Twilight*, the killings are depicted as romantic proof of Edward and Bella's love for one another as they (Edward, usually) knock off their enemies. In *The Hunger Games* teenagers kill each other to win a reality TV show. Sex, however, is anathema to these movies: in *Twilight* it is seen as dangerous, and in *The Hunger Games* it is an awkward inconvenience. Murder, though, is absolutely fine.

'One big problem is the [US] motion picture ratings system: it is much harder these days on sex than violence and so if you don't want to get an R rating [the US equivalent of an 18], which would kill the film, but to still attract the kids, you put in violence but leave out the sex. The ratings board is much harder on teen sex than violence and everyone knows it,' said one producer who works in teen films.

It's true, the Motion Picture Association of America (the MPAA) is easier on violence than it used to be for one big reason: computer-generated imagery (CGI). 'We are seeing different kinds of violence with the rise of CGI and parents feel their children are able to filter what's real and what's not,' says the MPAA's Joan Graves. As to whether it has become stricter about sex over the past thirty years, and especially teen sex, that, she says, is slightly trickier to say: 'There has never been a round table discussion saying, "OK, we'll change this, we'll change that." These changes happen over decades. But the ratings system is built to change. It's reflecting current standards rather than standards from twenty years ago. A movie that was made thirty years ago might well have a different rating today.' In Britain, if a film has an 18 rating, no one under eighteen can see it, but in America, a film with an R rating can be seen by a child as long as they are accompanied by an adult. This then puts the onus on American parents to decide whether or not their child should see the film and so the MPAA sees its role as equipping parents with the information to make that decision.

Thus, the US ratings system is built to 'reflect the standards of American parents', as Graves puts it, and if that sounds somewhat fluid, then it is. There is no strict rubric about what is and isn't allowed, only a sense of what 'American parents' will tolerate. But Graves is very clear that the ratings board does not offer instructions to filmmakers about what they can and can't film – that's the studio's job. All it's there to do is 'reflect [American] society', and in its angstiness about teen sex and relaxed attitude towards violence, in a country where three people are killed every hour by guns and abstinence is still part of many schools' curriculum, one can easily argue that it succeeds at that.

'The Americans have issues we don't have, mainly from the Bible Belt, and so as a result out of all the films we rate we give about 30 per cent a different rating than they get in the US,' David Cooke, director of the British Board of Film Classification (BBFC), explains in his plush office overlooking Soho Square, which feels more like the study of a grand literary editor than the workspace where the number of swear words and nipple counts in films are catalogued. Compared to the States, Cooke says, the BBFC is 'more relaxed about sex – but we're not as relaxed as Scandinavia!'. On the other hand, 'We are a bit tougher on violence than they are in the States.' Like the MPAA, the BBFC sees its role as being 'in line' with public opinion as opposed to leading it. Unlike the MPAA, it does this by surveying 10,000 members of the public every four years to gauge their opinions on what they do and don't think is appropriate in films for varying age groups. It has been doing these surveys since 2000; before, film ratings were, Cooke says, 'more capricious, more down to the whims of the [BBFC] president'. When Cooke looks back at movies from the eighties to check their ratings, he frequently thinks the ratings were too strict. In retrospect, they reflect how that decade in Britain was, as Sian Barber in *Behind the Scenes at the BBFC: Film Classification from the Silver Screen to the Digital Age*, sees it as 'filled with heightened debates about childhood and children which emerged from [the Thatcherite] right-wing political agenda'.

These days, the BBFC takes context into account 'as opposed to relying on an algorithm' when looking at sexual content and swearing, which the MPAA does not as much. As a result, a film like *The Invisible Woman*, which depicts Charles Dickens's adulterous affair, got a 12 in the UK but an R in the US, definitively proving that Americans are more likely to be led morally astray by the amorous adventures of a Victorian author than the Brits. There definitely hasn't, Cooke says, been a hardening of attitude – by the BBFC or the British public – towards abortion. 'There also hasn't been much of a shift about what's deemed acceptable for teenagers by adults. The only social issues the public have expressed greater concern to us about are teenagers harming themselves, the sexualisation of children and the glamorisation of drugs,' he says. 'So those are the issues we're probably tougher on now than we were in the past.'

While attitudes towards teenage sex in the UK have fluctuated a little over the past thirty years, there has been nothing like the big waves of hysteria that one sees in the US. The British government has never funded any abstinence-only sex education: 'Occasionally a Conservative minister will promote the idea, but they need to provide evidence that this would be beneficial and none has been provided. If anything, the opposite is repeatedly proven,' says Lucy Emmerson from the Sex Education Forum. For the past forty years in this country, contraception has been relatively accessible and – crucially for young people – free, especially since 1974 when what were then called Family Planning Clinics were allowed to prescribe the Pill. Despite occasional comments by various Conservative ministers, legalised abortion is generally accepted as a right. America is a much more conservative country than Britain because it is a much more religious one. But this does not mean British teenagers are immune to the changing winds from America. After all, the vast majority of their pop culture comes from that country.

When there was talk at the beginning of the twenty-first century of remaking *Dirty Dancing*, Bergstein wondered how the studios would deal with the abortion plot in the film, especially as she owns the rights to the script. After all, when *Fame* was remade in 2009 the abortion plot was simply dropped, which also happened when the 1966 film *Alfie* was pointlessly remade starring Jude Law and Sienna Miller. In the end, it became a moot issue because – perhaps unsurprisingly – the remake never happened. Instead, Bergstein turned the play into an international stage musical mega-hit and oomphed up the abortion plot, emphasising the risks Baby's father, Dr Houseman, took by helping Penny, endangering both his medical licence and his freedom. People, Bergstein says, need to remember what it was like before, and what it could all too easily be like again:

My feeling has always been that people who are anti-abortion are anti-sex and anti-pleasure for young women, and that's why I wanted to make a movie about both. That's why Baby and Johnny's first love scene comes after they've seen Penny nearly drowning in her own blood as a result of sex, and the song on the record player is [Solomon Burke's] 'Cry to Me'. It's not an idealised romantic scene, it's a scene about loneliness and terror and sex. But I wanted to say if you plunge into the physical world and if you do it with honour and without fear, you will attach yourself to a moral world.

More than that, *Dirty Dancing* taught my generation of women, and continues to teach generations of younger women, about their moral compass. We came for the sex, but we have stayed because it shows us something even more real and scary. It teaches us something about ourselves and the world. And, as Baby learns, only the best kind of sex can do that.

THE TEN BEST POWER BALLADS ON AN EIGHTIES MOVIE SOUNDTRACK

10 'Up Where We Belong', by Joe Cocker and Jennifer Warnes, from *An Officer and a Gentleman*

Technically, a love song, yes. But a Cocker-ishly POWERFUL love song.

9 'Glory of Love', by Peter Cetera, from *The Karate Kid II*

Say what you like about *The Karate Kid II* (it's rubbish, for starters), but this song is grade A singing into the hairbrush material.

8 'Shooting for the Moon', by Amy Holland, from *Teen Wolf*

The end scene when this song plays is so satisfying that I didn't even notice the first 10,784 times I saw it that an extra in the background drops his trousers at the camera.

7 'Let the River Run', by Carly Simon, from *Working Girl*

Total singing in the shower fodder, and that's the best kind of fodder.

6 'St Elmo's Fire (Man in Motion)', by John Parr, from *St Elmo's Fire*

John Parr tries as hard to get a St Elmo's reference into his song as the characters do in the film, and God bless them all for trying.

5 'Flashdance – What a Feeling', by Irene Cara, from *Flashdance*

The movie that made Hollywood decide to knock out films

that look like movie videos. And this is the song that convinced them.

4 'Purple Rain', by Prince, from *Purple Rain*

I've seen this film hundreds of times, and I still have no idea what this song is about.

3 'We Don't Need Another Hero', by Tina Turner, from *Mad Max Beyond the Thunderdome*

TIIIIIINAAAAAAAAA!!!!

2 'If You Leave', by OMD, from *Pretty in Pink*

The ultimate prom song, one that manages to combine Ducky's heartbreak with Andie's romantic triumph. No filmmaker understood better the power of synth music than John Hughes.

1 'Holding Out for a Hero', by Bonnie Tyler, from *Footloose*

Nobody does power ballads like Bonnie does power ballads.

The Princess Bride:
True Love Isn't Just About
the Kissing Parts

It feels downright inconceivable[1] to devote only one chapter in a book about lessons gleaned from eighties movies to *The Princess Bride*. Why, just off the top of my head, while standing on my head, I can name five life lessons that this movie teaches you that you don't learn anywhere else:

1. 'Never go against a Sicilian when DEATH is on the line!'
2. 'Love is the greatest thing – except for a nice mutton, lettuce and tomato sandwich when the mutton is nice and lean.'
3. 'Life is pain. Anyone who says differently is selling something.'
4. Eventually, you learn not to mind the kissing parts.
5. And most importantly, 'As you wish' = 'I love you.'

Such is the depth of wisdom in this film that in 2013,

---

[1] I'm using Vizzini's definition of the word here, of course.

twenty-six years after its release, BuzzFeed devoted a list[*1] to the lessons gleaned from it. A BuzzFeed list! Who needs the Oscars, *Princess Bride*, when you have that ultimate of modern-day accolades?

The Princess Bride is so adored that it's probably[*2] now a clichéd response on internet dating websites: walks on the beach, an open fire, sunsets and *The Princess Bride*. And yet, despite this, love for *The Princess Bride* is not seen as desperately hackneyed or cheesily safe. *The Princess Bride* is what you'd need a prospective love interest to cite as their favourite movie for the relationship to progress,[*3] it's the one film that would make you rethink a lifelong friendship if you found out your best friend 'just didn't get it' – not that they would ever say that because I honestly don't know a single person of my generation who isn't obsessed with this film. And not just my generation: in his very enjoyable book about the making of *The Princess Bride*, *As You Wish*, Cary Elwes – who played Westley the farm boy, of course – recounts being told by both Pope John Paul II and Bill Clinton how much they loved the

---

*1 '17 Important Life Lessons from *The Princess Bride*', Erin La Rosa, BuzzFeed, 15 May 2013. Seventeen! Pah! There are at least 1,374,978 lessons in that movie. Step it up with your listicles, BuzzFeed!

*2 I only managed to last a week on a dating website so I'm afraid my research isn't as thorough as it could be. You see, because of *The Princess Bride*, I have high standards when it comes to love and I just didn't believe that any beautiful farm boys would be on match.com. How would he have wifi up in his mountainous hovel?

*3 The US version of the TV show *The Office*, when it was still amazing, played on this idea in the second series when Pam (UK translation: Dawn) chose 'The Princess Bride' as one of her Desert Island movies choices, proving she is the right woman for Jim (UK translation: Tim). Jim's current girlfriend Katy (played by Amy Adams), on the other hand, chooses 'Legally Blonde', which definitively establishes her inferiority to Pam.

movie, proving that *The Princess Bride* appeals to saints and sinners alike.[*1]

Now, having said all that, I have a confession to make. I was not the big *Princess Bride* fan in my family when I was growing up. That title instead went to my sister, Nell. Our mother took us to see it at the cinema when I must have been nine and Nell was seven and even though the film was – incredibly – something of a commercial disappointment when it came out, the cinema was absolutely packed with kids like us. In my mind, everyone in the audience was utterly in thrall to this tale of Buttercup (Robin Wright), her true love Westley (Elwes), and their battles against Prince Humperdinck (Chris Sarandon), Vizzini (Wallace Shawn) and Count Rugen (Christopher Guest) and their eventual assistance from the brave swordsman Inigo (Mandy Patinkin), the giant Fezzik (the professional wrestler known as André the Giant) and Miracle Max (Billy Crystal).

Afterwards, we stood in the cinema atrium as our mother bundled us back into our coats.

'Did you girls like it?' she asked.

Standing there in her corduroy dungarees and T-shirt, Nell looked in a state of semi-shock. 'I LOVED IT. I WANT TO SEE IT AGAIN RIGHT NOW!' she practically shouted.

Now, *The Princess Bride* is wonderful, but in order to understand how unexpected this proclamation was, you

---

[*1] If you love *The Princess Bride*, which I'm assuming you do if you're reading this chapter, and because you're presumably a sentient human being, you really should read *As You Wish*. Any book with an index that includes the entry 'André the Giant: breaking wind, and, 123–126' should be on everyone's bookshelves by law.

have to know a little bit about my sister. Ever since she was old enough to throw a tantrum, my sister refused to wear dresses. She never played with dolls. She refused to let my mother brush her hair, and had apparently no interest in her physical appearance. She did not like mushy stories – she didn't even like reading books. In other words, she was the complete opposite to me. How much of that was a deliberate reaction against me, a younger sibling defining herself in opposition to the older one, and how much of it was simply an innate part of Nell was already a moot point when we went to see *The Princess Bride*: Nell's parameters were so firmly set by then that her nickname in our family was 'the tough customer'. She would only consent to drink one kind of fruit juice (apple), and only by one brand (Red Cheek), and only if it came out of a can (never a carton), so there was absolutely no negotiating with her about mushy princesses. Lord only knows how my mother got her to see the movie in the first place. She must have hidden the title from her.

And yet, like the grandson in the film, Kevin Arnold,[1] Nell found that, against all odds, she did enjoy the story, just as Kevin's grandfather, Columbo,[2] promises. I think Nell made my mother take her to see the film at the cinema at least three more times. As she wished.

When it came out on VHS, we bought it immediately and it was understood that the video cassette was officially

---

[1] So called (by me) for the obvious reason that the grandson was played by Fred Savage, who went on to play Kevin Arnold in *The Wonder Years*. But you already got that, and I apologise for condescending to you by spelling it out.

[2] Because Peter Falk plays the grandfather and – What? You got it? OK, cool. Just looking out for you, bro.

Nell's, just as the video cassette for *Ferris Bueller's Day Off* was officially mine. When she found out that the film had originally been a book by William Goldman, who also wrote the screenplay, she asked my amazed mother to buy that, too. Nell read it over and over until the pages fell out, so she stuck them back in and then read the book again. *The Princess Bride* was the book that taught her to like books, as much as the movie taught her to relax some of her other rules. She developed a lifelong crush on Westley and, not long after, she started wearing dresses, too.

The reasons why Nell loved this film so much exemplify, I think, why it is universally adored in a way that, say, the vaguely similar and contemporary *The Never-Ending Story*, is not. It's a fairy tale for those who love fairy tales, but it's also a self-aware spoof for those who don't; it's an adventure film for boys and – for once – girls, too, but without pandering to or excluding either; it's got a plot for kids, dialogue for adults and jokes for everyone; it's a genre film and a satire of a genre film; it's a very funny movie in which everybody is playing it straight; it's smart and sweet and smart about its sweetness, but also sweet about its smarts. It's a movie that lets people who don't like certain things like those things, while at the same time not betraying the original fans. But most of all, *The Princess Bride* is about one thing in particular: '*The Princess Bride* is a story about love,' says Cary Elwes. 'So much happens in the movie – giants, fencing, kidnapping. But it's really a film about love.'

This might seem like a statement of the obvious, but it isn't, actually. Yes, the film is ostensibly about the great true love between Buttercup and Westley, and their most perfect kiss which leaves all the other kisses in the world behind. Both Elwes and Wright were so astonishingly beautiful when they made the film that, watching them, it's hard to believe any love ever existed on this planet other than theirs. And they, rather pleasingly, were quite taken with one another. In his book, Elwes talks at length about how 'smitten' he was with Wright, and she says precisely the same about him: 'I was absolutely smitten with Cary. So obviously that helped with our on-screen chemistry . . . It doesn't matter how many years go by, I will love Cary forever.'

Disappointingly, however, Elwes insists that they remained just friends. 'Everyone asks if there was more!' he says, sounding a little exasperated, apparently unable to see what everyone else can: namely, that it seems against the laws of nature for two such beautiful people not to have had sex at least once. The last scene that Elwes shot was of him and Wright kissing on horseback, creating 'the most perfect kiss' of all time against a sunset. Surely that was romantic?

'Well, not really. Robin and I were friends by that point so we kept laughing, and [the director] Rob [Reiner] was going, "Touch her face, touch her face!"' He laughs.

But Westley and Buttercup's love is only a part of the film, and only one of several love stories in the film. There is also, for a start, the great love between Inigo and Fezzik. The scene in which a drunken and broken Inigo looks up into Fezzik's face in the Thieves Forest, and Fezzik says a simple, smiling hello, is much more moving than the moment when Buttercup realises the Dread Pirate Roberts is actually Westley (after, unfortunately, she's pushed him down a hill). Even if Inigo does become the Dread Pirate

Roberts at the end of the film, as Westley suggests he should, it is as impossible to imagine him going off without Fezzik as it is to imagine Buttercup and Westley being severed.

This love between the two men is at the root of one of the film's subtlest lessons. Bad guys teach audiences how to think of opponents in life, and this is especially true of bad guys in books and films aimed at kids. Because stories for kids tend to be relatively simple, villains in these films are almost invariably evil, and that's all there is to be said about them. Cruella de Vil, Snow White's stepmother, the witch in 'Rapunzel': WHAT a bunch of moody cows. This is also certainly true of movies for children in the 1980s, from the frankly terrifying Judge Doom (Christopher Lloyd) in *Who Framed Roger Rabbit?* to the enjoyably evil Ursula in *The Little Mermaid*. It's a pleasingly basic approach, and one that validates most kids' (and adults') view of the world: 'I am good and anyone who thwarts me is wicked and there is no point in trying to think about things from their point of view because they have no inner life of their own beyond pure evil and a desire to impede me.' *The Princess Bride*, however, does something different.

It's easy to forget this once you've seen the movie and fallen in love with the characters but Inigo and Fezzik are, ostensibly, bad guys. When we first meet them in the movie, they knock our heroine, Buttercup, unconscious and kidnap her for Vizzini. We are also told they will kill her. In the eyes of children, you can't get much more evil than that. They are hired guns in the revenge business, which is not a job for a good guy in any fairy tale. But Goldman flips it around. We quickly see Inigo and, in particular, Fezzik being extremely sweet with each other, doing their little rhymes together and trying to protect one another from Vizzini's ire. Their love for one another shows us there is more to these villains than villainy. Goldman then ups the ante even further by having Inigo describe to the Man in Black how he has devoted his life to avenging the death of his father, thus giving him the kind of emotional backstory kids can definitely understand, as well as adding another mission to the movie. Soon after beating (but not killing) Inigo, the Man in Black fights with Fezzik who we already know has a similarly sad past ('unemployed – IN GREENLAND').

Plenty of villains were once good before crossing to the dark side: Darth Vader, many of Batman's nemeses, Voldemort. The point in those stories is that the difference between true evil and true greatness comes down to one wrong decision, one wrong turn, and there is no going back from that. But *The Princess Bride* does something more subtle: it suggests that good people sometimes end up doing bad things, but are still good, have stories of their own and are capable of love. Inigo and Fezzik both killed people in the past for Vizzini, but they're all still good people. This is quite a message for kids (and adults) to take in: not everything is clear-cut when it comes to good and bad, even in fairy tales.

In the original novel, William Goldman goes into much greater detail about Fezzik and Inigo's friendship, and this is one of the reasons why I – in all honesty – prefer the book to the film.[*1] But the film alludes to it enough in

---

*1 Which is not to say I don't love the movie. I do, completely, love the movie. But I ADORE the book. Other reasons why I prefer the book are that Buttercup is allowed to be much funnier than she is in the film, and William Goldman's authorial interjections in the text are worth the price of the book alone.

order for audiences to understand the real bond between the men, and partly this happens through the script and partly through the actors, especially one actor in particular.

At one point, Arnold Schwarzenegger was considered for the role of Fezzik, but, thank heavens, he was already too expensive by the time the film finally started shooting. Where Schwarzenegger is all jarring rectangles and jutting jaw, André the Giant was all soft circles and goofy smiles. Where Schwarzenegger palpably punished himself to a superhuman extent to get the body he clearly wanted so badly, the man born André René Roussimoff suffered from gigantism due to acromegaly and had no choice about his size, just as Fezzik didn't, much to the latter's misery ('It's not my fault being the biggest and the strongest – I don't even exercise'). It would be a patronising cliché to say André was born to play Fezzik, but he was certainly more right for the role than Schwarzenegger.

By the time he made *The Princess Bride*, André was seven foot four inches and weighed over 540 pounds. Easily the sweetest stories in Cary Elwes's book come from the cast and crew's memories of the wrestler who died in 1993 at the age of forty-six, and this is not mere sentimentality. Quite a few of *The Princess Bride*'s cast have, sadly, since died, including Mel Smith, Peter Cook and Peter Falk, but none of them prompts the same kind of fondness as that felt for André. 'It's safe to say that he was easily the most popular person on the movie,' Elwes writes. 'Everyone just loved him.'

Partly this is due to the extraordinary nature of the man. Robin Wright recalls going out to dinner with him where he ate 'four or five entrees, three or four appetizers, a couple of baskets of bread, and then he's like, I'm ready for seconds. And then desserts. I think he went through a case of wine and he wasn't even tipsy.'

But it was André's innately gentle nature that made him so beloved. His 'compassion and protective nature', Elwes writes, helped Wallace Shawn overcome his almost paralysing fear of heights when they were filming the climb up the Cliffs of Insanity. When Robin Wright felt chilly when filming outdoors, André would place one of his huge hands on top of Wright's head. 'She said it was like having a giant hot water bottle up there. It certainly did the trick; he didn't even mess up her hair that much!' Elwes writes. When he died, William Goldman wrote his obituary in *New York* magazine. The last lines were as follows: 'André once said to Billy Crystal, "We do not live long, the big and the small."

Alas.

Next, on a smaller level, is the love between Miracle Max (Crystal) and his aged wife, Valerie (Carol Kane). Initially they seem simply like a squabbling old couple, playing purely for broad comedy (and their scene is the broadest comedic one in the film). But it soon becomes clear that Valerie is only needling Max because she wants him to get back his confidence in his work after Prince Humperdinck destroyed it by sacking them, and her little cheer when her husband agrees to make a miracle for Inigo is really very touching. By the end of their scene, they're working together, finishing one another's sentences, holding each other arm-in-arm and whispering little asides to one another. As a portrait of elderly marriage goes, this one is a pretty lovely one.

Finally, there's the great love story that frames the whole movie: the one between the grandson/Kevin Arnold (Fred Savage) and the grandfather/Columbo (Peter Falk). In the beginning of the movie, the grandson is irritated by his cheek-pinching grandfather and can hardly believe that he has to stop playing his adorably primitive-looking computer baseball game to listen to grandfather read a book.[1] As the film progresses, the relationship between the grandson and grandfather progresses almost like a traditional love story: the grandson slowly gets more interested, clutching his covers anxiously when Buttercup is almost eaten by the Shrieking Eels; then he gets angry, banging his bed with his fist when it seems like Westley has been killed; and finally, he comes round entirely and tells his grandfather to come back the next day to read the book again.

'As you wish.' His grandfather smiles, and the film ends.

'That wasn't actually in the script,' Elwes says. 'They came up with him saying that on, I think, the last day, and it really captures the love between the grandfather and grandson. You can also see the tenderness between Fred Savage and Peter Falk.'

In Elwes's book, Savage recalls how comfortable Falk made him: 'I don't even remember when we were shooting or when we weren't. He would sit in that chair, and I would be in the bed, and he would talk to me all day . . . He just kind of became my grandfather.'

This relationship feels especially significant because the reason this film exists is because of the bond between particular parents and their children. Rob Reiner first came across the book when it was given to him by his father, the

---

[1] This computer game is the one thing that dates the film. Other than those creaky graphics, the movie looks remarkably timeless – more so, really, than any other film from the eighties. This is partly because there aren't any eighties clothes in the film (other than the grandson's mother's weird mullet hairdo), and partly because instead of having a pop-and-synth soundtrack, Mark Knopfler wrote a simple instrumental piece.

comedian and actor Carl Reiner. Elwes, too, was given the novel when he was thirteen by his stepfather, and his love for the book made him especially determined to get the role. And most of all, the reason the book was written in the first place was because of the love one father felt for his children. Back in 1970, William Goldman decided to write a story for his two daughters, then seven and four years old, to entertain them while he was away in Los Angeles working on a movie: 'I said to them both, "I'll write you a story, what do you want it to be about?" And one of them said "princesses" and the other one said "brides". "Then that will be the title," I told them. And so it has remained.'

Goldman has written a frankly ridiculous number of acclaimed novels (*Marathon Man*), screenplays (*Butch Cassidy and the Sundance Kid*, *All the President's Men*, *Misery*) and memoirs (*Adventures in the Screen Trade*, *Which Lie Did I Tell?*). But his favourite thing he ever wrote, he has said, is *The Princess Bride*. He lovingly turned it into a script in 1973, and then watched it languish for thirteen years, rejected by studio heads who all said the same thing: they loved it, but it was unfilmable. When it was finally picked up by Rob Reiner, Goldman was so anxious that Rob had to reshoot scenes because Goldman, standing behind the camera, was praying that the film would turn out OK and his prayers were picked up by the microphone.

'Please understand that this is a very personal project for me. Normally I don't care much for any of my work. But this one is different. It is my favourite thing I've ever written in my life. So if I appear a little nervous, that's the reason,' Goldman told the cast.

The Princess Bride is funny, and exciting, and scary, and funny, and silly, and sweet, and funny (I might have mentioned that). But the reason it has endured is because it is such a warm film, one without cynicism or calculation, and a film as lovely as this one could only have been born out of love itself – all kinds of love.

And yet, this is also the reason the film was initially deemed something of a damp squib. While not a bomb, the movie was certainly not the commercial success it should have been – and would, eventually, become. But because the film isn't aimed at one particular demographic, exemplified by its multi-layered depiction of love, the studio simply had no idea how to market it, or even who to aim it at. After all, it features a simply fairy-tale love, but also a deeper love about friendship, one about grandparents and grandchildren, and then a pair of squabbling geriatrics: who on earth is it aimed at? The correct answer, of course, is 'everyone', but that is not an answer movie marketing departments understand. For all that I despair of the way movies are marketed and targeted today, it's not like they always got it right in the eighties either. Despite the movie being one of the most exciting films ever made, the studio marketed it with one of the most boring posters of all time, featuring a silhouette of Kevin Arnold listening to Columbo read a book. Not even I especially want to see a movie featuring just that.

'Rob unfurled the poster on the way back from the Toronto Film Festival on the plane and we all gathered around and we thought, Gosh, there's not even a sign of Fezzik! How can anyone know what the movie's about without Fezzik?' recalls Cary Elwes, understandably still bemused. How could any marketing department see a film featuring a real live actual giant, and then leave the giant off the film poster, for heaven's sake?

The theatrical trailer was even worse and was quickly pulled from cinemas, and if you look it up on YouTube you'll see why.

'The movie opened the same weekend as *Fatal Attraction* and nobody went. The cast and crew were all pretty surprised and bummed but Goldman had warned us this might happen,' says Elwes. 'He said, "Look, this is an oddball movie so it's going to be a tough sell. I won't lie to you, I've been through it, for more than a decade."'

'We were in dangerous terrain – because when you mix genres in a movie, that's where you end up,' Goldman writes in his delightful essay on *The Princess Bride*. It wasn't until the movie came out on VHS and audiences were able to discover the film for themselves, without the cack-handed meddlings of the studio, that it became the success it deserved to be.

The lesson that *The Princess Bride* taught the film industry is that it is possible to make a movie for kids and adults alike, and this is one it has remembered well. Modernised fairy-tale films such as *Enchanted* and pretty much the whole output of Pixar all owe an enormous debt to *The Princess Bride*. *Shrek* in particular can be seen as the next generation's take on *The Princess Bride*, with its toying with tropes and tongue-in-cheek humour. But as much as I love *Shrek*, *The Princess Bride* has a simple sweetness that *Shrek* doesn't. *Shrek* is more knowing than *The Princess Bride*, with more winks over the heads of the kids to their parents. Part of the joy of *The Princess Bride* is that kids and adults enjoy it on the same level. It doesn't differentiate between what kids get and what adults enjoy. There is no irony to *The Princess Bride*, no nudging nods to contemporary adult references. For this reason, *The Princess Bride* is a much more clever film than *Shrek*, which is no slur on *Shrek*. After all, *The Princess Bride* is one of the cleverest and most original movies ever made, and this is exemplified in its depiction of love.

There are plenty of reasons why *The Princess Bride* could not be made today: 'It would all be done by CGI, which would make the movie completely different,' says Elwes. 'Also, I seriously doubt that a studio would let a director cast two unknowns, as Robin and I were then, in the leads of such a big movie. They'd want a big box office draw, like Tom Cruise, or whoever.' But the most obvious reason is in its complex layering of different loves about different ages, emphasising how the film really is aimed at everyone.

Modern classic children's movies feature many kinds of love: the love between an elderly couple in *Up*; the love a boy feels for the plastic cowboy he is leaving behind in *Toy Story 3*; the love between a donkey and a dragon in *Shrek*. Ahh, love in its infinite varieties! But I can't think of another children's movie in which there are so many different kinds of love featured, and all aimed fully at the children to understand. *The Princess Bride* teaches children that the love their grandparents feel for them, and what they feel for their grandparents, and the love friends have for one another, is true love, as important as Westley and Buttercup's true love. This is why Kevin Arnold – and Nell – learned not to mind the kissing parts, thanks to *The Princess Bride*.

Decades after Nell shouted about how much she loved *The Princess Bride* in the cinema, I got a job assignment from work. My editor asked me to interview someone who had just written a book, and I eagerly agreed. I don't usually bring family members on job assignments, but in this case I decided to make an exception. I called Nell and told her to meet me at an office block next Monday. As it happened, she had just had her second baby but she instantly agreed. And so, on a cold December morning in north-east London, Nell, accompanied by her three-week-old daughter Edith, met Westley. His hair was a little shorter, and his accent a touch more transatlantic after having spent three decades in the States, but he was definitely Westley.

'Look at this most beautiful girl!' cried Cary Elwes, reaching towards Nell, but stopping a few inches short of her face and reaching down instead to the baby in her arms. 'This is just the most precious thing . . .' and his voice trailed away as he gazed at Edith, utterly rapt.

Nell got her moment of great love with Westley. If it wasn't quite as she'd imagined when she was seven, or seventeen, it was, ultimately, as she wished.

TOP TEN FASHION MOMENTS

**10 Kevin Kline's teeny tiny running shorts, *The Big Chill*
(see also: Tom Selleck in *Three Men and a Baby*)**
Coupled with some fine manly chest hair.

9 Tom Hanks's white tux in *Big*
Deliberately ridiculous, totally iconic.

8 Rob Lowe, *St Elmo's Fire*
Sweaty Rob Lowe wears a yellow vest top with black bats
patterned all over it, while playing the sax. Your life =
complete.

7 Michael J. Fox, *Back to the Future*
A T-shirt, a shirt, double denim and the 'life preserver'.
One of the jokes in this film is how people in the 1950s
don't get 1980s fashion. People in the 1950s were right.

6 Nicolas Cage, *Valley Girl*
Frosted hair, a leather waistcoat and a bare chest is a strong
look, Nicolas.

**5 Absolutely everything Michael Douglas wore in the
decade**
From his patterned blouson shirts undone to his mid-chest
in *Romancing the Stone* and *The Jewel of the Nile*, to his
braces in *Wall Street*, this man was eighties fashion in
human form.

4 The Heathers in *Heathers*
For services to shoulder-padded jackets and coloured tights.

3 Molly Ringwald and Jon Cryer, *Pretty in Pink*

God bless John Hughes and his belief that wearing weird clothes proves one is a sensitive soul. Extra points for Ringwald's hat, golden stars for Cryer's sunglasses.

2 Melanie Griffith and Joan Cusack, *Working Girl*

Where to start? Melanie's mullet and white trainers? Melanie's extraordinary lingerie? Actually, let's just say 'absolutely everything Joan Cusack wears in this film' and leave it at that.

1 *Desperately Seeking Susan*

The movie that proves everyone's life is improved by eighties fashion.

TOP FIVE COMMENTS ABOUT FASHION

5 'This jacket used to belong to Jimi Hendrix.'
'You bought a USED JACKET? What are we, poor?'
(Rosanna Arquette and Mark Blum, *Desperately Seeking Susan*)

4 'Pink is my signature colour.' (Julia Roberts, *Steel Magnolias*)

3 'Does Barry Manilow know you raid his wardrobe?'
(Judd Nelson, *The Breakfast Club*)

2 'This is a really volcanic ensemble you're wearing.' (Jon Cryer, *Pretty in Pink*)

1 'Six thousand dollars?! It's nawt even leatha!' (Joan Cusack, *Working Girl*)

Pretty in Pink:
Awkward Girls Should
Never Have Makeovers

Until Molly Ringwald met John Hughes, she'd always felt wrong.

'I was growing up on the west coast and just so self-conscious about my looks,' she recalls from her home in California, her two children shouting happily in the background. 'Back then I was surrounded by images of Cheryl Tiegs and Farrah Fawcett, and that was the look then – that California blonde look, which was the opposite of what I was.'

But Hughes – unusually, perhaps, for a thirty-something male director – recognised the appeal of the then fifteen-year-old Ringwald's looks from the start, and he saw something in her, something unconventional. As soon as he came across her headshot in his pack of photos while looking for young actresses for his next film, with her snub nose, slightly slack jaw and bright red hair, he stuck it up on his billboard and, without even meeting her, wrote *Sixteen Candles* for her in two days.

Hughes could see the value of Ringwald's unfashionable looks for the same reason he was able to write films about teenagers that felt so true to young people at the time, and still do today: because, at heart, he was still the sensitive teenage outcast he loved to write about. 'John was frozen in time emotionally in a way. He would not have been able to create the sense of truth in those characters had he not been so much like that himself,' says director Howard Deutch, Hughes's frequent collaborator.

This meant he didn't see teen films as an easy means to get sexy girls in bikinis up on the screen, as screenwriters for the hugely successful *Porky's* – which came out in 1982, two years before Hughes's first teen film *Sixteen Candles* – did. Rather, what he loved about teenagers was their complications as opposed to their cleavages.

'When I started to work with John, I realised my differences could work to my advantage because they made me stand out, but in a good way. So my skin got even paler and my hair got redder,' Ringwald says. He wanted his teenage actors to stay totally true to their teenage selves, to the point that they were encouraged to pick out their own clothes for the films. One of the few times Hughes ever chided Ringwald was when she turned up on set wearing eyeshadow: 'He thought I was trying to be someone else.' She smiles.

Hughes, more than any other filmmaker, made the 1980s the golden age of teen films because he realised that the trick to making good films about teenagers was to take them as seriously as they take themselves. 'One of the great wonders about that age is your emotions are so open and raw. That's why I stuck around that genre for so long,' he said in an interview. 'At that age it feels as good to feel bad

as it does to feel good.' It's only as a teenager, Hughes
believed, that you have this capacity for deep feeling, which
explains why his own work was divided between the
swoonily soulful teen films, including *Sixteen Candles*, *The
Breakfast Club*, *Pretty in Pink*, *Ferris Bueller's Day Off* and
Some Kind of Wonderful, and the slapstick 'dopey-ass
comedy,' as he put it, such as *National Lampoon's Vacation*,
The Great Outdoors and, in the nineties, *Home Alone*.'[1]
With the exception of *Weird Science* – which is a dopey-ass
teen comedy and as a result is Hughes's least memorable
teen film – he kept these two sides to his filmmaking separate, even going so far as to fire Rick Moranis from *The
Breakfast Club* as the janitor because he felt, rightly, that
Moranis's humour was too broad for that film, and that's
the only time I'll ever say a word against Moranis. Teen
films were about deep emotions, and deep emotions were
reserved for his teenage characters alone. 'When you grow
up,' one of his characters in *The Breakfast Club* says, 'your
heart dies.'

Even though Hughes wove plenty of autobiographical
details into his films, he was a lot less interested in his own
youth than he was in that of contemporary teenagers. Not
many adults can say that. He would hang out with his
teenage actors on the set, make them mix tapes, take them
to concerts (Hughes genuinely loved music and, unlike a
lot of eighties filmmakers, didn't just see it as merely a
means to sell soundtracks), and he would infuriate his crew
by corpsing along with the kids during embarrassing

---

[1] This is not intended as an all-encompassing diss of Hughes's comedies.
Personally, I would fight to the death for *Planes, Trains and Automobiles*
and fight at least until grievous injury for *Uncle Buck*.

scenes. Hughes's teen films feel so heartfelt because they were written with such honest respect for his teenage actors, and the one with whom he felt the closest affinity was Ringwald: 'We just instantly connected. He felt more like a friend than a director. We talked about everything,' she says. So it is not surprising that the truest character Hughes ever wrote was one he created for her: Andie Walsh from *Pretty in Pink*.

By the time Hughes and Ringwald made *Pretty in Pink*, they knew each other pretty well after having already worked on *Sixteen Candles* and *The Breakfast Club*. Ringwald's character, Sam, in the former is sparky, but the film is pretty unwatchable today due to being weirdly racist[1] and a bit rapey.[2] Hughes then cast Ringwald as popular and posh Claire in *The Breakfast Club*, because it amused him to cast her against type, and he gave the more interesting female character, Allison, to Ally Sheedy. It wasn't until *Pretty in Pink* that he created for Ringwald the role she deserved. 'John always wrote best when he was writing for someone, and his real muse was Molly,' says Howard Deutch, who directed *Pretty in Pink*. 'A lot of who Molly was became the character he wrote for her in *Pretty in Pink*. So Molly inspired John to write that character and the writing of the character also impacted on Molly.'

Like all Hughes's teen films, *Pretty in Pink* has a laughably simple premise: Andie, a high school girl from the wrong side of the tracks (literally, she lives next to the train

---

[1] The Chinese exchange student character, Long Duk Dong, is a caricature so crude he makes the scenes feauturing the Chinese villain in *The Hangover* look like an educational video from the UN.

[2] The awful Caroline and Geek ending, as ranted about in the Introduction.

tracks – no one could ever accuse Hughes of subtlety), wants to go to the prom with a wealthy boy called Blane, to the horror of her lifelong and fellow lower-middle-class friend, Duckie.

'When we were filming I remember thinking, This is about a girl going to a dance? Seriously? Who's going to want to see this? Really had my finger on the pulse there!' laughs Andrew McCarthy, who, thirty years on, has yet to escape the shadow of the film (although we fans of the 1989 comedy *Weekend at Bernie's* also associate him with near necrophilia. But that's a different story).

The Breakfast Club is more original as an eighties teen film in that it pretty much takes place in just one room (truly, this is one eighties film that is begging to be turned into a play) and DOESN'T EVEN HAVE A PROM, whereas *Pretty in Pink* ticks off all the classic clichés: pop song title, scenes in crowded school hallways, big music number, climactic prom. But it is in many ways a more satisfying film, partly because it features some of the best acting ever to appear in any of Hughes's films, especially from James Spader who nearly steals the whole movie, bringing his delicious Spaderish creepiness unlike anything seen in any other teen film ever. Jon Cryer as Andie's heartsick and nerdy friend Duckie is great, too, full of frustration and fury that the girl he always revered turns out to lack the wisdom to fall for him, and who among us has not felt so let down by a love interest? But what really makes the film stand out is the character of Andie.

Before the eighties, young women didn't tend to do too well in teen films. In the fifties they were generally ignored as movies focused instead on the agonised plights of young men (*The Wild Ones*, *Rebel Without a Cause*). In the sixties filmmakers realised that making movies about teenage protagonists made it even easier for them to shoot endless scenes of young women in minimal amounts of clothing without having to bother too much about things such as plot or logic. So young women were ostensibly given leading roles, but star billing really went to their bikinis (the hugely popular Frankie Avalon and Annette Funicello films). By the seventies, teen films were synonymous with horror movies (*Halloween*, *Carrie*) or movies sentimental-ising teenagers from an earlier era (*American Graffiti*, *Grease*), and, blood-soaked prom queens aside, they were utterly devoid of admirable female characters. But then Hughes arrived in the eighties, and suddenly the girls started getting the good roles.

Hughes loved to write about awkward kids, but unlike too many male filmmakers, then and now, he didn't only write about awkward boys: he also grasped the extraordi-nary idea that teenage girls were humans – not sex objects or icy bitch temptresses – and his close friendship with Ringwald doubtless helped him with this. He said that some of Ringwald's roles in his films were 'really a portrait of myself', and the fact that he gave the two best roles he wrote for her male names – Sam and Andie – further suggests his identification with them.

'When I first read John's scripts, I couldn't believe someone could write such amazing parts for young women. There had been movies with strong female protagonists before, but not ones with a strong female teenage protago-nist', recalls Ringwald.

Hughes's teen films are peppered with awkward, trucu-lent, even difficult young female characters: Jeanie, the patron saint of unhappy siblings everywhere, in *Ferris Bueller's Day Off*; Allison, making her dandruff blizzard out of her hair in *The Breakfast Club*; Watts, who proudly wears men's boxers instead of women's underwear in *Some Kind of Wonderful*; Iona, Andie's delightfully mouthy boss in *Pretty in Pink*, played by Annie Potts, aka Janine from *Ghostbusters*. In *The Breakfast Club*, Hughes showed he recognised one of the great plights of being a teenage girl when the two female characters discuss how to answer the question of whether or not you've 'done it': 'It's kind of a double-edged sword, isn't it?' Allison says to Claire. 'If you say you haven't, you're a prude. And if you say you have, you're a slut. It's a trap. You want to but you can't, and when you do, you wish you didn't, right?' It's not only boys, Hughes knew, who struggle with sex. But of all Hughes's great female characters, there is none greater than Andie.

I first saw *Pretty in Pink* when I was nine, and while I did, like every other heterosexual female, promptly develop a lifelong crush on McCarthy, it was Andie with whom I fell in love. She was the first girl I'd ever seen on screen who felt recognisable to me. While I pretended sometimes I was Sloane from *Ferris Bueller*, all pretty and confident and with a boyfriend who picked me up from school in a car, I recognised that the teenager I would be was the awkward girl who drove herself to school. At the time, I lived in a Jewish enclave of Manhattan, meaning my life looked so different from the suburban white bread ones depicted in John Hughes's films that I may as well have grown up in a different country. Yet even if the details of my life looked nothing like Hughes's movies, they nonetheless taught me something important: that I, a weird girl who lived too much inside her own head, whose looks somehow never seemed to coincide with the fashions of that day and wouldn't even kiss a boy until well into her third decade, deserved to be the star of my own movie.

This is not a message girls and young women can take for granted any more. Until the *Twilight* series and *The Hunger Games* came along, studios had assumed for years that young women couldn't front franchises for teenagers. 'Teenage girl [audiences] just weren't even in the equation until *Twilight* came around. When people talked about the teen market, they meant the male teen market,' says film producer Lynda Obst. 'This is because studios look at a movie's takings from the first weekend and teen boys tend to go out in packs on a first weekend, whereas girls didn't. Also, teen boys tended to match the international market, so studios would market to them, because the international market is so much more important these days. It wasn't until *Twilight* that it was the girls who came out in droves.'

But Bella in *Twilight* and Katniss in *The Hunger Games* are, obviously, very different kinds of heroines to Andie. For a start, Bella is as passive and blank and tedious as the most retro of Disney heroines, always requiring the services of males to save her. She puts herself at risk for her creepy, cold and dangerous boyfriend, and this is depicted as romantic. Whereas Andie refuses even to change her hat for Blane, Bella enthusiastically changes entire species in order to stay with her boyfriend, going from human to vampire, which is some makeover.

'Passive' is not a charge one would ever lay at the feet of Katniss Everdeen, one of the most admirable female characters to be seen in a teen film for some decades, albeit one who kills other teenagers. Many reviewers praised Katniss as a rare example of a strong female hero in modern movies, but strength doesn't always have to be demonstrated physically, despite what today's superhero-loving Hollywood might think. Katniss also lives in a completely different world from that of the audience. A film doesn't have to look familiar to inspire teenage audiences – after all, Hughes's high schools looked downright exotic to me – but at least there was a pretence of realism there. Audiences might sympathise with Katniss, and maybe even Bella, but they could empathise with Ringwald and her contemporaries.

But the real difference between Bella and Katniss and Andie is the kind of movies they are in. For a start, they are self-consciously dark films, reflecting a common belief among Hollywood filmmakers today that darkness equals depth and serves as a compensation for throwaway, forgettable scripts. It's easy to make a movie feel dramatic when the stakes are as high as the characters' lives, as they are in *Twilight* and *The Hunger Games*. It is trickier in a film that features comedy and focuses on people's real lives.

John Hughes understood that while American teenagers in the eighties didn't have the problems their parents had endured in their youth – Vietnam, namely – their daily anxieties felt no less pressing. He knew that one doesn't need to soup up the daily minutiae of a teenager's life in a film in order to make it feel important to teenagers. This lesson was already forgotten by the nineties when the biggest teen films winkingly used plots from classical texts, such as Jane Austen's *Emma* (*Clueless*), *The Taming of the Shrew* (*10 Things I Hate About You*) and *Les Liaisons Dangereuses* (*Cruel Intentions*), simultaneously to mock the teen film genre and give it ironic credibility, as opposed to relying on the films to stand up for themselves (and thinking up their own plots, although, for the record, I do love *Clueless* and *10 Things I Hate About You*). These films didn't believe that the mundane details of the average teenager's life were interesting or important enough to make a film about, as eighties teen films definitely did, and Hughes especially did.

This reduced interest in female audiences has led to the rise of that dreaded stock (read: lazy) female film character whose presence has become such a given in certain types of films aimed at young people that she was eventually given a name. The Manic Pixie Dream Girl is a 'bubbly, shallow cinematic creature that exists solely in the fevered imaginations of sensitive writer-directors to teach broodingly soulful young men to embrace life and its infinite mysteries and adventures', as journalist Nathan Rabin, who coined the term, put it. Many successful teen films very much feature the trope, such as 2009's *(500) Days of Summer* and 2012's *The Perks of Being a Wallflower* in which, respectively, Zooey Deschanel and Emma Watson play attractively damaged pixies whose eyeliner and spontaneity rejuvenate their male leads while they themselves apparently have no inner lives (the vast majority of films featuring Manic Pixie Dream Girls, including these two, are written and directed by men). Most of all, they are not the star of their movie.

Stories serve as guides about how to live and what to expect from life, and if you're a girl who grows up believing that the most you can expect is to be a supporting character to a man, that's all you'll ever ask for. Rabin has since disowned the term, claiming, correctly, that misappropriation of the name has become as much of a cliché as the trope itself and the misappropriation tips into precisely the kind of sexism the term is supposed to satirise. But as Ben

Beaumont-Thomas wrote in the *Guardian*: 'Rabin is rightly uncomfortable in thinking about women in terms of stock subgroups, and yet this is exactly how a male-dominated film industry thinks about them – and after a trickle-down process, how ordinary men will end up thinking about them. By lampooning it in a tangy phrase like MPDG, a trope which has creeped along suddenly gets the light shined on it, and its ridiculousness becomes so well articulated that it's difficult to get away with it again.'

Andie is pretty much the opposite of a Manic Pixie Dream Girl. She exists totally in her own right. She is confident and insecure, wise and foolish, happy and furious, mature and childish, lustful and fearful, savvy but gauche. She is, in short, a teenager, and often unsure if she's worth what she wants. But as much as she doubts herself, she always stands up for herself: she screams in disarmingly unabashed rage at Blane when he lets her down, and she snaps back when Steff bullies her. I always liked that Hughes took the trouble to slip in the reason for Steff's hatred of Andie, and it has nothing to do with her being poor, or a nerd, or different – it's because she knocked him back. In other words, it's not about her, it's about him, and as messages to young female audiences go, telling them that misogyny often stems from male insecurity is a pretty good one. Most of all, Andie learns never to change herself for anyone.

When we first meet Andie in *Pretty in Pink*, there's a very big part of her that does want to be part of the popular and moneyed set, as much as she hates them. She drives down a street in the wealthy part of town and looks, longingly, at the big houses, much to Duckie's bemusement. There's no question that part of Blane's appeal to her is that he represents entry into that world, which is precisely why she's so conscious of him being from a different social class from her, despite her father reassuring her that it doesn't matter. It's only when she and Blane start dating that she realises how much she values herself, and she refuses to change an iota for him.

All the men have to change in the movie: Blane, Andie's dad, Duckie, even Steff. The one person who doesn't change is Andie, and she still gets her dream boy – although that wasn't quite what Hughes intended, because in the original ending of the film Andie ends up with Duckie.

When he wrote the script, Hughes pictured Blane as fratty and obnoxious, and Charlie Sheen – unsurprisingly – was seriously considered for the role. Another Jake from *Sixteen Candles*, in other words, but with Ringwald getting together with The Geek in this film. Instead, he and Howard Deutch decided to cast the more sweetly soulful McCarthy, thereby making Blane seem more like a plausible boyfriend for Andie, despite his wealth.[1]

As any straight woman could have told them beforehand, McCarthy was so damn cute – his delicate looks so perfect for the beautiful but weak Blane – that there was no way female audiences were going to accept any ending other than one in which Andie gets together with him. But Hughes and Deutch, not being straight women, were

---

[1] The criminally underrated 1986 teen film *Lucas* later cast Sheen as the unexpectedly sensitive popular boy and, despite Sheen's under-appreciated acting skills, and despite my deep love for this film, the truth is, he's not exactly plausible in the role. Every time he stands up for a nerd in the movie, I half expect him to turn around and give him a wedgie.

'completely shocked' when test audiences affirmed this after seeing the film with the original ending: 'The teenage girls were very clear about this: they wanted Andie to get what she wanted and to get with the cute boy, forget the frog, and I resented that,' recalls Deutch. Speaking as a former teenage girl, teenage audiences would probably have found Robert Downey Jr – who they initially considered for the role of Duckie instead of Jon Cryer – to be a more acceptable consolation prize than Cryer, but that was no longer an option, and so, reluctantly, Hughes rewrote the ending.

Thus, the film now ends with Blane turning up at the prom and informing Andie that the reason he stopped calling her is because, while he believed in her, 'I didn't believe in me.' Duckie tells Andie to go with Blane, and he heads off into the sunset with Kristy Swanson, the original Buffy the Vampire Slayer (try to keep up). Andie and Blane then kiss happily ever after.

Hughes and Deutch absolutely hated this revised ending: 'The movie became something else. Something that was not what the movie was supposed to be. It felt immoral,' says Deutch. My only real problem with the revised ending is that McCarthy had to wear a wig during the re-shoot as he had since shaved off all his hair for a new movie and the obviously synthetic nature of this tonsorial monstrosity is a downright insult to his youthful, beautiful bouffant. But in all honesty, I don't mind that Andie ends up with Blane. After all, why shouldn't the awkward girl get the beautiful boy if that's who she lusts for? (And boy, does Andie lust for him – she practically eats him when they kiss.) Also, as Hughes shows through the storyline of Andie's heartbroken and abandoned father, women should not get together with nice men if they don't actually love them. That is a too little noted but important message.[1]

But I think what I love most about this final scene, revised or otherwise, is what Andie's wearing which is – by anyone's measurement – the ugliest prom dress of all time, which she made for herself. 'Oh my God, that dress!' groans Ringwald. 'That is one thing in the film I won't take responsibility for. I remember thinking at the time that it was really funny because Andie wants to be a fashion designer, and she makes that dress. Pick a new career, Andie!' But in defence of this dress, it does encapsulate one of the truly great things about girls in eighties teen movies: they dress like shit.

When girls in eighties movies go on dates, they dress as demurely as the Amish: in *Valley Girl*, Julie's (Deborah Foreman) party outfit is a high-necked Victorian blouse and a pair of slacks; in *Lucas*, Maggie (Kerri Green) woos Cappie (Charlie Sheen) away from sexy cheer-leading captain Alise (Ally McBeal's future nemesis Courtney Thorne-Smith) while wearing full-length skirts and shapeless jumpers; Chris (Elisabeth Shue) in *Adventures in Babysitting* attracts the attention of a college boy – a college boy! – while wearing her dead grandfather's coat; Boof (Susan Ursitti) in *Teen Wolf* dresses like a middle-aged suburban mother and she gets her dream boy; Watts (Mary Stuart Masterson) wears boys' clothes and still gets Eric Stoltz at the end of *Some*

---

[1] 1987's *Broadcast News* is also very smart about this, with Holly Hunter's character, Jane, falling for the shallow handsome newsreader (William Hurt) instead of the schlubby and nice producer (Albert Brooks), and that's just the way it is.

Kind of Wonderful; in *St Elmo's Fire* – strictly speaking, a twenty-something movie as opposed to a teen movie, but a Brat Pack movie so, scientifically, it still counts – Leslie (Ally Sheedy) is every man's sexual fantasy despite dressing like a Quaker and sporting an amazing pudding-bowl haircut, while Wendy (Mare Winningham) pulls Rob freaking Lowe despite wearing her great-grandmother's wardrobe, right down to the underwear; Molly Ringwald's wardrobe in all her teen movies is a testament to the power of one's imagination if one apparently does not possess a full-length mirror.

These outfits are not actually a reflection of eighties fashion – in fact, it's usually the mean popular girls who wear the typically eighties clothes, from rah-rah skirts to cropped tops. Chris, let alone Watts, would never wear a puffball skirt. Instead, they reflect a female attitude that has been absent from teen films since the early nineties: dressing for oneself as opposed to dressing to look sexually available. Unlike teens in post-eighties movies, even good post-eighties teen movies, girls in eighties teen films don't dress to show off their 'big boobs' (*Easy A*) or 'to show a little skin – this reminds boys of being naked, and then they think of sex' (*Clueless*) – they dress entirely for their own pleasure, even their own comfort.

By contrast, in 1999's *She's All That*, Laney (Rachel Leigh Cook) has to take off her glasses (obviously) and show off her breasts (OBVIOUSLY) in order to go from school joke to potential girlfriend for the popular boy, Zack (Freddie Prinze Jr). Zack's sister even comes over before their date to pluck Laney's eyebrows, thereby ensuring that the date would be credible in the eyes of others, and the film blatantly approves of this, with the sister making 'hilarious' comparisons between Laney and Bert from *Sesame Street*. Natural body hair on women: GROSS-A-RAMA. And this brings us to a central teen movie issue: the makeover.

Eighties teen movies aren't averse to the occasional pointless makeover. One of the most misguided cinematic makeovers of all time takes place in *The Breakfast Club* when Allison (Sheedy) wins the glorious prize of Emilio Estevez's attention – but only after she swaps her fabulous eyeliner for pink blusher and a quite lame alice band. And I like alice bands. (This makeover is why Allison, in the pantheon of great Hughes female characters, is something of a disappointment. Sheedy herself was unsure about her makeover: 'I didn't want it to be a makeover scene, as if somebody painted a face on Allison and suddenly she became acceptable. But I thought if she wore this heavy black eyeliner, then it would be like wiping off the mask to reveal the person underneath. I could have done without the bow in the hair, but it was a compromise.' [1]) Looking further back, one of the most famous movie makeovers took place in a 1970s teen movie when Sandie in *Grease* swaps her lovely 1950s bobby soxer clothes for the wardrobe of roller derby groupie and wins back her boyfriend in the process (fistpump! Go women!).

Some of the most popular makeovers in movies, from

---

[1] 'How could that have been allowed to happen?' wailed the badass actress Ellen Page in an interview with *New York* magazine when discussing *The Breakfast Club*. Films like that, Page tells the magazine, make tomboys like her 'start judging ourselves, just because, you know, we'd rather climb trees than give blow jobs'.

1958's *Gigi* to 1990's *Pretty Woman*, have involved courtesans and prostitutes, emphasising that cinematic makeovers are invariably about making the female characters look more sexually available. But it wasn't until the nineties that they became such a staple of teen movies that the stereotype was later satirised in 2001's *Not Another Teen Movie* in which nerdy Janey (Chyler Leigh) is rendered slo-mo sexy simply by taking off her glasses and loosening her ponytail. In 1995's *Clueless*, Cher (Alicia Silverstone) makes Tai (Brittany Murphy) Beverly Hills-ready by reapplying her make-up and swapping her loose trousers for tiny miniskirts. In 1999's *Never Been Kissed*, Josie (the always lovely Drew Barrymore) is rescued from (undercover) high school hell thanks to some fashion and social help from her cooler brother Rob (David Arquette). Kat (Julia Stiles), the feminist protagonist in 1999's *10 Things I Hate About You*, endures a makeover from her little sister before the prom because everyone knows feminists are just too ugly to be seen at social occasions unless heavily overhauled.

What a makeover means for women in a movie is: 'Conform and show off your boobs', and all the examples cited above say just that. Change for men, in other words. By contrast, in the vast majority of eighties teen films, girls are celebrated for being their own gauche, unique selves, and this is a common theme in almost all eighties teen movies for all teenagers, from *Teen Wolf* to *Say Anything*. This celebration of the unique explains, I suspect, why so many kids in eighties teen films have such weird names (Boof and Styles in *Teen Wolf*), and especially in Hughes's teen films (Ferris, Bender, Sloane, Duckie, Blane, Watts). With the exception of the makeover scene in *The Breakfast Club*, Hughes celebrates his leading ladies' quirks, and

Andie's vintage clothes – which she wears because she can't afford new ones – are depicted as proof of her admirable creativity. If she does then wear the ugliest prom dress of all time, that's a price worth paying for individuality. *Pretty in Pink* is the anti-makeover movie.

Andie stays so true to her style, no matter how much she likes a boy, that Blane doesn't even realise she's dressed for their date when he picks her up from the record store and he suggests that she should go home and change (in true Andie style, she refuses). Laney Boggs in *She's All That*, by contrast, gets so overhauled before her date that her paramour doesn't even recognise her – and he likes her more for it. Nineties teen makeover scenes are all about stamping out a teenage girl's awkwardness and unique personality whereas the girls in eighties teen movies celebrate those two qualities. Even Diane Court in *Say Anything*, the girl with 'the body of a gameshow host', dresses undeniably, unapologetically and gloriously badly, with her frumpy skirt suits that she wears to house parties. And it was the very weirdness of these eighties girls, the Andies and the Dianes, that attracted the boys to them. They didn't even have to get out the tweezers.

Celestia Fox, a casting agent who discovered and worked with some of the most successful British and American teen actors in the eighties, says the reason teen films and teen characters are so much glossier today than they were thirty years ago can be summed up in one word: '*Clueless*. That changed everything. And, to a certain extent, *Beverly Hills 90210* did, too. These shows completely altered the look of American films and TV shows aimed at teenagers. Not so much in Britain – British film has always been and is still mainly period pieces and gritty films. But in

America, everything made after *Clueless* immediately became much more aspirational and glamorous, and it still is.'

'*Clueless* was never meant to be a teen film exactly – it was a comedy of manners,' says the film's director, Amy Heckerling, who also directed the 1980s teen film *Fast Times at Ridgemont High*. 'I saw it as a satire, almost, whereas *Fast Times* was about how teenagers actually lived.' But what was once satire soon set the standard, and not just in terms of how teenage actresses dressed.

Actresses in teen films and teen TV shows have also become progressively thinner over the past few decades, especially in the past decade. A comparison between the original cast of the TV show *Beverly Hills 90210* (1990–2000) and the cast of the revived series *90210* (2008–2013) is so jarring it's eye-watering: the actresses on the recent series look – and this is barely an exaggeration – half the size of those on the old show, and, shockingly, the original cast look almost chubby in comparison when they were seen at the time as very slim. Even the young actresses on the Disney Channel (aimed at nine- to fourteen-year-olds) are getting thinner as a brief comparison between Hilary Duff (a star on the channel in 2000) and Bella Thorne (2010) proves. Not only are teenage girls seeing fewer representations of their lives onscreen, they're seeing fewer actresses who even vaguely resemble them.

Again, some of this can be traced back to *Clueless*, with its deliberate gloss and glamour. But the actresses in that film look almost chunky compared to the ones in films today. (The one *Clueless* actress who continued to work in popular movies after that film, the late Brittany Murphy, became, notoriously, much skinnier in her later films, thus

fitting in with the new and increasingly limited aesthetic.)
But really, this change has largely come from the fashion
world. Films, especially films aimed at young women and
teenage girls, have always taken their cues from fashion
trends and there is no question that the fashion industry
venerates a much skinnier look now than it did in the
eighties, as the most skirting comparison between eighties
supermodels and today's jarringly attenuated models
proves. Fashion editors invariably say that models today
look 'much healthier' these days than they have of late, and
this is true, but only if one thinks that looking better than
the pale and miserable-looking eastern European models
popular at the beginning of this century – let alone the
half-starved teenage Kate Moss of the nineties – is a
triumph for health in itself as opposed to a decidedly
minor and relative improvement.

'When I started in this business thirty years ago, teenage
actresses were always about a size 6 [10 in the UK], maybe
a 4 [UK 8]; now they're always a size 0, or even a 00,' one
fashion stylist who works for teen magazines told me. A
costume designer who has worked on one of the biggest
teen films of this century adds, 'When I get clothes for
these girls, I often have to shop in the children's section,
even though they're sixteen. Teen actresses are not expected
to look like teenagers any more – they're expected to look
like models, and this is because female celebrities have sort
of taken the place of models. Just look at the covers of
fashion magazines today and who do you see? Actresses
and celebrities.' When asked if Ringwald would get work
today as the romantic lead in a teen film, the costume
designer rolled her eyes.

Ringwald is one of the most successful teen actresses of

all time, but her influence proved a lot shorter-lived than her fame. If *Pretty in Pink* were made today, the film would be told from Blane's point of view and Andie would be relegated to being a Manic Pixie Dream Girl, about two stone lighter with heavy eyeliner and blow-dried hair (see: *Along Came Polly*. Or, rather, don't). Ringwald says:

> I feel like the films and TV shows today for teenagers are all about wanting to be famous and rich, and the girls are so skinny and sexualised in them, I just don't have the stomach for them. The kind of roles I played in teen films just don't seem to exist any more. My elder daughter is almost ten and I wanted to show her something that would make her feel better so I was thinking and thinking and I thought, Oh my God! I made it! So we sat down together and watched *Pretty in Pink*. It was wonderful to watch it now but it also feels really sad that the only movie that hit the spot was made thirty years ago. But ever since my daughter watched *Pretty in Pink*, she doesn't want to watch those other shows any more. She knows there's something else out there.

Plenty of awesome and weird heroines appeared in eighties teen films after *Pretty in Pink*. There's self-righteous and fearless watermelon carrier Baby in *Dirty Dancing*, which was released the following year; dorky and courageous Thor-obsessed Sara in *Adventures in Babysitting*; and most of all, Veronica in *Heathers*, the film that didn't just make female aggression scary, *Carrie*-style, but also triumphant, and really, really cool. By the end of the decade, audiences had become so used to teenage girls getting the good parts that Cameron Crowe was able to make one of the most sophisticated and feminist teen films of them all, *Say Anything*, in which the teenage boy, Lloyd (John Cusack), says specifically all he wants to do with his life is to support his brilliant girlfriend so she can shine. 'This is a very different kind of knight and white horse. It's not, "I'll take you away", it's "I'll enable you to be you." If you're a terrific girl and you're brilliant, that's what you'd hope for,' said *Say Anything*'s executive producer, James L. Brooks.

Thanks at least partly to Hughes, young actresses enjoyed lead roles in teen movies for a brief period in the nineties, such as Julia Stiles as the fuming feminist in *10 Things I Hate About You* and Alicia Silverstone in *Clueless*, as well as a brief flurry of independent films about tough girl heroines, such as 1996's *Girls Town*, 1998's *The Opposite of Sex* and 2000's *Girlfight* and *Bring it On*. But the return of raunchy comedies and superhero films pushed them to the back again. There have been occasional teen films starring young women in the twenty-first century, such as, most obviously, 2004's *Mean Girls*, but these are the exceptions. From a Hollywood studio's point of view, it makes more sense to have a male lead in the belief that they're more likely to attract a wider audience. (The closest raunchy nineties teen movies came to creating an Andie-like character is Michelle in *American Pie*, Alyson Hannigan, the goofy flute player who is always utterly herself, even when consumed with lust. But she is played in the movie for laughs, and is really just a side character to the male lead.)

But Ringwald herself would never get to play another great Hughesian heroine because by the time *Pretty in Pink* came out, she and Hughes were barely talking. During the making of *Pretty in Pink*, Hughes told Deutch to ask

Ringwald if she would appear in their next film, *Some Kind of Wonderful*, which Deutch also directed, as Watts, another awkward girl. But Ringwald felt it was time to grow up. She knew the film was just too similar to ones she'd done before, as *Some Kind of Wonderful* is really just a gender-reversed *Pretty in Pink*, with the original ending reinstated. (Deutch insists that Hughes didn't write it as a reaction to having had to rewrite *Pretty in Pink* and somewhat improbably suggests that Hughes didn't see a connection between the two films.) So she turned it down, and Hughes stopped speaking to her and, after *Some Kind of Wonderful*, he never made another teen film. It turned out there was a downside to working with a director so in touch with his inner teenager: sometimes he really acted like a teenager.

'John could be very sullen – if his feelings were hurt, he'd shut down and not speak to you for days,' says Matthew Broderick, the star of *Ferris Bueller's Day Off*.

Ringwald later wrote in the *New York Times*: 'We were like the Darling children when they made the decision to leave Neverland. And John was Peter Pan, warning us that if we left we could never come back. And, true to his word, not only were we unable to return, but he went one step further. He did away with Neverland itself.'

'There was a tremendous sense of loss for him when she moved on, as I think there was for her, too. They were very, very close and it was really sad to see that end,' says Deutch.

Hughes died in 2009, at the ridiculously premature age of fifty-nine, of a heart attack: 'When you grow up, your heart dies.'

Reporting his death, newspaper coverage barely mentioned *Home Alone*, which was his most financially successful film by a hefty mile. Instead, the media focused on his teen films, especially those he made with Ringwald. In the *New York Times*, chief film critic A.O. Scott wrote: 'Molly Ringwald was for Mr Hughes what Jimmy Stewart was for Frank Capra: an emblem, a muse, a poster child and an alter-ego.'

But Hughes and Ringwald never spoke again, and she instead pursued an acting career without him. There was no final tearful make-up scene between her and her former mentor, no Hughesian climactic final scene. But that's the thing about awkward girls: they might get their happy endings, but they don't always follow the script.

TOP FIVE BRITISH BAD GUYS

5 Charles Dance, *The Golden Child*
Charles Dance, phoning it in and all the funnier for it.

4 David Bowie, *Labyrinth*
One of the weirdest villains of the eighties and one of the weirdest songs, too. I expect nothing less, David Bowie.

3 Steven Berkoff, *Beverly Hills Cop*
It's the law for Berkoff to appear in any list of top villains: Shakespearean, James Bond, you name it. He clocked up a few in the eighties, including in *Rambo First Blood Part II*. But obviously this one's my favourite.

2 Terence Stamp, *Superman 2*
'KNEEL BEFORE ZOD.' For his facial hair alone, Stamp comes zooming in at number two.

1 Alan Rickman, *Die Hard*
No competition. Unbelievably, this was Rickman's first film role, and with his debut, he became the uber-Brit villain (albeit playing a German). Unbettered by anyone until Rickman played the Sheriff of Nottingham in 1991's *Robin Hood Prince of Thieves*.

When Harry Met Sally:
Romcoms Don't Have to Make You
Feel Like You're Having a Lobotomy

Come closer, children, come closer, and sit by your old granny's knee. I'm a-gonna tell you a tale from times of yore, of what life was like back in the olden days. Oh, it was all very different back then, I can tell you! Back then, we didn't have things like mobile telephones – good gracious, no! If you wanted to walk around with a phone that had a photo of you and your friends on the front, you'd have had to cut a handset off the wall and tape a Polaroid on to the back of it. What's that you ask? 'What's a handset on a wall? What's a Polaroid?' Oh dear, I'm using old world language. Let's try again. So as I was saying, back when your granny was a young child, we didn't have mobile phones, we didn't have the internet and, perhaps most shockingly of all, romcoms weren't synonymous with mind-numbing retrograde crap that made you think all women were insane and all men horrible human beings. I know! It's like hearing about a time when people didn't have indoor plumbing, isn't it?

Those of us who were born before 1995 know that

romcoms didn't used to be terrible, but we know this in the way that we know we used to love Michael Jackson and Bill Cosby in a manner wholly uncomplicated by their personal lives. We accept that time did exist, even if it does feel impossible today. The low status of the romcom today makes me very sad because it is so wrong. What's more fun to watch than romance and comedy, for heaven's sake? The answer is 'ANYTHING' if by 'romance and comedy' we now mean 'misogynistic bullshit starring Katherine Heigl and Gerard Butler', as apparently we now do, judging by 2009's *The Ugly Truth*. And the result is, romcoms have been declared dead.

'RIP Romantic Comedies: Why Harry Couldn't Meet Sally in 2013,' blared the *Hollywood Reporter*. 'Why Are Romantic Comedies So Bad?' mused the *Atlantic*. 'Death of the Romcom,' read a graph on Box Office Mojo, showing how the romcom has tanked while movies about super-heroes have soared.

Do we really want to live in a world in which *Captain America* is considered to be more universal than romance and comedy, for heaven's sake? Nobody, goes the theory, wants to see romcoms any more, because they are terrible. The end. But the truth is, the only reason romcoms are terrible these days is because Hollywood stopped giving a shit about women. Fin.

Romcoms were once amazing. In fact, the romcom genre encompasses some of the finest – and most feminist – films ever made, from *The Philadelphia Story* in 1940 to *Annie Hall* thirty-seven years later. There were so many great romcoms in the 1980s that I feel like there should be a collective noun for them: a delight of romcoms, a swoon of romcoms. And they weren't just good – they were critically respected: romcoms such as *Moonstruck* and *Working Girl* won Golden Globes and Oscars. Sure, the Oscars are stupid and ultimately meaningless, but the only romcom of the past fifteen years that has been comparatively lauded was 2012's *Bridesmaids*, which – uniquely for today – was written by and starred women. Which brings me to the next point.

What marks eighties romcoms out is that so many of the best ones starred women. Whereas Woody Allen made himself the protagonist of his great seventies romcoms, such as the wonderful *Annie Hall* and the now pretty much unwatchable *Manhattan*, in the eighties he made his then-partner Mia Farrow the focus, and his movies became sweeter, more varied and more interesting for it. She is very much the star in films such as *The Purple Rose of Cairo* and *Hannah and Her Sisters*. Cher was forty-one when she starred in *Moonstruck* and Nicolas Cage, her romantic opposite, was twenty-three, and no one in the film ever comments on this (fairly obvious) disparity.[*1] *Working Girl* transplanted the romcom to zeitgeisty eighties Wall Street, with a vague (very, very vague) feminist spin, and has three fabulous actresses at its core: Melanie Griffith, Sigourney Weaver and Joan Cusack. Kathleen Turner proved that women can front romantic action films when she co-starred with Michael Douglas in the sweetly screwball *Romancing the Stone* and *The Jewel of the Nile*.

'I was the first! The first female lead of an action movie.

[*1] Possibly because everyone was too distracted by Cher and Cage's awesomely hammy acting and even more awesomely hammy lines, e.g.: 'I ain't no monument to justice!' 'A WOLF WITHOUT A FOOT!' Seriously, go watch this movie, it's just the business.

I knocked up a lot of firsts,' hoots Turner. 'But I don't remember that being discussed at the time – certainly no one expressed to me that they had any concerns. You know, I'm a strong woman and I was a terrific athlete so the only thing that they were worried about was they had to stop me from doing my stunts: "No Kathleen, you can't swing across the gorge on a vine, insurance doesn't cover that." Ah, come on!"[1]

All these films attracted not just female audiences but (gasp! Shock! Amazement!) men, too. *The Princess Bride* proved that romcoms didn't just have cross-gender appeal, they had a cross-generation one, as well, because only people without souls don't enjoy romance and comedy and men, women and children alike all generally have souls.

The wonderful *Tootsie* showed that you could have a romcom that looked at love from both gender sides simultaneously. When aspiring actor Michael Dorsey (Dustin Hoffman) dresses up as a woman and redubs himself Dorothy Michaels, in order to get a role on a soap opera, this former selfish asshole finds himself helping to empower the women on the show against the sexist director (Dabney Coleman, everyone's favourite sexist in the eighties). So far, so early eighties comedy. But Hoffman plays the part much more tenderly than audiences have come to expect from movies featuring actors cross-dressing. In an emotional interview with the American Film Institute in 2012, a tearful Hoffman described how shocked he was when he first saw himself made up as a woman because he wasn't beautiful. He then went home and cried and said to his

---

[1] Can we please have a moment of respectful silence for the hot tamale of awesomeness that is Kathleen Turner?

wife that he had to make this movie. When she asked why, he replied: 'Because I think I am an interesting woman when I look at myself onscreen. And I know that if I met myself at a party, I would never talk to that character. Because she doesn't fulfil physically the demands that we're brought up to think women have to have in order to ask them out. There's too many interesting women I have . . . not had the experience to know in this life because I have been brainwashed.'

To the film's credit, it does show various men in the movie learning to appreciate Dorothy, despite not being conventionally attractive, including her co-star John (played by George Gaynes, better known to eighties movie fans as dippy Commandant Lassard from the *Police Academy* films), the father of a friend and even, to a certain extent, Coleman. You can tell that Hoffman truly did respect both the character and the film because he managed to make a whole film about a man cross-dressing without once coming across as even slightly transphobic – a downright marvel, considering the film was made thirty-five years ago, and this is why it feels as timeless as the similarly transphobia-free *Some Like it Hot*. Nothing dates a film quicker than bigotry (that, and giving a cameo role to Paris Hilton). At most, the movie has a small plotline about his co-star Julie thinking that Dorothy's a lesbian, but even this is done rather sweetly: when Michael-as-Dorothy tries to kiss her, Julie reels away in shock but, instead of being shocked or even horrified, she burbles apologetically, 'I'm sure I've got the same impulses. Obviously I did . . .'

But the movie flakes out when it ends with Michael getting together with Julie, played by the astonishingly beautiful Jessica Lange, whereas it would have been much more interesting if Michael himself had learned to see the appeal in women who don't necessarily look like goddesses – such as, for example, his best friend Sandy who likes him, played by Teri Garr, but who he dumps. Still, at least the point of the film is that women shouldn't date assholes, and if it take Michael dressing as a woman to become the non-asshole that Julie deserves, fair play to them all. And at least Hoffman himself took something away from the movie (even if all I took away from it was that even five-foot-five-inch schmucks with big Jewish noses only want gorgeous blonde shiksas). (Incidentally, I really do love this movie.)

Then, in the final year of that decade, the greatest of all eighties romcoms was released which looked at love from the men's and women's points of view in a far more credible, funny and moving way than *Tootsie*: *When Harry Met Sally* . . .

Along with *Ferris Bueller's Day Off*, *When Harry Met Sally* . . . is the most quotable film of the 1980s, the most quotable of all the decades. Nora Ephron wrote so many great lines in it that the self-restraint needed not to type them all out in one giant quote binge is actually giving me finger cramp.

'Thin. Pretty. Big tits. Your basic nightmare' – No! Stop it!

'Someone is staring at you in personal growth' – Stop! You promised you wouldn't do this!

'You know, I'm so glad I never got involved with you. I just would have ended up being some woman you had to get up out of bed and leave at three in the morning and go clean your andirons, and you don't even have a fireplace – not that I would know this.'

Ah well. It takes a stronger woman than me to resist the pithy power of the Ephron.

But as funny and wise as *When Harry Met Sally . . .* is – and it is so funny and wise, and we'll return to this – the funniest thing about it is that it was dismissed by the critics when it was released. The *New York Times* described it as 'the sitcom version of a Woody Allen film' (critics can be real idiots) and it was only nominated for one Academy Award, Best Original Screenplay – and it lost that to *Dead Poets Society.*[1] *Dead Poets Society*! Well, I did tell you the Oscars were stupid.

I get the surface comparisons with Allen – the white on black opening credits, the adoring shots of New York City, the privileged uptown world, the hat-wearing women – but *When Harry Met Sally . . .* is nothing like a Woody Allen movie, even though plenty of critics still beg to differ on that point (writer Mark Harris memorably described it as 'not *Annie Hall* but a movie about people who have seen *Annie Hall*').

Like the best of Ephron's writing – her journalism, *Heartburn*, her essays – *When Harry Met Sally . . .* has the precision of a personal story but is actually interested in drawing out universal truths. Allen, by contrast, is only ever interested in his stories and would never dream of suggesting that they somehow say something about anybody but him, and sometimes that's great and sometimes it's less so. When people talk today about the message of *When Harry Met Sally . . .*, they think of Harry's claim

---

[1] Other screenplays that lost that year to *Dead* freaking *Poets Society*: *Do the Right Thing*, *Crimes and Misdemeanours* and *Sex, Lies and Videotape*. The Oscars were completely hilarious that year.

that 'men and women can't be friends', and how the movie seems to confirm that. But Ephron said she didn't believe that at all. Instead, she wrote:

> What *When Harry Met Sally . . .* is really about is how different men and women are. The truth is that men don't want to be friends with women. Men know they don't understand women, and they don't much care. They want women as lovers, as wives, as mothers, but they're not really interested in them as friends. They have friends. Men are their friends. And they talk to their male friends about sport, and I have no idea what else. Women, on the other hand, are dying to be friends with men. Women know they don't under-stand men, and it bothers them: they think that if only they could be friends with them, they would understand them and, what's more (and this is their gravest mistake), it would help.

Gender generalisations are, as a generalisation, abhorrent, but it takes a truly po-faced pedant not to delight in this one. Imagine a romcom today being built on this kind of subtle wisdom. And as abhorrent as gender generalisations are, I think only a man could ever claim that *When Harry Met Sally . . .* feels like an Allen movie. Sally and her female friends are so different from the kinds of women you find in Allen's movies they may as well be aliens, because the women in *When Harry Met Sally . . .* were written by someone who didn't just like women, but under-stood them.

Unusually for a romcom – or any movie, for that matter – *When Harry Met Sally . . .* is equally interested in the women in the film as it is in the men, and the reason for this is Ephron was writing about real people. Harry was based on Rob Reiner, the film's director, and Sally was based on Ephron herself: 'I realized that I had found a wonderful character in Rob Reiner. Rob is a very strange person. He is extremely funny, but he is also extremely depressed . . . but he wasn't at all depressed about being depressed; in fact, he loved his depression,' Ephron wrote. 'And because Harry was bleak and depressed, it followed absolutely that Sally would be cheerful and chirpy and relentlessly, pointlessly, unrealistically, idiotically optimistic. Which is, it turns out, very much like me.'

Incidentally, the best female character Allen ever wrote was also based on a real person – Annie Hall, which was a straight-up homage to his ex-girlfriend Diane Keaton (real name: Diane Hall). Anyone who thinks that an author is cheating if they use real life in their fiction is a fool. Real life is often what gives fiction its truth, and good fiction in turn helps us understand real life. Ephron knew better than anyone that real life is the stuff great fiction is made of: 'Everything is copy,' was her mother's mantra and this attitude turned her into a legend when she turned her brutal divorce from Carl Bernstein into one of the funniest novels ever written, *Heartburn*. So it seems like the best way to honour her memory would be to write a little bit about the personal relationship I have to this movie.

I first saw *When Harry Met Sally* . . . when I was a teenager, almost a decade after it came out. I must have watched it in London, where we moved to from New York in 1989, in our living room on our dying VHS, and the character I related to immediately wasn't Sally, the female lead who wants to be a writer, but Harry, the miserable and proud-of-his-misery Jew. Harry was the first character I'd ever seen in a film who was Jewish the way I was Jewish: if someone was asked what religion they thought Harry and I are, they'd probably say 'Jewish', but it wouldn't be the first personality attribute you'd list about either of us (that would be 'self-absorbed'). This was Jewishness the way I knew Jewishness – being Jew-ish – and not the self-conscious outsider and faintly minstrel Jew-y-ness that Woody Allen portrayed. Also, like Harry, I was miserable, in a way that only an extremely privileged, middle-class teenage girl from a very nice family can be miserable. And like Harry, I made the mistake of thinking that made me deep.

It wasn't – and it still isn't – easy being a female movie fan. Movies tend to be written and directed by men, which means that the female characters are generally insane or boring. I only began to notice this when I moved on from eighties teen films, where I had Molly Ringwald, Ally Sheedy, Winona Ryder and Jennifer Jason Leigh for companionship, to nineties movies for grown-ups, where my options felt hugely reduced. So when I was a teenager and I wondered who would play me in the biopic of my life (I told you I was self-obsessed), I settled on Bill Murray. Only he had the qualities of humour, cynicism and lovableness that I was sure would be appreciated in me one day. Until I saw *When Harry Met Sally . . .*, that is, and then I thought Billy Crystal might just make the cut. After all, he was Jew-ish. And miserable. And deep.

But as I grew older, I began to see a different strength in the movie, one I had entirely missed when I was younger because, like Harry, I was too self-obsessed: I began to see Sally. And this is when my life began to change thanks to

When Harry Met Sally (I'm going to skip the ellipses hereon: I get the point of them in the title but they're annoying to type and even more annoying to read, and I don't think Ephron would mind. She never even liked the title).

So as I was saying, it's not always easy to be a female movie fan, especially a female fan of comedies. Men are generally the protagonists of comedies, because comedies tend to be written by men, so it's easy to grow up resenting your gender, a little. Why do you have to be a woman? Women are boring. Women are there just to laugh at the men's jokes, or be the disapproving shrew. Women don't get the good lines. Women are Margaret Dumont and men are the Marx Brothers, and I like Margaret Dumont (especially when she was wearing a swimming costume – her swimming costumes in the Marx Brothers films were amazing), but I prefer clowning to making moues of disapproval at Groucho. Worse, when you grow up watching men play leads in films, as I increasingly did, you get used to wanting everything to work out well for men, because you've been trained to be on their side. I spent years staying in relationships with men who were not worth my body, let alone my time, because I worried that if I broke up with them they'd be sad like Lloyd Dobler was in *Say Anything* (it turned out, they weren't, because Lloyd Dobler is fictional) (and also, those guys were all idiots).

Until, that is, *When Harry Met Sally*. It's written by a very funny woman and therefore features many funny women. Sally is not just Harry's straight sidekick – the Sigourney Weaver to Dr Venckman, or the Buttercup to his Westley. Sally doesn't even have to perform any of the three functions women are usually lumbered with in romcoms:

pine desperately for the man, make the man grow up by being a nagging shrew, or be liberated from her frigid bitchiness by the power of his amazing penis. In fact, for the first half of the film it's Harry who's heartbroken after his ex-wife left him for Ira the accountant, making him the vulnerable, humiliated, needy one. Sally supports him – helping him lay carpet, singing songs from *Oklahoma!* with him – because she is seemingly over her ex-boyfriend Joe ("'I am over him," Sally says, when she isn't over him at all; I have uttered that line far too many times in my life, and far too many times in my life I have believed it was true,' Ephron wrote).

Here, I realised, was an adult female character who wanted love, but wasn't pathetic, and was loved, but also human. She wasn't just Harry's romantic quarry – she was her own person. I was thrilled when I read that Ephron based Sally on herself because that meant Sally must be Jewish. I'm not some cinematic Zionist who can only enjoy her characters if they're kosher, but this proved that the film doesn't follow that insufferable template of having a goyish woman fall for a Jewish man because of his allegedly adorable Jewish qualities, and the Jewish man falls for her in turn because she is not (mazel tov, sir!) a Jewish woman. Woody Allen populated the cliché and Judd Apatow has since flogged it to death (while Larry David has waved the flag for it on TV). In Sally, Ephron coined that rare-to-the-point-of-non-existent film character: a desirable Jewish woman. A Jew-ish woman. Sally also pointed out to me that being miserable didn't mean I was deep. It meant that I was just ruining my own life.

Sally's relationship with her girlfriends, especially Marie (Carrie Fisher), is one of my favourite things about the movie. Her friends are portrayed as a source of support, but also have lives of their own (an extreme rarity in a movie, in which friends usually exist merely to be friends with the protagonist). This makes their friendship feel utterly, utterly real. 'You're right, you're right, I know you're right,' Marie chants in self-recrimination whenever Sally tells her, for the ten thousandth time, that Marie's married lover will never leave his wife for her.

Like Sally and Marie, I lived in New York City in my early thirties and, like them, I dated some absolute shockers who I should have been smart enough to avoid. It turned out, much to my surprise, that even those of us who grow up hoping to be as wise and cynical as Dr Venckman make the same grim, boring, sad mistakes as so many other women, and for exactly the same reasons: we're hopeful, we're suckers, we're lonely. Ephron knew that, but didn't mock women for it, or depict them as pathetic for wanting companionship; rather, she regarded them with fond affection, and that made me do the same about myself, eventually. Bad romcoms stigmatise and deride feelings of heartbreak and loneliness, and make me feel like I'm being a shameful cliché for desiring love, like some subnormal character in a Kate Hudson or Katherine Heigl movie. Good romcoms, like *When Harry Met Sally*, reassure me that this is what it's like to be a human being. Every time my best friend Carol made these mistakes we'd call each other for reassurance, just as Sally and Marie do, and the other one would say, 'You're right, you're right, I know you're right.' And eventually, the point would sink in: don't beat yourself up about this, but get yourself together and move on.

Writing good romcoms is hard. You can't fake them because most people recognise when something is funny and most people have been in love, whereas no one is a superhero so you can do whatever you want there. I was amazed when I read in an essay that Ephron 'struggled' with the screenplay for *When Harry Met Sally* and that 'it was really hard' ('I was just doing it for the money,' she cheerfully admits), because it reads as smoothly and effortlessly as a bunch of friends talking.

It makes me laugh when I hear male screenwriters today insist they don't write female characters because, well, how can they possibly understand women, what with them just being dumb lugs? In an interview with the *Guardian*, Evan Goldberg, writer of the bro-heavy comedies *Superbad* and *This is the End*, offered what he thought was a reasonable explanation for why there are so few female roles in his movies: 'I'm a guy! I'm not as good at writing about women. Kristen Wiig [who wrote *Bridesmaids*] is way better. I don't fully understand my wife's emotions – and I'm supposed to write an excellent female character and unravel the secret of women?'

And he learned this mentality from his mentor, Judd Apatow, who that same year said the following to the *New Yorker*: 'The reality is, I'm a dude and I understand the dude thing, so I lean men just the way Spike Lee leans African-American.' Imagine how different movies would be if more men realised that women are humans and not an entirely different species. Because insisting you can't write dialogue for the opposite gender is not being gender-sensitive, it's being lazy.

So what happened after Harry and Sally's ellipses? Well, there was an absolute glut of romcoms in the nineties, starting with the mighty behemoth of *Pretty Woman*, the timeless and romantic tale of what happens when a rich asshole picks up a hooker in LA for a blow job. Some nineties romcoms were a complete delight (*Four Weddings and a Funeral, Groundhog Day, The Wedding Singer*), but even Ephron's romcoms had diminishing returns, going from the magic of *When Harry Met Sally* to the sweetness of *Sleepless in Seattle* to the meh-ness of *You've Got Mail*. By the late nineties and early noughties, the trend had switched to raunch with male leads, kick-started by *There's Something About Mary*. Hollywood made more romcoms with male leads (*Along Came Polly, Garden State*), which were increasingly tired and formulaic and were written solely from a male perspective.

'Audiences aren't tired of romance, they're tiring of formulas,' one director told the *Hollywood Reporter*, a claim that would make a lot more sense if Hollywood wasn't subsisting on *The Avengers 7* and *Batman 22*. And without wishing to state the obvious, maybe if audiences really are tired of formulaic movies, Hollywood could make romcoms that are, you know, less formulaic. Just a thought, guys! Even if no one had ever before made a romcom, audiences still wouldn't want to see awful pap like *He's Just Not That Into You, Love Actually* or *Valentine's Day*, because they're terrible. And people definitely don't want to see them now because they know that romcoms can be good. Whereas if *When Harry Met Sally* was released today, people would want to see it. But it probably wouldn't get released today because movies like that struggle to get made now.

'Women's films, like weepies and romcoms, don't get commissioned any more because they don't work overseas. There's a different kind of funny today – less wit. Wit and nuance doesn't travel,' says producer Lynda Obst, who worked in the romcom market for years before having to move on to sci-fi due to what she describes as 'lack of windows for rom-com'. 'Funny is an Asian man who's going to blow up your car. Comedies take place in the same style as action movies and they go from set piece to set piece – you don't see that in Cameron Crowe or Nora Ephron's films. You see writing and dialogue. Now it's about dialogue moving you to another set piece where something big will happen. Comedy writers are taught to write set pieces,' she says.

'There is also a creeping sexualisation of women in recent romcoms, particularly in those starring Jennifer Aniston,' says film writer Melissa Silverstein, and she's right. It's amazing to see how 'frumpy' (i.e., normal) Sally looks, with her shaggy hair and baggy clothes, compared to the glossy female stars of today's romcoms.

Christopher Orr in the *Atlantic* argued that the reason romcoms struggle today is because, well, love is too easy now: 'Among the most fundamental obligations of romantic comedy is that there must be an obstacle to nuptial bliss for the budding couple to overcome. And, put simply, such obstacles are getting harder and harder to come by. They used to lie thick on the ground: parental disapproval, differ-ence in social class, a promise made to another. But society has spent decades busily uprooting any impediment to the marriage of true minds. Love is increasingly presumed – perhaps in Hollywood most of all – to transcend class, profession, faith, age, race, gender, and (on occasion) marital status.'

Well, if Mr Orr thinks love is easy these days, I'll have what he's having. Love is a freaking nightmare today, as it always was and always will be, and that's because human beings are ridiculous. There was no real impediment to Harry and Sally's love – they're the same age, often single at the same time and they like each other – but it took them twelve years and three months to get together, because that's what people are like. Ephron knew that, and she was smart enough also to know that love wasn't about set pieces, or schticks, or clichéd impediments – it's about people. Jane Austen knew that, too, and even though so many of the relationships in her books seem to be rooted in issues about money (Darcy is richer than Elizabeth in *Pride and Prejudice*, Edward is richer than Elinor in *Sense and Sensibility*, and so on), the only real impediment to them is the characters themselves: Darcy is too proud, Elizabeth is too prejudiced; Edward is too loyal to his commitments, Elinor is too self-effacing; Anne Elliot in *Persuasion* was too easily persuaded by bad advice, and Captain Wentworth's pride was hurt; Emma in her eponymous novel is too immature and spoilt to see what is in front of her face. This is why her novels have lasted, and it's why *When Harry Met Sally* has lasted: because stories that are about human emotions don't date. But it's hard to translate complicated human emotions for overseas sales, I guess, and car explosions are a lot easier to write anyway.

As to whether it's simply too hard in this modern world to translate real modern life into romcoms, it would help if romcoms weren't so scared of real modern women. I can't remember the last time I saw a romcom where a woman's job wasn't seen as some kind of freaky extension of her personality. Sally has a job, but unlike, say, Sandra Bullock in *The Proposal*, this doesn't mean she's a ball-breaking bitch, nor is it the reason she's still single in her thirties. And unlike, say, Kristen Wiig in *Bridesmaids*, who in that film plays a failed pastry chef, or Wendy in the appalling *What to Expect When You're Expecting*, who plays the manager of a baby clothing store, Sally doesn't have an unthreatening 'feminine' job: she's a journalist, and she's apparently just as successful as Harry, who works as a political consultant. In fact, Sally has exactly the same job, a journalist for *New York* magazine, as Jess, Harry's male best friend, played by Bruno Kirby. There is no distinction in this movie between Jobs for the Boys and Jobs for the Little Ladies. Ephron understood, as bafflingly few filmmakers do nowadays, that a woman's job doesn't have to define her or diminish her – it's just something she does. Like a man does. Fancy that!

The depiction of women with high-powered jobs wasn't always perfect in the eighties – Sigourney Weaver's bitch boss character in *Working Girl* probably won't go down as a feminist classic – but it was a lot better than it is now, and no one seems to talk about this. Women in 1980s romcoms didn't just work, they were often even more successful than their male co-stars. Kathleen Turner's character in *Romancing the Stone*, Joan Wilder, is far more successful and famous than Michael Douglas's character, Jack Colton, and this ultimately saves their lives when potential killers recognise her and profess themselves to be fans: 'Ha ha! Poor Michael doesn't get much credit in that movie, does he', cackles Turner delightedly.

Cher in *Moonstruck* plays an accountant while Nicolas Cage is a baker. Holly Hunter in *Broadcast News* is more senior to both Albert Brooks and William Hurt, and they both fall for her, and even though she ends up with neither of them, she doesn't end up alone. In *Raising Arizona*, Holly Hunter (again) is so much more successful than her doting husband (Nicolas Cage, again) that she is the cop who takes his mugshot every time he's arrested. In *Baby Boom* Diane Keaton is forced to give up her high-powered job on Wall Street when she inherits a baby because the men in her office can't handle it, including her boyfriend, played by Harold Ramis (for shame, Egon). So she then moves to the country-side, becomes a successful baby food magnate and, once again, is much more successful than her vet boyfriend (Sam Shepard). And nowhere – nowhere – is this seen as an issue.

Thanks to the eighties movies I grew up watching, this is how I imagined as a kid my adult life would be: every day I'd walk into a steel and glass office building in a skirt suit, pantyhose, high heels and a camel-coloured coat, fresh from a 7 a.m. salon appointment, clutching a briefcase in one hand and sipping my black coffee in the other, while two men who looked like catalogue models in Brooks Brothers suits would walk alongside me, talking urgently about how we had to close the Del Monte deal that day. I'd then go to my corner office, handing my coat to my secre-tary Tom on my way in (Tom would then bring in a cappuccino, on my orders), and I'd go through my various urgent messages before meeting my silver-haired boss, Chesterton, for lunch at a new French place 'downtown' with white tablecloths and white wine. The afternoon would be taken up with meetings, which I would run, of course, and I'd close the Del Monte deal and everyone would cheer for me. Then in the evening, my camel coat and I would meet my not-quite-as-high-powered boyfriend for dinner at a darling Italian place 'uptown', but we'd have to stay at mine as my personal trainer was coming over the next morning at 6 a.m. I couldn't WAIT to be a grown-up.

That world isn't really shown in movies today, partly because the corporate world isn't quite as aspirational as it was in the eighties, but also because the role of women in movies has changed. Now, if a woman is more successful than a man in a movie, it means she's a bitch and will have to be broken down, as in *The Proposal, The Ugly Truth* or *The Devil Wears Chauvinistic Stereotypes*.[1] What makes this mentality even more ridiculous is that women are now the primary money-earners in America. 'To make a woman adorable you have to defeat her at the beginning. It's a conscious thing I do – abuse and break her, strip her of her dignity, and then she gets to live out our fantasies and have fun. It's as simple as making the girl cry, fifteen minutes into the movie,' one successful female screenwriter told the *New Yorker*.

'This is the backlash. The backlash comes when women make strides. The studio convention now is that movies work better when the women characters have unthreatening jobs. They say audiences think it's cuter,' says Obst. But audiences, of course, aren't even given the option. It's the studios and filmmakers who decide.

Another factor is the lack of women working today behind the camera on movies. Women have been running studios in Hollywood since 1980 when Sherry Lansing became the president of 20th Century Fox and Cheryl Boone Isaacs is currently president of the Academy of Motion Picture Arts and Sciences, the group behind the Oscars. But as the *New York Times* film critic Manohla

---

[1] In fact, to compare how much attitudes have changed to women working from the eighties to now, you just need to look at the era-defining family sitcoms from these two eras. In *The Cosby Show*, Claire Huxtable (Phylicia Rashad) is a lawyer, on a professional par with her doctor husband, Cliff (the fallen idol, Bill Cosby), and she is the calm, wise centre of the family. In *Modern Family*, the two women in the show, played by Sofia Vergara and Julie Bowen, are both housewives and clearly professionally inferior to their husbands, and both slotted into the usual clichés for women: the over-emotional sexy minx (Vergara) and the nagging shrew who gives her adorable husband a hard time (Bowen).

Dargis notes: 'trickle-down equality doesn't work in Hollywood, even when women are calling the shots and making the hires.'

In 2013 women constituted just 10 per cent of the writers working on the 250 top grossing films. If the remaining 90 per cent of working screenwriters are too lazy to write a movie from a woman's perspective, then the result is what we see now: an absolute dearth of movies written about women and for women. Amy Pascal, Sony's then co-chairman, said, 'You're talking about a dozen or so then female-driven comedies that got made over a dozen years, a period when *hundreds* of male-driven comedies got made. And every one of those female-driven comedies was written or directed or produced by a woman. It's a numbers game – it's about there being enough women writers and enough women with the power to get movies made.'

Not that studios especially want these female-driven movies anyway: they want franchises, and romcoms and female comedies aren't seen as blockbuster material. 'Studio executives think these movies' success is a one-off every time,' Nancy Meyers, who wrote and directed *Something's Gotta Give* and *It's Complicated*, said. 'They'll say, "One of the big reasons that worked was because Jack was in it," or "We hadn't had a comedy for older women in forever."' According to Melissa Silverstein, editor of *Women and Hollywood*, 'Whenever a movie for women is successful, studios credit it to a million factors, and none of those factors is to do with women.'

Romcoms aren't heart surgery, but they – at their best – explore and explain the human heart, and that's why great ones are so great and terrible ones are so very, very terrible. This is also why it feels like such a shame that studios simply think they're not worth their time any more. To be fair, writers as wise and funny and fair as Ephron – and Austen, for that matter – don't come along every day. But things have reached a pretty pass when film trade publications admit that *When Harry Met Sally* wouldn't even get made any more.

Anyway, I grew up and the more I grew the more I became a mix of Harry (Jew-ish) and Sally (journalist, dependent on my friends, wanting love) and, like them, I eventually found the right person for me, although, also like them, I took my sweet time about it, and I sure didn't make it easy for myself along the way. Like Harry, I waited for someone who made me laugh, and like Sally, I waited for someone who wanted me to make them laugh. But the person in this movie who I learned the most from was Ephron, because she taught me everything I know about, not just men and women, but love and marriage and friendship and funniness and good writing. And I know that's a lot to ask for from a movie but I don't think it's too much to ask for occasionally. I'm right, I'm right, you know I'm right.

TOP FIVE RICK MORANIS MOMENTS

Ahhh, sweet Rick Moranis. He was the uber-nerd in the eighties and then, suddenly, he was nowhere. This bothered me for years, so finally I decided to ask the man himself: 'Hey Rick! What the hell happened?!'

And this is what he said: 'I took a break because I was a single parent[1] and it got too hard, working and looking after my kids,' he says. 'The break got longer and longer and I realised I didn't miss what I had been doing, keeping in the mind that the last films I'd done weren't as gratifying as they weren't collaborative comedies.'[2] Movies were changing, my kids were changing, so I decided just to stop doing it and one thing led to another. I didn't grow up wanting to be a performer or an actor. It was only after I had a pretty high degree of success and became a marketable commodity and was asked to act in other people's projects and to function as an actor and not comedian, and I didn't find it that enjoyable. So I just stopped.'

Does he miss it?

'Oh goodness, no.'

So very Moranis, don't you think? It makes me miss his sweet nerdy face even more. Still, at least we have his finest moments.

5 Wayne Szalinski, *Honey, I Shrunk the Kids*

Moranis enters franchise hell. He clearly enjoyed the first

---

[1] Moranis's wife, Ann, died from cancer in 1991.

[2] Moranis's later films included *The Flintstones* and, er, *Honey, We Shrunk Ourselves*. So, you know, fair enough.

one the best and he's (unsurprisingly) great as the batty scientist.

4 Nathan, *Parenthood*
A rare non-nerdy role for Moranis, and he's adorable in it. Bonus points for singing a Carpenters' song, too.

3 Dark Helmet, *Spaceballs*
Rick Moranis as Darth Vader! For God's sake, what's not to love?

2 Seymour, *Little Shop of Horrors*
OK, so he's not Pavarotti but the man can sing! He really can sing!

1 Louis Tully in *Ghostbusters*
He is hilarious as the accountant throwing the worst party ever ('Everybody, this is Ted and Annette Fleming. Ted has a small carpet cleaning company in receivership, but Annette is drawing a salary from a deferred bonus from two years ago . . .'), and adorable as the demonic Key Master. Moranis at his most Moranis-ish.

Ghostbusters
(With a Segue into *Top Gun*): How to be a Man

I read a lot of film books while researching this (sort of) film book and they've taught me a few things about how film books should be written if they are to be taken seriously, and these are lessons that I feel are as useful in life as they are in film books:

1. Drop in random French phrases wherever possible so it looks like you're quoting from the French film magazine, *Cahiers du Cinéma*, because even if you don't know what the hell you're talking about, nobody will be able to tell;
2. When in doubt, start banging on about Godard;
3. Never describe a film as your 'favourite film'. This looks unprofessional and childish. Instead, claim – in ringing tones *comme les écrivains de Cahiers du Cinéma* – that it is the Greatest Film.

Zut alors! Malheureusement, not all the French in the world could convince anyone that I am more interested in Godard than *The Goonies*, so that's a non-starter. But I shall make use of one of these handy life lessons and state that the best, most brilliant, most extraordinary, the most deftly created piece of auteur film work of all time is *Ghostbusters*.

For pretty much most of my life, I'd assumed that this was a fact accepted by everybody: *Ghostbusters* is the greatest movie ever made. Sure, people tended to say random words like '*Citizen Kane*!' and '*Vertigo*!' and '*Return to Oz*!'[1] when asked by *Cahiers du Cinéma* for their favourite film. But I thought they did this just as, when asked who they'd like to have at their dream dinner party, they say, 'Mother Teresa and Nelson Mandela!', as opposed to who everybody would actually like which is, obviously, Madonna and Bill Murray.

Now, one could take my massive assumption that my tastes reflect those of everyone else on the planet two ways:

1. I have an ego the size of Asia coupled with a narcissist's complex and incipient sociopathic tendencies;
2. *Ghostbusters* is so good that even if it's not everyone's FAVOURITE movie, it is probably in their top ten and so whenever I mention my love of *Ghostbusters* people say, 'Oh yeah, everyone loves *Ghostbusters*.'

For the purposes of this chapter, we will go with option two.

I never thought of my *Ghostbusters* obsession – and it is, I fully admit, an obsession – as remarkable. If anything, I saw it as a perfectly natural response to a great work of art. Devoting an entire shelf to books and articles by or about the people involved, however tangentially, in the

---

[1] The true maverick's choice.

making of this movie? Commendable intellectual curiosity. Spending £150 on a book about *Ghostbusters* that came out the year the film was released, just because it finally explains why the character of Winston is squeezed out of the movie? Hey, that's an investment piece! Refusing to go on a second date with someone because they failed to recognise a completely random (and not, to be honest, wildly relevant) *Ghostbusters*' quote over dinner?[*1] Well, why waste time with losers? It wasn't until I found myself awake at 2 a.m. at the age of thirty-three on a Tuesday scrolling through eBay in search of a rumoured copy of Bill Murray's original *Ghostbusters* script, which obviously was not going to be on eBay, that I felt it might be time to look at what, precisely, was going on here and why, after all this time, *Ghostbusters* still feels so special, maybe even more special, to me.

There is sentimentality, for sure, not exactly for my childhood but for the city of my childhood. *Ghostbusters* is as much of a love letter to New York as anything by Woody Allen, and a less self-conscious one at that, showing New Yorkers reacting with relative normality to an invasion of the undead.[*2] Many of the jokes in *Ghostbusters* stem from the idea that, ghosts aside, Manhattan itself is an out-of-control Wild West place, a Gotham city where a man could collapse against the windows of the Tavern on the Green, the ritzy restaurant that used to be in Central Park, and the diners

---

[*1] Failure to recognise quotes from *When Harry Met Sally* and *Indiana Jones* were also date dealbreakers. It really is astounding I was single until the age of thirty-five.

[*2] The very English comic horror film *Shaun of the Dead* (2004), which depicts a north London overtaken by zombies, owes a pretty hefty debt to *Ghostbusters*.

would simply ignore him. Trash is piled on the sidewalks and Checker cabs whizz round corners: this recreation of New York, 1984 – the New York of my childhood – is still how I think of the city, even though it has, for better or worse, changed a lot since then.

Even the hilarious anachronisms give me a sentimental frisson: Louis being mocked for his love of vitamins and mineral water; Ray and Peter chuffing down fags while toting nuclear reactors on their backs; Larry King in a cloud of cigarette smoke while chatting drily on the radio; the bad guy being the man from the Environmental Protection Agency. These all look particularly out of date in the Manhattan of today, and I can't help but feel the city is a little poorer for it. But my absolute favourite New York-y moment in the film is at the end, when a doorman brings Ecto-1 round after the Ghostbusters have saved the world – or at least Central Park West – from destruction. Despite having battled a giant marshmallow man, Dan Aykroyd still has a couple of dollar bills in the pocket of his ghost uniform with which to tip the doorman. You cannot get more New York than that.

But there is something else in *Ghostbusters* that makes me sentimental, something else that I love in it that doesn't exist any more. That is, its depiction of how a man should be.

Just in terms of sheer variety, one could do a lot worse than turn to eighties movies for lessons in how to be a man. When most people think of masculinity in eighties movies, they probably think of that strange genre that sprouted and bulged up in that decade like Popeye's biceps after eating spinach, consisting of men who look like condoms stuffed with walnuts[1] speaking their lines in confused accents and emphasising random syllables, strongly suggesting they'd learned the words phonetically: Schwarzenegger, Lundgren, Stallone[2] and, towards the end of the decade, Van Damme. Chuck Norris, too, can be included here, despite his lack of walnut-ness, but he earns membership of this group with his similar lack of obvious acting talent and strong fondness for right-wing messages in his films.[3]

But there is more to eighties men than that. For a start, there are the men who raise babies and children (*Mr Mom*, *Three Men and a Baby*, *Uncle Buck*), which some feminist critics argued at the time was a backlash against feminism because they seemed to mock the idea of feminised men. In fact, in retrospect, these films look more like movies awkwardly coming to grips with feminism (*Tootsie*, too, can be included here, with a man pretending to be a woman, and occasionally looking after a child, and becoming a better person for it). *Mr Mom* (1983), in which Michael Keaton loses his job and looks after the kids while his wife works, is clearly none too sure what to make of this 'feminist' thing: the movie's message is that the swapping of traditional gender roles will probably destroy the marriage and almost certainly the house (somewhat dismayingly, the film was written by John Hughes).

But by 1987, *Three Men and a Baby* was getting much

---

[1] Copyright: the great Clive James.
[2] Technically, if not obviously, a native English speaker.
[3] During the 2012 US election, Chuck Norris and his wife Tina made a video in which they issued a 'dire warning' to America, suggesting that were Barack Obama to win the presidency, we would be sentencing 'our children' to 'a thousand years of darkness'. Eighties stars never fade away – they just become more themselves.

more of a handle on things. The men (Tom Selleck, Steve Guttenberg and Ted Danson) are unexpectedly lumbered with a baby girl and, by the end of the film, very much want her to stay with them in their bachelor shag pad, even after the baby's dippy English (foreigners – tchuh!) mother turns back up. It turns out that, unlike Mr Mom, they are capable of looking after a baby without causing havoc to domestic appliances (men – amirite??). The men in *Three Men and a Baby* are notably much less obnoxious than *les mecs* in the original French version, *Trois Hommes et un Couffin*, who have a pact never to let a woman stay more than one night in their flat and have a tendency to call the baby 'a swine' when it has an accident on the sofa. *Ahh, les Français – ils sont tres masculins, ooh la la!*[1]

Which is not to say that the American version is without its anxieties. *Three Men and a Baby* goes to such lengths in order to reassure audiences of the uber-masculinity of the three guys, despite their TERRIFYINGLY FEMINISED baby-raising skills, that they become hilariously camp. Peak camp is reached, for me, when Selleck goes out jogging wearing little more than a tiny pair of shorts and an enormous moustache, and he picks up a sports magazine full of photos of muscled-up half-naked men. Now, if that isn't the definition of throbbing heterosexual masculinity, I don't know what is.

Yes, the eighties were a different time and American movies in that era seemed to think that 'homosexual' was merely Latin for 'psycho killer or flouncy interior decorator'. But nonetheless, whenever I watch this movie (which is more often than I'm going to commit to print) I think it's

---

[1] See? Random French words. They always work.

a shame the filmmakers didn't just go with the obvious option here and make the guys gay, living in a happy yuppie *ménage à trois*. After all, this would explain why three apparently very solvent guys in high-flying careers[*1] in their thirties would choose to share an apartment in midtown Manhattan as opposed to getting their own *American Psycho*-style bachelor pads. And for heaven's sake, have you looked at that Broadway-themed mural Steve Guttenberg paints of the three of them in the atrium of their apartment? No amount of references from Selleck to his love of sport can obscure the fact he and his two friends are living in the campest New York apartment north of 14th Street. These guys – the actor! The architect! The cartoonist! – are basically the eighties yuppie version of the Village People.

And let's talk about that homoeroticism! Accidental homoeroticism is yet another one of the great joys of eighties movies, and it was the last decade that would be blessed with the pleasure because from the nineties onwards gay culture and references would be too mainstream and recognisable to slip past studios unnoticed.

The plethora of eighties buddy movies easily and frequently tip into accidental homoeroticism, with the female characters being explicitly excluded from pretty much the whole film and all sorts of intense emotion between the two male leads. *Lethal Weapon* is one example and an even more obvious one is *Stakeout*, in which Emilio Estevez and Richard Dreyfuss spend an entire movie living together in faux domesticity and, in the case of Estevez,

---

[*1] More high-flying, incidentally, than the characters in the French version. Typical Americans! So career-obsessed! So competitive! *Bof*.

voyeuristically spying on his male partner's sexual encounters.

The Lost Boys is the most blatantly homoerotic mainstream movie ever made for teenage boys. In this film, young Michael (charisma vortex Jason Patric) is initiated into the manly life of a new town by going into a cave with Kiefer Sutherland and his male buddies (none of whom seem the least bit interested in the fact that a half-naked Jami Gertz is wandering around drunkenly in front of them) and drinking their body fluids. Sure, why not, right? Vampires are inherently homoerotic and the director Joel Schumacher (who later homoeroticised *Batman* – not difficult, admittedly – by sticking nipples on the batsuit) revels in the connection in this movie in a way *Twilight* later determinedly, somewhat dismayingly avoids. Michael does at some point have what looks like deeply unsatisfying sex with Jami Gertz, but the person he gazes at with the most intensity is young Jack Bauer. And I haven't even mentioned that Michael's little brother Sam (Corey Haim), who dresses like he's trying out for Wham!, has a poster on the door of his closet of Rob Lowe lifting up his shirt. Because sure, why not, right?

The Lost Boys is not the only eighties movie to suggest that the way a man becomes a man is by rejecting the world of women and gazing lustfully at other men. *Top Gun* is, clearly, the camp king here, with men in uniform staring passionately at one another and offering – and this is an actual quote from the movie – to ride one another's 'tail'. *Top Gun* is officially the most homoerotic thing that has ever existed, and I say that as someone who spent eight years covering men's fashion shows in Milan.

Most of uber-producers Jerry Bruckheimer and Don

Simpson's films – including *Flashdance*, *Top Gun*, *Beverly Hills Cop* and, in the nineties, *Days of Thunder* and *Bad Boys* – are, at the very least, camp because they are, as producer Julia Philips put it, 'a series of soundtracks in search of a movie'. More simply, they are extended music videos – in fact, some of the scenes are nothing but music videos, with montages set to a power ballad – and, to my mind, that is not a criticism. I love eighties music videos, I adore montages, and anyone who doesn't thrill to a power ballad is lying to themselves. These movies are fun (well, except for *Days of Thunder*) because they are about pure sensation. But they also easily become camp because camp is about exaggeration and surface aesthetics, which is a perfect description of Simpson and Bruckheimer's films.

Simpson himself was known for the kind of exaggerated macho posturing similar to that of his films: the drinking, the hedonism, the voracious use of call girls. And so, as is always the way with self-consciously macho men, there was something extraordinarily camp about him. This is especially true of macho men in the eighties, when straight men dressed like members of Duran Duran, blow-dried their hair and took an open interest in bodybuilding. Simpson himself was the Liberace of eighties heterosexual Hollywood: he was obsessed with plastic surgery and body image, he spent ridiculous amounts on clothes and cars, and he cultivated a self-image that included fabricating stories about his own childhood. His films almost invariably feature an especially close and yet emphatically platonic male friendship – in *Top Gun*, most famously, there's the tortured triangle of Maverick's (Tom Cruise, obviously) intensely loving relationship with Goose (Anthony Edwards) and his lustful one with Iceman (Val

Kilmer). Even Maverick's alleged girlfriend, Charlie (Kelly McGillis), has a male name.[1] All of this, unsurprisingly, reflected Simpson's life offscreen. His relationship with Bruckheimer was extremely close and while neither was or is gay, there was something bizarrely camp about them as a duo. During the making of *Top Gun*, they bought matching black Ferraris and matching black Mustang convertibles, they designed their houses to match and, as if to ensure

---

[1] In the best moment in the otherwise deservedly forgotten 1990s film *Sleep With Me*, Quentin Tarantino expounds on this theory, first mooted by film critic Pauline Kael, at pleasing length: '*Top Gun* is a story about a man's struggle with his own homosexuality. It is! That is what *Top Gun* is about, man. You've got Maverick, all right? He's on the edge, man. He's right on the fucking line, all right? And you've got Iceman, and all his crew. They're gay, they represent the gay man, all right? And they're saying, go, go the gay way, go the gay way. He could go both ways. Kelly McGillis, she's heterosexuality. She's saying: no, no, no, no, no, no, go the normal way, play by the rules, go the normal way. They're saying no, go the gay way, be the gay way, go for the gay way, all right? That is what's going on throughout that whole movie . . . He goes to her house, all right? It looks like they're going to have sex, you know, they're just kind of sitting back, he's takin' a shower and everything. They don't have sex. He gets on the motorcycle, drives away. She's like, "What the fuck, what the fuck is going on here?" Next scene, next scene you see her, she's in the elevator, she is dressed like a guy. She's got the cap on, she's got the aviator glasses, she's wearing the same jacket that the Iceman wears. She is, okay, this is how I gotta get this guy, this guy's going towards the gay way, I gotta bring him back, I gotta bring him back from the gay way, so I'll do that through subterfuge, I'm gonna dress like a man. All right? That is how she approaches it. But the REAL ending of the movie is when they fight the MIGs at the end, all right? Because he has passed over into the gay way. They are this gay fighting fucking force, all right? And they're beating the Russians, the gays are beating the Russians. And it's over, and they fucking land, and Iceman's been trying to get Maverick the entire time, and finally, he's got him, all right? And what is the last fucking line that they have together? They're all hugging and kissing and happy with each other, and Ice comes up to Maverick, and he says, "Man, you can ride my tail, any time!" And what does Maverick say? "You can ride mine!" Swordfight! Swordfight! Fuckin' A, man!'

they definitely looked like evil camp villains, they hired identical twin secretaries. They revelled in super-macho displays, ones that frequently seemed to disguise their own insecurities or outright lacks: every Friday night during the making of *Top Gun*, the cast and crew would throw a huge pool party to which Simpson would bring dozens of young women he picked up on the beach. One particular Friday, the cast and pilots working on *Top Gun* decided to throw Bruckheimer and Simpson into the pool. Bruckheimer relented – but only after he prissily took off his expensive cowboy boots. Simpson clung desperately to metal railings but he could not fight off the pilots and they threw him into the pool. Simpson promptly 'sank to the bottom, having been too embarrassed to tell anyone he could not swim'.

Bruckheimer loyally remained colleagues with the increasingly out of control Simpson, until even he could no longer tolerate his friend's excesses. And then, like that other image of camp American heterosexuality, Elvis Presley, Simpson eventually died, bloated and battered and far too young, on his own toilet.

In fact, if anyone wanted to learn how to be the ultimate eighties movie man, the obvious place to start would be, not *Ghostbusters*, but *Top Gun*. As well as homoeroticism, this movie features the two other major takes on masculinity in movies from that decade: a fist-pumping love for the American military, and the celebration of the maverick – and male = lone wolf.

The eighties was the decade when American politicians, led primarily by President Reagan, began to rewrite the story of the Vietnam War, pitching it not as a tragic and wasteful period in America's history, but rather as 'a noble cause', to use Reagan's favoured phrase. Reagan followed up this revisionism by launching a series of military ventures in Central America and Libya, acting as palate cleansers to wash away the old taste of Vietnam loss and replace it with, instead, newfound American militarism.

Hollywood happily reflected this switch, with movies such as *Red Dawn* and *Top Gun*. Even films like *Rambo: First Blood Part II* and *Predator*, which are ostensibly about the failure of the American military top brass in Vietnam, celebrate the strength of individual soldiers over dubious natives. These films looked like pure propaganda, which is precisely what they were: many were made with assistance from the military in exchange for script approval, as the Pentagon saw these movies as an excellent means of recruitment. Which, again, they were: according to David Sirota, recruitment went up 400 per cent when *Top Gun* was released, thanks in part, as the *LA Times* reported at the time, to the navy's clever wheeze of 'setting up manned tables outside movie houses during *Top Gun* premieres to answer questions from would-be flyboys emerging with a new-found need for speed from an F-14 warplane'. Of course, most of these young people didn't realise that they were watching what were little more than adverts for the military, nor did their parents, whose taxes were partially subsidising the tanks and guns featured in these movies to tempt their children to enlist.

Hollywood had collaborated with the military plenty of times before the 1980s, going all the way back to 1927 with the film *Wings*, the very first winner of a Best Picture Oscar, which the military helped to produce. But given *Top Gun*'s enormous success, the number of collaborations between Hollywood studios and the military increased exponentially in the eighties, with studio bosses convinced that churning out pro-war propaganda in exchange for access to military equipment was a guaranteed winner of a formula, and the military was now fully persuaded that recruitment through movies was the way forward. And so, alongside anguished films about Vietnam such as *Platoon*, *Full Metal Jacket* and *Good Morning, Vietnam*, came what Movieline describes as 'hyper-macho, bazooka-toting fantasy fare', like *Top Gun*.

This is one movie lesson from the eighties that is still very much alive today. Michael Bay's deadening *Transformers* franchise, the laughable 2012 flop, *Battleship*, which starred Rihanna as a weapons specialist and the 2012 film *Acts of Valor* (which Movieline describes as 'Navy SEAL porn flick') were all underwritten by the Pentagon, and all dutifully present a defiantly macho, determinedly pro-military message. Nor is it just bad films that get made this way: 2013's *Captain Phillips* starring Tom Hanks as a captain taken hostage by Somali pirates was also made with the military's cooperation and it, too, presents an utterly sterling view of the Americans in uniform. 'When you know that you're going to need the military's assistance, and you know they are going to be looking at your script, you write it to make them happy right from the beginning,' writes David Robb.

But of course, *Top Gun* isn't just about falling in line with the military. Hell no! It's about (somewhat contradic-torily) rebelling against it, too! Because that's what real men are like, you see. A real man isn't a pencil pusher – he's the lone wolf, the renegade, the MAVERICK. Real men ride their motorcycles against a sunset into the danger zone. Women have sex with the mavericks, but men ARE the mavericks. High five low five! Yeah! And just in case that isn't entirely clear in the script, Cruise's character's name is, of course, Maverick (real men also don't bother with fey subtlety).

The idea of the male rebel outsider was hardly coined in the eighties, but the idea of the rebel outsider fighting against the inept or even evil American government was one that not only gained enormous traction in the eighties, but was encouraged by, of all things, the American government – or, to be more precise, President Ronald Reagan. 'I've always felt that the nine most terrifying words in the English language are, "I'm from the government and I'm here to help,"' Reagan said in 1986. Reagan had cannily picked up on this national mood that had been burgeoning in the seventies in the wake of the disaster of the Vietnam War and the humiliation of the Watergate scandal. Anti-government moral mavericks started to emerge in films of that time, including Han Solo (another character who, like Maverick, was blessed with nominative determinism), the sexy outsider who made money working against the Empire, and, of course, Clint Eastwood's Dirty Harry. Tellingly, Reagan – a B-list actor through and through – was especially fond of using references from the films of both those characters, referring to the Soviet Union as 'the evil Empire', much to George Lucas's horror, and notoriously telling tax increasers in 1986 to 'go ahead – make my day.' Movie nerds like myself around the world sympathise with this tactic of Reagan's: if you can't get cast in the movie, quote the movie.

Thus, the mentality of the eighties in America began to take shape: government and social collectivism is bad, the male renegade outsider is good, and it was a mentality that was instantly reflected in TV shows (*The A-Team, Knight Rider, The Dukes of Hazzard, Moonlighting*) and movies. Wild buccaneer-for-profit Jack Colton (Michael Douglas) in *Romancing the Stone* and *The Jewel of the Nile* is a straight rip-off of Han Solo. So is Indiana Jones, for that matter, the renegade archaeologist, trying to save cultural and religious artefacts from collectors and Nazis. As if Spielberg wanted to make this point extra clear, he then cast the same actor who played Han to play Indy. *Lethal Weapon, Die Hard* and *Beverly Hills Cop* also play on this idea of the rule-breaking maverick, with, respectively, crazy ol' Riggs (Mel Gibson), sweaty ol' John McClane (Bruce Willis) and wisecrackin' Axel Foley (Eddie Murphy) determinedly giving ulcers to their fat superiors with their maverick – and ultimately CORRECT – ways.

E.T. is probably the most obvious and – for those who saw it as kids – most formative example of a movie that pitches the US government as actually nefarious. In the film, faceless government agents tear through Elliott's home like zombies rampaging through the family's sleepy suburbia, in a classic horror movie trope. The government then doesn't just kidnap sweet and innocent E.T. (and, ostensibly, Elliott) – it nearly kills them both, and they are only saved by Elliott's pure childlike nature, not the clumsy oafish ways of the evil government. *Splash* and *Project X* completely ripped off I mean paid heavy homage to *E.T.* with their distinctly similar plots featuring, respectively, in place of an alien, a mermaid and monkeys which had to be kept safe from meddling government agents.

But it's in *Top Gun* where this trope that the rule-breaking maverick is awesome is at its most ridiculous because it is so heavily and paradoxically tied to that other ultimate eighties movie trope about masculinity: that the military is awesome. And this means the movie's ending is utterly bonkers. Maverick's brash arrogance and reckless selfishness turn out to have been the correct instincts all along, meaning there is really no message. Music videos feature more interesting emotional journeys than *Top Gun*. In fact, the filmmakers were so averse to making Maverick's maverickness seem in any way misguided that they refused to give the movie the story arc it so obviously needed: for him to be the reason his partner Goose dies. But despite Maverick's guilt after the crash, Goose's death has nothing to do with him – it was due to faulty equipment. The only lesson Maverick (and audiences) learn from this incident is that Maverick should not have let the death of his best friend cause him to lose his confidence, because that is when he is at his least manly, repulsive both to his girlfriend (Charlie) and his boyfriend (Ice). It is only when he gets his confidence back that he becomes a triumphant 'fly boy' again and Ice invites him to ride his tail, again.

This, the movie suggests, is how the military will survive, just as the police are dependent on rule-breakers like Riggs in *Lethal Weapon*, McClane in *Die Hard* and Axel Foley in *Beverly Hills Cop*. These movies aren't arguing for the dismantling of institutions, just for the triumph of the unleashed individual within, and that's because these movies were made in the eighties: the era of selfish individualism, yes, not full-on revolution.

Being a man the *Top Gun* way is still very much a popular message in today's American movies and, for that matter, politics. The Tea Party is explicitly based on the premise that the federal collectivism is deeply suspect and individualism is the way of the future. If the US government nearly killed E.T., no wonder millions of Americans don't trust them to look after the national healthcare system. Has President Obama forgotten how E.T. turned a crusty shade of white when the government got their hands on him? White, for gawd's sake! It's not natural for an alien!

But there was another way to be a man, according to eighties movies, and it had nothing to do with homoeroticism, the military or howling lone wolves. It might have something to do with looking after kids, but that wasn't its main point. And yet, unlike the *Top Gun* way, it's one that's hardly endorsed at all by today's movies, or, indeed, any American pop culture at all, even though it is far, far preferable. And that is, the *Ghostbusters* way.

Ever since I saw this movie at the age of six, sharing my fold-down seat in the cinema with my mother's big purse for added weight so the seat wouldn't snap back up and swallow me up like the killer plant in *Little Shop of Horrors*, the Ghostbusters have represented to me an ideal of masculinity. This is not just because I fancy all of them, which I definitely do – the Ghostbusters are all total hotties, although this fact is rarely noted, for some mystifying reason. Young Aykroyd, for a start, is very much in my top five, maybe even my top three, and the only thing hotter than him greeting the crowds at the end of *Ghostbusters* with a fag in his mouth on Central Park West is him looking all sweet and poor and forlorn in *Trading Places* (mmm, sweet poor forlorn Aykroyd . . .). ANYWAY, I digress.

It might seem odd, this idea that a bunch of dudes running around Manhattan wearing cartoon insignia on their uniforms and car represent masculine goodness, and some people would disagree with me.'[1] In fact, some dark souls have accused the Ghostbusters of sexism, and to be fair to these people and their souls it's not wildly difficult to see why: the ghosts are all female (minus Slimer, of course) and are either trying to kill the Ghostbusters (Zuul, Gozer) or give them oral sex;'[2] Venkman sexually harasses or patronises any woman in his path; the general air of male clubbiness to the whole film. Read this way, the film sounds like a terrible precursor to a terrible Adam Sandler film – and it could have been, had it starred and been written by anyone else (just imagine if it was a Gene Wilder and Richard Pryor film. Or, you know, don't). While defending the movie from such accusations, writer and *Ghostbusters* mega-fan Adam Bertocci writes that the confusions come from the fact that the film is actually about 'ancient power struggles in which the boundary was between two worlds, masculine and feminine, and all that they represented: Apollo versus Dionysus, yang versus yin, sun versus moon, fire versus water, ego versus id, reason versus emotion, science versus magic.' This is sweet, but it does also emphasise the alleged gender distinctions in the film. Journalist Noah Berlatsky puts it a little less forgivingly, describing *Ghostbusters* as 'totally sexist' because it 'denigrated and (literally) demonized women' and 'bodily

---

*[1] Crazy people.

*[2] The scene in which Ray (Aykroyd) dreams a ghost is going on him in the film is, by some measure, the weirdest and worst moment in the film. It makes absolutely no sense, mainly because it was part of another scene that was cut. That it was written at all, and stayed in the film, serves as a handy little reminder that Aykroyd is, as we shall discuss, kind of an odd fellow.

fluids are viewed as ectoplasmic ick'.

Now, leaving aside the fact that it isn't, last time I checked, only women who produce bodily fluids, I can (just about) see Berlatsky's point – but he's wrong. Damn wrong! To accuse *Ghostbusters* of sexism is to apply a very basic algorithm to determine its sexual politics. This means, then, that the subtle and very sweet ways *Ghostbusters* subverts the sexist tropes of male-led comedies, made both in the eighties and still very much made now, are overlooked. There is a reason, in my personal and objective experience, why women love this film as much as men, and it isn't because they've been possessed by Zuul and turned into dogs.

First, there's the depiction of male friendship. The three primary Ghostbusters – Peter Venkman (Bill Murray), Ray Stantz (Dan Aykroyd) and Egon Spengler (Harold Ramis) – are all friends. Good friends. They like each other, they're amused by each other and they stick together when they're fired at the beginning of the film from their university jobs. There's nothing eroticised about their friendship, no overcompensation of macho-ness, no competitive banter. No cruelty, in other words (although Venkman is a little cavalier about making Stantz mortgage his parents' house to fund the business). Nor is there any suggestion that male friendship is so special it must be protected from all outsiders who threaten it – namely, women.

In *Ghostbusters* and *Ghostbusters II*, Ray and Egon are nice to Dana: they welcome her into their group and they try to protect her from Peter's excesses. Compare this to the treatment meted out to the female love interests in modern-day equivalent movies such as *The 40-Year-Old Virgin*, *Anchorman* and *Knocked Up*, or less broad bromance films such as *Sideways*, in which the male friends are all, without fail, horrible to the women (read: INVADERS). While Venkman might tease some of the women in his orbit (mocking Janine for her 'bug eyes', lusting after Dana), he always immediately apologises, and neither the film nor his buddies praise him for his foolishness. This strikes me as a lot more significant than the gender of ghosts.

The Ghostbusters also never fall out with one another. This, too, is appealing and makes them rarities in the world of male friendship in movies. In today's more recent male-led comedies, such as *I Love You, Man* and *Anchorman*, the male friends always fall out at some point, followed by an emotional reunion. That's because, in those films, the friendship between the male leads has become so celebrated that it is a (barely) platonic romance and therefore the trajectory of the friendship is like that of a clichéd film love story: boy meets boy, boy loses boy, boy gets boy back. The Ghostbusters never fall out with one another, because they are friends – just friends – and they are grown-ups. I'll return to this point later.

Just as the overly close friendships in *Top Gun* were a reflection of the one between the filmmakers off-camera, so the relationships in *Ghostbusters* were an expression of those behind the movie. The original idea for the film was born out of one particular friendship: the one between Aykroyd and his best friend and former *Saturday Night Live* fellow cast-mate, John Belushi. By the time Aykroyd sat down to write what would be the first draft of the movie, the bearishly sweet but wildly self-destructive Belushi had been flailing around in film flops and drug addiction since the pair's last film, 1980's *The Blues Brothers*, and Aykroyd pictured his ghost film as the dual project his best friend needed: 'Abbott and Costello,

Dean Martin and Jerry Lewis – everyone did a ghost picture,' Aykroyd said. And yet, despite those comic precedents, Aykroyd did not envisage the film as a comedy.

Instead, he saw it as a semi-serious look at the paranormal and parapsychology, an idea that makes a tiny bit more sense when one takes into account that Aykroyd is a spiritualist and member of the American Society of Psychical Research. In fact, some of his ancestors were mystics and his father wrote what *Vanity Fair* describes with an apparently straight face as 'a well regarded history of ghosts'. For Aykroyd, this was a deeply personal project on several levels: on the one hand, he was exploring what he calls 'the family business'; on the other, he was trying to rescue his best friend. But on a warm and bright March afternoon in 1982, just as Aykroyd was at home in New York writing a line for his friend, the phone rang. It was Belushi's manager, Bernie Brillstein, calling from Los Angeles: Belushi had died in the Chateau Marmont after overdosing on cocaine and heroin. He was thirty-three years old.

Aykroyd was devastated. Photos from Belushi's funeral on Martha's Vineyard show a shocked-looking Aykroyd leading the procession on a motorcycle – and a young Bill Murray, who revered Belushi, grimacing while placing a flower on the dead comedian's coffin. Aykroyd soon after decided that his fellow *Saturday Night Live* castmate, Murray, should play the part he had written for Belushi, and it was the part that ultimately truly made Murray's name, just as Aykroyd once hoped it would make Belushi's. But he would still keep his late friend in the film in his own way: Slimer is a direct homage to Belushi who, like the green blob, would steal food off room service trays in hotel hallways and generally cause chaos. More obliquely, the movie would be made by Black Rhino Productions, which is Aykroyd's production company – named in honour of a dream he had after Belushi died, in which his friend's face was on a charging rhino.

It's easy to overstate the influence of Belushi on 1980s American comedy, just out of sentimentality and sadness for his premature death. But it's equally easy to underplay it because he died so young and so long ago. But the impact of it heavily affected the movie that would soon become the most successful comedy of all time, giving it a sweetness that other comedies from that same era, starring the same actors and made by the same director, do not have. 'Belushi's death was the soul of the film for Danny, and it played into my own sensibilities of friendship and humanity,' says the film's director, Ivan Reitman. 'I went in knowing that what was important was that the audience had to care about these guys, they had to want to be friends with them and to care about their friendship.'

Aykroyd's original script, which he showed to Reitman, was set in the future, on various planets and over several dimensions. 'My first draft,' Aykroyd later said, 'was written in a way that your basic acceleration physicist might have enjoyed more than the mass audience.'

'Danny's first draft,' Reitman recalls, 'was basically unfilmable.' But Reitman loved the script's basic premise: a bunch of guys acting like firefighters but catching ghosts. So he took Aykroyd out to lunch and suggested some changes, such as setting it in present-day New York ('It became my New York movie,' Reitman says with a smile). The always amenable Aykroyd agreed to all the changes. Murray had already told Aykroyd that he liked the script and made characteristically vague noises about maybe committing to it. Reitman then suggested hiring Harold Ramis, with whom he'd made the 1981 army comedy *Stripes*, which also starred Murray. After getting Columbia to commit to a $25 million budget – which was seen then as an obscene amount of money to invest in a comedy – Ramis, Aykroyd and Reitman decamped to Martha's Vineyard to rewrite Aykroyd's script. All these men were already old friends and would soon become even better ones. 'Those weeks on Martha's Vineyard,' Reitman recalls, 'were two of the most fun weeks of my life.'

First, they created the different character traits for the three Ghostbusters who before had, in Aykroyd's original script, been pretty much interchangeable: 'Put [the characters of Peter Venkman, Raymond Stantz, and Egon Spengler] together, and you have the Scarecrow, the Lion, and the Tin Man,' Aykroyd said.

'For actors, especially in group comedy, those kinds of archetypes always seem to work,' said Ramis.

They also used character traits from each other, with Venkman taking on Murray's already well-honed sarcastic outsider tone and Stantz becoming the paranormal nerd, just as Aykroyd was and is. It is impossible not to take delight in watching an actor play a role that he was seemingly born to play, whether it's Clark Gable as Rhett Butler or Humphrey Bogart as Rick. With *Ghostbusters*, you get that three times over: Murray as the wise-ass, Ramis as the egg-head and Aykroyd as the lunkish geek. From then on, any time any of them branched out of these types – Murray as the depressed father in *Rushmore*, Aykroyd as the southern good ol' boy in *Driving Miss Daisy*, Ramis as the stoner dad in *Knocked Up* – it felt to me both daring and unsettling, as though I'd caught my father cross-dressing.

Next, they jettisoned all the inter-planetary time travel from Aykroyd's script, wisely cutting out all the spiritual woo-woo stuff but keeping in all the geeky science: the proton packs, the containment units, the streams that must never be crossed. Geeky science was already becoming one of the defining characteristics of eighties movies, particularly in male-led comedies, and would feature in films such as *Mad Science* to *Short Circuit* (aka E.T. as a robot) to *Batteries Not Included* to Bill and Ted's time-travelling phone box in *Bill and Ted's Excellent Adventure* to the greatest eighties film science experiment of them all, the DeLorean with the flux capacitor. This is my kind of sci-fi, and my kind of masculinity: gleefully, nonsensically, sweetly nerdy.

Notably, this kind of sci-fi and accompanying special effects – the nerdy nonsense kind – has endured a lot better than the more grandiose visions of, say, *Star Wars*, with all those tediously phallic lightsabers. At times the film makes fun of its shonkiness, such as Egon using a colander to read Louis's (Rick Moranis) mind. But with the exception of the demon dog that crashes Louis's party, which was done using stop-motion puppets, the special effects in *Ghostbusters* still look just as good today as they did in the eighties, just as they do in *Back to the Future*, *Bill and Ted's Excellent Adventure* and the grievously under-rated *Young Sherlock Holmes*. And this is at least partly why these movies have lasted so well and why they still attract viewers who weren't even born when DeLoreans were being manufactured.

Murray, meanwhile, was in India filming another movie. The day he arrived back in New York, Reitman and Ramis met him at LaGuardia airport and took him out to a restaurant in Queens to show him the script. But Murray trusted his friends so much he barely looked at it, said 'about two words about the script' Ramis later recalled, and flew back out again. 'It was trust. *Ghostbusters* was the first film he committed to without fighting like crazy,' Ramis said.

But of course, *Ghostbusters* does not only star the Ghostbusters themselves. Other actors and actresses had to work within this already existing strong friendship. When Aykroyd wrote the script, he envisaged a role for John Candy, and Reitman approached him to play Louis. When Candy suggested playing the role with a heavy accent and two dogs, Reitman decided he was going too broad, even for *Ghostbusters*. So instead, he cast the Canadian comedian Rick Moranis, then little known to American audiences.

'My career was completely luck,' says Moranis. 'Different things would come up and I would pick what I felt was the most fun and who would be the most interesting to work with. I wasn't being offered a lot of the Schwarzenegger parts: you have a round Jewish face and you don't wear contacts and you're five foot five, you're going to get certain parts. People always thought of me as the nerdy guy, even in non-nerdy parts.'

Because the part of Louis had been written for Candy, Moranis set about shaping it more to his image: he suggested that Louis be an accountant and be more nerdy and less lecherous over women, as they'd written originally. 'Ivan let me work with my character, which was wonderful. They were all extremely friendly and supportive guys and really encouraged my input, even though they'd all known each other for years and I was really the outsider,' says Moranis.

Sigourney Weaver also ended up shaping her role to the

benefit of the film. She came in to audition for the part of Dana, 'which I know sounds ridiculous – we made Sigourney audition, when she'd already done *Aliens* and *The Year of Living Dangerously*,' says Reitman with a laugh. 'But she'd never done comedy. Little did I know that comedy was her true love.'

Weaver proved her comedic skills by opening her audition with the suggestion that Dana become a dog in the movie, and she promptly climbed up on Reitman's coffee table, got down on all fours and howled.

'And I was just fascinated – it was so goofy!' says Reitman, sounding very much like he's still recovering from the encounter over thirty years later. 'And I thought, you know, that's a good idea, we should look at it.'

Weaver also suggested that Dana be a musician instead of a model, as was originally written in the script, and she made similar suggestions throughout the shoot in order to make her character more than a cipher. In the scene when Venkman first goes to Dana's flat to check out her haunted refrigerator, Dana was written as very passive in the script: she doesn't get it when Venkman is making salacious come-ons to her, and she seems scared of him, threatening to scream at one point. In the film, Weaver rolls her eyes at Venkman and clearly just finds him ridiculous and, in doing so, makes the scene a lot less creepy than it could have been – after all, Venkman is basically sexually harassing Dana in her own apartment. But because Dana stands up to him, and Murray himself looks and acts like such a tongue-tied nebbish next to Weaver's patrician, cool glamour, the power tips more in her favour. The scene becomes sweet instead of stupid, therefore proving the rarely acknowledged fact that when female characters are allowed to be stronger than a wet rag, it does everyone in the movie a favour.

'Sigourney insisted, without being obnoxious in any way, on making her character real,' said Ramis. 'Often in comedies, you see characters doing all these outlandish things while the people around them are acting like stooges, as though nothing out of the ordinary is happening. And so when Sigourney was able to stand there like a real person and say to Bill [in that scene], "You are so odd," it was totally genuine – and she came up with that line herself. I loved it, because it let the audience off the hook and allowed them to say, "Yeah, he IS odd."'

Ramis also admitted, 'We [Ramis and Aykroyd] had never written women very well,' which is a disappointing cop-out from him. *Ghostbusters* does, sadly, fail the Bechdel test, and is a classic example of Katha Pollitt's Smurfette Principle. But at least they had the sense and ego strength to take Weaver's suggestions and allow the main female character more agency than they'd written, which is a helluva lot more than the filmmakers behind today's male-led comedies do.[1] Dana is more interesting than a generic love interest, largely due to Weaver, and the fact that Reitman cast the lead actress from *Alien* strongly proves he wanted an actress who the audience would recognise as powerful. The film even tweaks and literalises what is now an infamous trope in comic books and comic book movies, Women in Refrigerators, referring to the tendency for female characters

---

[1] When actress Katherine Heigl later – and rightly (if somewhat belatedly) – complained about the female characters in *Knocked Up*, her male co-star Seth Rogen sneered on Howard Stern's radio show in July 2009, 'It's not like we're the only people she said some batshit crazy things about. That's kind of her bag now.' The depiction of female characters in Apatow and Rogen's films have remained unchanged ever since.

to be killed or injured as a plot device. (The name derives from a storyline in the *Green Lantern* comic books in which a female character is killed and stuffed into a fridge, for no reason.) In *Ghostbusters*, Dana becomes imbued with the powers of her actual refrigerator, and lives to tell the tale (and snog Murray on Fifth Avenue).

Another factor here is Murray who has been, from the beginning of his career in *Meatballs* (1979), the master of taking awful characters and tweaking them just enough so that their creepiness is undercut and they become palatable. Even in the opening scene when we meet him at the university and he is trying to seduce the pretty female student, with his mugging and hesitancies he comes across as more laughable than a predatory creep. The fact that he is literally electrocuting a male student in order to get his quarry emphasises that the film wants us to see this guy as, not cool, but a jerk. Later, Venkman refuses to sleep with Dana when she's possessed and begging him to do so, proving there are, in fact, moral depths to this formerly lecherous university professor, and this is reiterated by his look of heartbreak when he thinks Dana is dead. *Ghostbusters* is a male-led comedy, for sure. But it's one that doesn't only respect men by any means.

In fact, the cast member who found it hardest to penetrate Aykroyd-Ramis-Reitman-Murray's wall of white male friendship was not a white woman, but a black man: Ernie Hudson, who plays Winston Zeddemore, the fourth Ghostbuster, and this led to the biggest flaw in *Ghostbusters*, and in their depiction of masculinity. Back in the eighties, Hudson was a jobbing actor and a single dad, working hard to support his two sons. 'As soon as I read the script I thought, Wow, this is really cool, this could change everything for us,' he remembers.

In the version Hudson read, Winston becomes part of the Ghostbuster team from almost the beginning of the film, but in the version that they ended up shooting he doesn't appear until nearly the end, meaning most of his lines had been cut out. For years, *Ghostbusters* fans speculated that Winston's part was cut because Eddie Murphy turned down the role to make *Beverly Hills Cop* and they didn't want to give so many lines to a relative unknown like Hudson. Others suggested that racism played a part, with white Hollywood, once again, stiffing the black guy. Reitman has denied the Murphy rumour ('Murphy was never a consideration'), but Aykroyd has said that he originally wrote the film with Murphy in mind as a Ghostbuster. Reitman also hastily dismisses accusations that Hudson's crunched-down role feels uncomfortably like the Token Black Guy: 'It was always written for these three guys, we grew up together, so this was the comedy troupe, so to speak. I cast Ernie because he was really different in his energy from the other guys.'

Hudson was devastated by the script change, but tried to stay pragmatic about it: 'I think the studio thought they could sell the guys as they were from *Saturday Night Live*, and they wanted to include Winston marginally. I don't know. I blame the studio because in my mind it's easier for me to say "some exec" rather than the guy sitting next to me. I don't think it came from the guys [Aykroyd, Ramis and Reitman], the guys are great, but what do I know?' He tried, he says, 'not to go to the racial side of it', because he didn't want to send a defeatist message to his sons.

The studio was almost certainly less excited about the bankability of Hudson compared to Aykroyd and Murray. But the truth is, it was Ramis and Aykroyd who cut down Winston's part, for the precise reasons that Hudson feared – race and star power, but not quite as he imagined. According to Ramis:

> As writers, we'd never done a black character. The Writer's Guild sends out letters about this regularly – 'Let's see more women and minorities.' So when we wrote Winston, I think we had our own little reverse backlash going. We bent over backwards to make Winston's character good – and in doing so, we made him so good that he was the best character in the movie. We looked at it and said, 'Jesus! He's got all the good lines.' At the same time, everybody was saying Bill's character was a little weak. So, little by little, we started shifting Winston's attitude to Bill's character – which made perfect sense – and we also ended up delaying Winston's introduction until much later in the film.

This explains why there are two sceptical outsiders among the Ghostbusters – Venkman and Winston – which always felt like an overkill to me. It's only because Murray plays the part 'so odd', as Dana says, that he doesn't feel like an everyman, as Winston does, and the overlap isn't more obvious than it already is.

Once they started shooting, Reitman says that they realised Hudson was so funny they decided to re-expand his part, but only up to a point. Winston does still get some good lines ('I've seen shit that'll turn you white!' 'I love this town!'), but his role is unquestionably squeezed. And Hudson's disappointments continued after the movie: he was turned down to voice his own character in the cartoon of *Ghostbusters* (they gave it to Arsenio Hall instead), and his part was, once again, nearly pushed out of the (pretty meh) sequel to the film. 'That was difficult for me because that I really didn't understand. But once you get angry, it's all over. So I stayed positive and kept working. And I can also say that the original *Ghostbusters* is a perfect movie as it is,' says Hudson.

Ham-fisted handling of racial issues aside, it is, really. But what makes it feel especially perfect today, particularly in regard to the subject of masculinity, is the fact that the guys in it are grown-ups.

It's extraordinary watching eighties comedies now, especially ones starring men and featuring male friendships, such as *Ghostbusters*, *Trading Places*, *When Harry Met Sally*, *Three Men and a Baby*, even *Three Amigos!*, for heaven's sake, because as silly as the men are in those movies – and they are often very silly – they still behave like adults. Not stunted adolescents, not misogynistic overgrown babies, but adults. They like women, they usually have jobs, they don't wish they were nineteen, they don't sit around smoking bongs all day and they're not jerks. This distinguishes eighties comedies strongly from today's male-led comedies. Yes, contemporary male-led movies all show that this is because the guys are immature and need to grow up, but what they also show is that guys are a lot more fun whereas women are tedious shrews whose only function in life is to drag the poor menfolk, wailing and wanking, away from their PlayStations and into the sad, drab world of maturity. These movies accept that men have to grow up, but they don't like it.

'I don't know anyone who wants to grow up,' says Judd

Apatow, who, along with Adam Sandler[*1] and filmmaker Adam McKay (*Anchorman*, *Step Brothers*), has been at the forefront of popularising the trope of the overgrown man-boy. 'For me it's natural to tell stories about people who are resisting the maturation process – there's nothing that's fun about having responsibilities and dealing with real world problems. I'm always fascinated by the moment people are expected to define themselves as an adult. I also like stories about feeling time pressure. Everyone feels they need to get things done by certain stages – getting married, having kids. We all hear this ticking clock all the time and it drives us crazy so I write about that a lot.'

Even though Apatow cites eighties movies as his most formative source of inspiration, especially *Ghostbusters*, *Fast Times at Ridgemont High*, *Say Anything* and the John Hughes films, he concedes that there are no films from that era that feature men resisting growing up. With one exception – *Diner*, Barry Levinson's 1982 film set in 1959 about a bunch of young men hanging out in the run-up to a friend's marriage. 'One of the things I love about *Diner* is that it shows the moment they have to grow up and get married. I don't know why, but it is a moment I keep going back to in my movies because so much happens in that transition,' Apatow says. But in that film, Levinson takes care to emphasise the cruelty of the young men's immaturity, showing how much they hurt their wives when they scream at them for not putting their records back correctly. This, the movie suggests, is a form of spousal abuse. When Pete is caught

---

[*1] In fact, Sandler and Apatow shared an apartment when they were both starting out. Ladies, we can only look back and regret that we never got to hang out in Sandler and Apatow's woman-repelling bachelor pad.

lying to his wife so he can play sports games, in Apatow's *Knocked Up*, he's just having, the movie says, immature, male-bonding fun. The men are not fun in *Diner* when they behave like jerks, and there's no intimation that they'd be happier if they stayed that way for ever – they're just mean.

The guys in *Ghostbusters*, by comparison, behave like recognisable adults, and seem far more grown up than men in most pop culture today. And when the Ghostbusters seem like relative paragons of maturity, then something weird is going on.

'Yes, exactly!' cries Reitman excitedly, as though he has been waiting to make this point for years.

> As silly and as raw as those eighties films are, they're not coarse. I think now, with the last few generations, these things have evolved. Kids stay in school as long as they can these days, and especially with the masculine gender, there seems to be a desire to put off settling down for as long as possible. So many of the ideas that go into these movies are about that – the childishness of young adult males. I think it's funny enough for a while but I've seen it already and it's time for something else. It's one of the reasons I think those films don't tend to hold up in multiple viewings in much the way that I keep hearing about those [eighties movies] that people tend to view over and over again.

Yes, kids do tend to stay in school longer and, yes, there is a melding between the generations that has never heretofore existed, with grandparents poking their grandkids on Facebook and mothers and daughters shopping together in Topshop. Never has it been easier to stay part of the youth culture for longer. But as much as I'd like to blame Facebook for absolutely all evils in the modern world, the truth is that young men today are no more like Adam Sandler in *Billy Madison* than they ever were (thank God). The telling thing here is that it's men who are depicted as stunted adolescents, not women.[*1] And this is because the trope of the over-grown man-boy is simply the laziest and lowest answer to a question that has been building up in pop culture for decades: how to incorporate male-based storylines into a society that is increasingly enlightened by feminism.

Despite still getting the vast majority of starring roles and storylines, men do not get a great deal in pop culture today. A particularly popular trope for fathers on TV shows today, from *The Simpsons* to *Modern Family* to *Peppa Pig*, is to depict them as incompetent man-boys, haplessly trying to keep up with their far more mature wives. Compare, say, useless Phil Dunphy in *Modern Family*, always getting things wrong, always buying the wrong kind of car, always mocked by his kids, with Cliff Huxtable in *The Cosby Show*, the patrician doctor whose kids respected him despite his wildly questionable taste in knitwear. In American movie comedies today, men are not sweetly silly, as they were in the eighties, keen but not desperate for female attention – they are overgrown teenagers who regard women as bitches to humiliate or mother figures to worship. Women, bromance movies suggest, are a necessity in life, but it's

---

[*1] *Bridesmaids* and the HBO show *Girls*, both produced by Apatow, depict young women struggling to grow up. But these remain anomalies and the amount of attention both these projects received, when they were merely showing women do what men had been doing onscreen for decades, underlined the different expectations placed on male and female fictional characters.

only by hanging out with one's male friends, swapping porn films with them, taking mushrooms in Vegas with them, and making homophobic gags while playing computer games with them, that a man is truly at ease with himself.

Why this has happened can be gleaned, not from films, but TV. The most celebrated recent TV blockbusters all depict the erosion of patriarchy: 'Tony [Soprano], Walter [White] and Don [Draper] are the last of the patriarchs,' writes the *New York Times*'s film critic A.O. Scott. '[But] it seems that, in doing away with patriarchal authority, we have also, perhaps unwittingly, killed off all the grown ups . . . In my main line of work as a film critic, I have watched over the past 15 years as the studios committed their vast financial and imaginative resources to the cultivation of franchises that advance an essentially juvenile vision of the world. Comic-book movies, family-friendly animated adventures, tales of adolescent heroism and comedies of arrested development do not only make up the commercial centre of 21st century Hollywood. They are its artistic heart.' This genre of film, Scott continues, is 'a cesspool of nervous homophobia and lazy racial stereotyping. Its postures of revolt tend to exemplify the reactionary habit of pretending that those with the most social power are really the most beleaguered and oppressed.' The man-boy, in other words, is a petulant temper tantrum about the demise of simple patriarchal structures, a giant shrug of confusion about how men should be if they can no longer act like Don Draper without being arrested. It is a form of rebellion when the only thing to rebel against is women and them-selves, and it is a giant step backwards from the compara-tively enlightened likes of *Three Men and a Baby*.

One could easily argue that it was the eighties that started this trend of infantilisation and especially infantilised men, which makes sense as this was the decade of the so-called backlash against feminism. After all, it was the eighties that saw a huge rise in youth culture, with MTV and teen movies dominating the pop culture, as well as the growth of high-concept movies, which are the definition of an infantilised artform. In his both fascinating and charmingly pretentious essay on 1989's *Indiana Jones and the Last Crusade*, Peter Biskind argues that George Lucas and, in particular, Steven Spielberg popularised in the seventies and especially the eighties 'the echt lesson of the sixties: don't trust adults, particularly those in authority.' *Star Wars*, most obviously, is a film about kids versus parents (i.e., the Empire), with the kids being very much on the side of the good. Lucas then described *Close Encounters of the Third Kind* as a movie 'for the kids in all of us', and movies like *Star Wars* and *Indiana Jones* encourage a childlike unquestioning sense of awe in audiences of all ages ('I want a movie to overwhelm me,' Spielberg once said), bludgeoning them with spectacle and old-fashioned derring-do, replacing the more complex and anguished post-Vietnam films of the 1970s with something far more simple with clear-cut good guys and bad guys.

Spielberg has been fond of the-wisdom-of-children versus the-obtuseness-of-adults trope in his films for decades, and this is perhaps most obvious in the films he made in the eighties. In *E.T.*, Elliott is shown to be the one who should control the situation, not his mother and certainly not the US government. In *Indiana Jones and the Last Crusade*, Indy is emphatically in the child's role, locked in an Oedipal battle with his father (Sean Connery), who he resents but also wants desperately to please, like the neediest of adolescent boys.

The eighties saw a weird flurry of actual man-boys in a

slew of utterly disposable films about fathers, grandfathers and sons swapping bodies: *Vice Versa* (Judge Reinhold and Fred Savage), *18 Again!* (George Burns and Charlie Schlatter), *Like Father, Like Son* (Dudley Moore and Kirk Cameron) and *Dream a Little Dream* (Jason Robards and Corey Feldman – not, I suspect, a film Robards looked back on with much pride). Yet all these movies show that being an adult is preferable: you get to have sex, drive cars, not go to school and not listen to your parents. Being a kid, in these films, sucks.

The wonderful if deeply, deeply weird 1988 film *Big* comes closer to the current mentality that idealises man-boys. When thirteen-year-old Josh Baskin asks the arcade game Zoltar the Magnificent to make him big, he becomes Tom Hanks, replete with Tom Hanks's chest hair and Tom Hanks's penis, which is more than I ever got from an arcade game. As an adult but with a child's mentality, he charms women and work colleagues at his new job at a toy manufacturer, the insinuation being that his delightful innocence is just what the world of adulthood needs. This theory works well enough in the arena of Josh's job – who better to come up with ideas for toys for kids than a kid? – but gets decidedly icky when it comes to Josh's love life. The intimation here is that what a jaded thirty-something career woman needs in her life is a man who is – and acts like – a prepubescent virgin. If I ever went back to a man's apartment with him, and he suggested we sleep on different levels of a bunk bed, as happens to Susan (Elizabeth Perkins) when she goes to Josh's loft for the first time, I wouldn't think, Wow, what a sweet guy! I'm so girlishly excited about his innocent way of seeing the world! Instead, I would pick up the phone and say, 'Hello? Operator? Put me through to the Weirdos on the Loose Unit.' This, however, is not Susan's reaction and she eventually sleeps with and moves in with the chap Carrie Bradshaw would refer to as Bunk Bed Guy, which is weird in itself, but even weirder for the audience who knows that Josh – I repeat – is thirteen years old.

'It's emphasised in the screenplay that it was a secret he was a little boy,' says Tom Hanks, a little defensively when asked about this. 'And when we shot the scene when they're about to be intimate for the first time and there's that bit when he turns the light back on because I thought, well there's no way a thirteen-year-old boy wouldn't want to see this.'

Sure, the sex scene is believable but that doesn't mean it's not weird, right? He's THIRTEEN.

'Yeah,' he agrees. 'It was weird.'

But at least in the case of *Big* and all the body swap films, the reason the man is acting like a boy is because he is, actually, a boy. In none of these films, no matter how much they celebrate George Lucas's 'the child within us all' is there any suggestion that men should resist growing up, or that this is even their natural inclination. The reason the Ghostbusters represent an idealised sort of masculinity to me is because they're neither patrician nor man-boys – they're just funny, friendly guys whose funniness doesn't depend on misogyny or insecurity. Is that really too much to ask for these days?'[1] They were enough like my father when I was a kid to feel reassured by them (Harold Ramis), they were enough like me so that I wanted them to be my friends and giggle with them (Bill Murray), and they were handsome enough so that I wanted to do things to them I was only starting to understand (Aykroyd, obviously[2]). And

---

[1] Yes.

[2] I'm sensing that I'm not really convincing you of my whole 'Aykroyd = total hottie' argument.

those things still hold true, onscreen and, it turns out, off.

In early 2014 I was sent by the *Guardian*, where I work when I'm not watching eighties movies, to Los Angeles to cover the Oscars and the *Vanity Fair* party, the famous post-ceremony event. It so happened that Bill Murray had presented an award and had made an impromptu tribute to Harold Ramis, who'd died that year. When I saw him at the party, I didn't even stop to think or take the time to feel shy. I just instinctively ran up to him in an unashamedly starstruck way.

'Mr Murray, *Ghostbusters* is my favourite movie in the world. What is the secret of *Ghostbusters*' everlasting appeal?' I burbled breathlessly, simultaneously terrified and elated in that way you are when you meet your heroes.

He looked down at me (Murray is surprisingly tall), his hair now grey, but still as skew-whiff as Peter Venkman's after a ghost shoot-out. For a mortifying second, I thought he'd tell me to get lost.

'Friendship,' he replied without a pause. And then he gave me a noogie.

TOP FIVE MONTAGES
(yes, I left out the Rocky training montage. Too easy)

5 The volleyball game, 'Playing with the Boys' by Kenny Loggins, *Top Gun*

Topless sweaty men playing sport and a song called 'Playing with the Boys' by Kenny Loggins – seriously, what else can you possibly want from an eighties montage?

4 The Ghostbusters get successful, 'Ghostbusters' by Ray Parker Jr, *Ghostbusters*

Classic montage with newspaper front pages spinning across the screen, and a VERY cute photo of Aykroyd on the cover of *Time* magazine.[1] The cameos from real eighties DJs, such as Casey Kasem and Larry King, make me go a little weepy.

3 Alex practises dancing, 'Maniac' by Michael Sembello, *Flashdance*

She welds – and then she dances! And when she dances there are a thousand close-ups on her arse. This is pure Bruckheimer and Simpson as they were hitting their stride.

2 Baby learns to dance, 'Hungry Eyes' by Eric Carmen, *Dirty Dancing*

So sexy, so adorable. I just love the bit when her trainers suddenly morph into dancing shoes. I could watch this montage a million times, and I probably have.

---

[1] Yes, I am still going on about how cute young Aykroyd was.

1 The trip to the Chicago Institute of Art, 'Please, Please, Please' by the Dream Academy, *Ferris Bueller's Day Off*

John Hughes's self-described 'self-indulgent' scene, and all the more moving for it. This is the scene that confirms *Ferris Bueller* to be the most poetic of all the eighties teen films, and perhaps of all teen films ever.

Ferris Bueller's Day Off: The Impact of Social Class

The eighties, goes the general thinking, was the decade of venality. No one in America – heck, in the WORLD – had been interested in making money before the 1980s came along and corrupted us all. It was, apparently, the era in which everyone walked around in gold lamé and regarded Ivana Trump as the last word in understated chic. Seriously, you couldn't take the dog for a walk in the eighties without tripping over a giant Versace gold logo. And a pair of giant shoulder pads. And a massive pile of cocaine. And cocaine plays absolute HAVOC with one's Armani stilettos.

Maybe it was – far be it from me to cast aspersions on lazy descriptions of an era – but a little-remarked-upon truth is that this is not, in fact, the mentality depicted in many mainstream eighties movies. Many Hollywood movies argued for, if not actual class warfare, then certainly a suspicion of wealth. Repeatedly, wealthy people are depicted as disgusting, shallow and even murderous, while working-class people are noble and good-intentioned, such as in not exactly niche films like *Wall Street*,[*1] *Beverly Hills Cop*, *Ruthless People*, *Raising Arizona* and *Overboard*. Contrast this with today's films like *Iron Man*, in which the billionaire is the superhero (and is inspired by actual billionaire Elon Musk), and the deeply, deeply weird *The Dark Knight Rises*, in which the villain advocates the redistribution of wealth – HE MUST BE DESTROYED. But the eighties films that were the most interested in issues of class were, of all things, the teen films.

The motivating force of almost every single classic eighties teen film was not, in fact, selling soundtracks, watching an eighteen-year-old Tom Cruise try to get laid or seeing what ridiculous hairdo Nicolas Cage would sport this time round, but social class. There's *The Karate Kid*, in which the son of a single mother unsuccessfully tries to hide his poverty from the cool kids at school who make fun of his mother's car; *Dirty Dancing*, in which a middle-class girl dates a working-class boy, much to her liberal father's horror; *Can't Buy Me Love*, in which a school nerd gains popularity by paying for it; *Valley Girl*, in which an upper-middle-class girl dates working-class boy; *Say Anything*, in which a privileged girl dates lower-middle-class army brat and her father turns out to be a financial criminal; *The Flamingo Kid*, in which a working-class kid is dazzled by a wealthy country club and starts to break away from his blue-collar father; and all John Hughes's teen films.

[*1] *Wall Street* is pretty much the film equivalent of 'Born in the USA' in the way it was misunderstood and reappropriated by precisely the people it was satirising: just as Gordon Gekko's mantra 'Greed is good' was adopted by Wall Street bankers, so Springsteen's protest against the Vietnam War was clunkily adopted by Ronald Reagan's 1984 campaign for the presidency.

Of course, issues of class can be found in the undercurrents of pretty much any American movie, from *The Philadelphia Story* to *The Godfather*. The difference with eighties teen films is that they were completely overt in their treatment of it: class is the major motivator of plot, even if it's easy to miss next to the pop songs and Eric Stoltz's smile. All these films stress emphatically that the money your family has determines everything, from who your friends are, who you date, your social standing in school, your parents' happiness and aspirations and your future. They, to varying degrees, rage against the failure of the American Dream. They stress that true class mobility is pretty much impossible, and certainly interclass friendships and romances are unlikely, for the simple reason that rich people are assholes and lower-middle-class and working-class people are good. Which was unfortunate because according to the vast majority of eighties teen movies, the only way a teenager could truly move up out of their socioeconomic group was if they dated someone wealthier than them, Cinderella-style.

The one exception to this rule is *Back to the Future*, which definitely does not rage against the American system; instead, it concludes that, yes, money does buy happiness and that's just great. When Marty returns from 1955 to 1985, he realises that he has inadvertently changed history so that now his parents, formerly poor and therefore miserable and barely on speaking terms, are now rich and therefore happy and cheerfully smack each other's backsides: 'I remember how upset Crispin [Glover, who played George McFly] and Eric [Stoltz, who was originally cast as Marty] were about the ending of *Back to the Future*: now that they have money they're happy,' recalls Lea Thompson, who played Lorraine Baines McFly. 'They thought it was really outrageous. It went right over my head, of course. Maybe because I was poor and when I got wealthy I was happy!'

'The point was that self-confidence and the ability to stand up for yourself are qualities that lead to success,' says Bob Gale, co-writer of *Back to the Future*. 'So we showed George and Lorraine had an improved standard of living, we showed them loving toward each other, and we showed that George was a successful author. It was the way to show the audience that George had indeed become a better man. And, of course, in the beginning, we depicted George as a loser, Lorraine as a drunk, with a terrible car and a house full of mismatched and worn-out furnishings.'

Back to the Future is such a charming film that it's easy to be swept along by it and not notice this equation of lower-middle-class status with being a 'loser'. But it does echo precisely the same message that other eighties teen films sent: the class you are born into dictates every aspect of your life.

'Class has always been the central story in America, not race – class,' says Eleanor Bergstein, the writer and producer of *Dirty Dancing*. 'And when you're a teenager you really start to notice this.' And there was no teen film-maker who felt this as deeply as Hughes.

David Thompson complains in his majestic *Biographical Dictionary of Film* that in Hughes's teen films 'the fidelity of observation, the wit and the tenderness for kids never quite transcend the general air of problem solving and putting on a piously cheerful face. No one has yet dared in America to portray the boredom or hopelessness of many teenage lives – think of Mike Leigh's pictures to see what could be done.' The first thing to say is that to complain that John Hughes isn't enough like Mike Leigh is like getting annoyed that a chocolate cookie is not trying hard enough if it's not a roast dinner. But it isn't fair to dismiss Hughes's movies as devoid of 'hopelessness' as his repeated depiction of class issues in his films definitely shows the 'hopelessness' in these American teenagers' lives. *Pretty in Pink* (lower-middle-class girl falls for wealthy boy) and *Some Kind of Wonderful* (lower-middle-class boy falls for lower-middle-class girl who has gained acceptance among the rich kids through her looks) are the most obvious examples of Hughes's teen films that were obsessed with class injustice and how difficult it is for kids from different classes to connect (Hughes, despite his inherently romantic nature, apparently thought they couldn't really). But it's there in all his teen films, including *Sixteen Candles* (Jake's house is notably bigger and flashier than Samantha's) and *The Breakfast Club* (Bender's somewhat implausible-sounding home life[1] is compared to pampered Claire's world in which she can give out diamond earrings on a whim). But the film that really emphasises how unfair he thought the system is *Ferris Bueller's Day Off*.

There are many reasons to love *Ferris Bueller's Day Off*, and I've gone through all of them. As a kid, I loved it because I thought Ferris was so cool – he was cute, he was funny and, most thrillingly of all, he could drive a car. When I finally, contrary to all my expectations, became a teenager and realised driving a car wasn't quite as rare a skill as I'd believed as a nine-year-old, I decided that the real reason to love this film was that it was so weird. Like

---

[1] Although to be fair to Hughes, the implausibility may be more of a reflection on Judd Nelson's acting than Hughes's writing.

all of Hughes's teen films, it has a simple premise (boy skips school and brings his best friend, Cameron, and girlfriend, Sloane, along for the ride) and takes place over a tiny period of time (like *The Breakfast Club*, *Ferris Bueller's Day Off* doesn't even cover twenty-four hours). But it is a much stranger beast than anything else Hughes ever wrote. While all Hughes's other teen films deal with the emotional minutiae of being a teenager, *Ferris Bueller's Day Off* doesn't make even the slightest pretence to realism. The characters are all surreal exaggerations of recognisable characters – the teenager, Ferris, is just that little bit too cocky, the principal, Ed Rooney (Jeffrey Jones), is definitely too demented – and the situations it depicts are, quite clearly, impossible.

'John always meant for the movie to be a fable,' says Matthew Broderick. 'In the original, longer version of the film there were some sombre Hughesian musings about how when you're an adult nothing matters any more. But when he was editing he decided to make it clear that it was a comedy fantasy and so cut all that out. From the start, he knew it wasn't going to be a message-y movie, like *The Breakfast Club*. He wanted it to be about having a good time.'

For years I had a theory – and I was very proud of this theory – that *Ferris Bueller's Day Off* isn't about Ferris at all: it's about his miserable best friend, Cameron, and the whole movie is actually seen through Cameron's eyes.[1] This is why we see Ferris as this golden boy, the one who can do no wrong, the one for whom everything always goes right

---

[1] There is a popular internet conspiracy theory that says Ferris is actually a figment of Cameron's imagination, and there is merit in that. But personally, I don't want to live in a world where Ferris doesn't exist, albeit only onscreen.

and the one who everyone loves: because that's how Cameron sees him. Everyone had a friend in high school – and some still later in life – who, to their mind, exists within some kind of gilded halo, who is always funnier, smarter, cooler and more popular than they could ever be, and that is who Ferris is for Cameron. While Ferris happily makes out with his girlfriend by the stained-glass windows in the Chicago Art Institute (in what is the second best montage scene from an eighties movie), Cameron has a mini nervous breakdown while staring at Georges Seurat's *Un Dimanche Apres-Midi à l'Ile de la Grande Jatte*, as he realises that he, like the child in the painting, is nothing more than a series of meaningless dots. Nothing comes easy for Cameron, who thinks too much about everything, but everything comes easy to Ferris, who thinks deeply about nothing. The clinching piece of evidence to my theory is that it's Cameron who goes through an emotional change during the movie. He learns that, in order for him to achieve happiness at last in his life, he's going to have to stand up to his father, for once. Ferris, by contrast, is as blithe and content at the end of the film as he is at the beginning.

I liked this theory a lot, mainly because I came up with it, but also because it explained all the things in the movie that I treasured. I loved the movie's dreamy surrealism, with Ferris frequently breaking the fourth wall (Hughes loved to have his teen characters break the fourth wall but nowhere did he do it better, or as much, as in *Ferris Bueller's Day Off*) and the strange characters with their strange peccadilloes: Grace, the school secretary, pulling pens out of her enormous hair; Charlie Sheen as the druggy punk dispensing life advice in the police station; the teachers whose classes are so boring they feel like a lobotomy.'[1] They are all exaggerations, and that feels right if the movie is seen through a teenager's eyes because teenagers do exaggerate everything as they feel everything so intensely. And most of all, I loved Cameron, Ferris's miserable best friend, who increasingly felt like the heart of the film to me. Ferris, I realised, was kind of a jerk: he borrows his best friend's dad's vintage car, much to his best friend's horror (licence plate: 'NRVOUS'), just because he wants to borrow it. He manipulates his parents' blind love for him, he torments his younger sister, and he lies to pretty much every single person in the movie.

'It was definitely a concern when we were making the movie – is Ferris actually just an asshole?' Broderick laughs. 'But I saw him as the maître d' of the movie, and it's right that he shouldn't have emotional development. He's hosting the film.'

---

[1] The economics teacher, who roll-calls 'Bueller . . . Bueller . . .' was played by Hughes's friend and noted economist Ben Stein who has said that acting in *Ferris Bueller's Day Off* was the happiest day of his life: '[My obituary will] have a picture of me and above it will say "Bueller . . . Bueller." The fact that I went to Yale Law School, was a columnist for the *Wall Street Journal* and the *New York Times*, wrote thirty books, that will all be washed away and it'll just be, "Bueller . . . Bueller." And that will be just fine' (from *You Couldn't Ignore Me If You Tried*, Susannah Gora). Stein omits from his list of achievements that he was also a speechwriter for Nixon, a game show host, an advertising spokesperson (which led to him being sacked by the *New York Times*) and wrote a famously laughable defence of Dominique Strauss-Kahn, the former head of the IMF who in 2011 was accused of raping a hotel maid. Stein pooh-poohed the allegation with the ironclad argument that 'people who commit crimes are criminals', and not rich, important men like Strauss-Kahn. Maybe those achievements didn't feel as noteworthy to Stein as his attendance at Yale Law School? But no matter. In this book at least, a good *Ferris Bueller's Day Off* appearance can wash away all sins.

All these issues further convinced me of the rectitude of my theory: of course the film must be Cameron's fantasy because only a teenager like Cameron (or a kid like me) would think that Ferris was cool. All adults think he is a prat. Of course the movie was seen through Cameron's eyes.

But as an adult, I've realised none of this is right either. What makes *Ferris Bueller's Day Off* feel so special and warm isn't that it's about Cameron or the relationships behind the camera: it's that it's about John Hughes and, in particular, a subject especially close to his heart – social class.

Hughes wrote all his teen scripts quickly and with seeming Ferris-like ease, writing it in just two nights: 'You know how Salieri looked at Amadeus with rage when he'd pulled it out of thin air?' his collaborator Howard Deutch said, remembering Hughes working on Ferris, and using another eighties classic film as an analogy. 'That was me looking at John writing a script. I'd be like, "How?! How?!"'

The reason Hughes was able to write his teen scripts so quickly was because he wrote so much of himself in them, both emotionally and in the details. It's easy to mock the homogeneity of the world presented in these films, a world in which everyone's white and everyone's straight. But Hughes never meant his films to be seen as universal – they were utterly personal portraits of his own childhood, growing up as a teenager in the suburbs of Illinois (almost no one made movies set in Chicago until Hughes came along). Yet the emotions in the film universalised the movies, and with their simplistic narratives and familiar tropes, their clean divisions between good and bad, Hughes's teen films have become to the latter half of the twentieth century what Western films were to the first: they are as central to the way Americans raised on them see their own lives, and the way non-Americans raised on them see America. There is a part of me that still feels, and probably always will feel, that I didn't go to a REAL high school because mine – private, all girls, urban – looked nothing like the public, co-ed suburban schools I grew up watching. At my school in New York, we didn't even have a high school – we had an 'upper school'. So whenever people ask me about my 'high school' experiences, for a few initial seconds I envisage myself at Shermer High School, Hill Valley High School or even Westerberg High School. And then I remember the boring truth.

To cite all the references Hughes put into his films that came straight from his own life would take up a whole book but a few select ones from *Ferris Bueller's Day Off* alone include Ferris's home address (his house number is 2800, Hughes grew up in 2800 Shannon Road); the 'Shermer High' school scenes were shot in Hughes's old high school, Glenbrook North High School; Hughes and his high school best friend used to talk their way into fancy restaurants, as Ferris does when he takes his friends to Chez Quis (a punning reference, as writer Susannah Gora points out, to the American pizza chain Shakey's). But probably the most autobiographical moment in the film comes when Ferris takes Cameron and Sloane to the Chicago Art Institute. When Hughes was in high school the museum was, he said, 'a place of refuge for me' (in *Some Kind of Wonderful*, the male protagonist, Keith, describes the museum as 'my sanctuary') and 'this was a chance for me to go back into this building and show the paintings that were my favourites'. But whereas Hughes would go to the museum alone as a teenager, here he has the teenage male lead of the film bring his girlfriend and best friend (and Hughes himself now brings his entire audience with him).

Ferris Bueller's Day Off isn't Cameron's fantasy about Ferris – it's a former teenage outsider's self-fantasy about what their teenage life should have been like, and this is why it appeals so much to Hughes's audience which is largely made up of current and former teenage outsiders. *Ferris Bueller's Day Off* presents a nerd's idealised view of teenage life: sanitised, safe and sweet, in which you are universally adored for being your own weird self and can do whatever you damn well want. This is a vision that would appeal enormously to a former teenage outcast (Hughes) and a future one (me as a child).

'I sort of saw Cameron and Ferris as the two sides to John Hughes, because he could be moody and quiet, John. But he had another side to him that didn't give a damn about anything and could be really funny,' says Broderick

Hughes wrote *Ferris Bueller's Day Off* after *Pretty in Pink* and during his reworking of *Some Kind of Wonderful*, and both of those films feature archetypal Hughesian outcasts: Duckie (Jon Cryer) and Keith (Eric Stoltz). Ferris, by rights, should fit into this group, seeing as he is odd, has no interest in doing what people in authority tell him to do and likes New Romantic English singers. Like Duckie, he favours animal print (Duckie: shoes; Ferris: waistcoat), he talks to himself and he dances to old-school singers.[*1] And

---

[*1] Ferris and Duckie's dance styles are pretty similar, too, which is not that surprising as the man who choreographed Ferris's parade dance, the great Kenny Ortega, also choreographed Duckie's dance to 'Try a Little Tenderness' in *Pretty in Pink*. He later went on to choreograph *Dirty Dancing* and, somewhat less excitingly in this book's opinion, *High School Musical*.

also like Duckie, he would be insufferably annoying if he weren't so sweet. (That Jon Cryer looked almost identical to Broderick as a teenager further encourages identification between their characters.) But there are two key differences between Ferris and Duckie and Keith: Ferris is rich and popular and Duckie and Keith are poor and outcasts and, in an eighties teen movie, these issues are inextricably connected.

Hughes grew up in a lower-middle-class family in an upper-middle-class neighbourhood, an artistic outsider in a typical suburban high school, and he never forgot how it felt to be 'on the lower end of a rich community', as he told the *New York Times*. The divisions he draws between the wealthy and poor kids is done with a hand so heavy it could only belong to a man who once felt himself to be the victim of class snobbery. To be rich, in Hughes's films, means that you are a jerk but granted instant popularity, while the noble working-class kids muddle through in the shadows.

So when Hughes decided to write a film about – for the one and only time in his career – a popular but likeable kid, he simply took the nerd from his previous film, Duckie, and made him rich. This, in Hughes's world, was how a kid, even one as odd as Duckie/Ferris, was guaranteed popularity. The Buellers definitely have money, enough to give their son a computer and their daughter a car. Where Duckie apparently sleeps on a mattress in a bare room in *Pretty in Pink*, his alter ego Ferris sleeps in a room surrounded by computers and a giant stereo system. Where Duckie pines hopelessly after his female best friend and fantasises in vain about marrying her, Ferris dates the prettiest girl in school and she is desperate to marry him. And where Duckie seems to have no parental figures at all in his life, Ferris's parents think he's wonderful, even when the school principal tells them he really isn't. *Ferris Bueller's Day Off* is like Duckie's fantasy, which it is, to an extent, because it's Hughes's fantasy. But because this is a Hughes film, there is, inevitably, a dig about wealth in it and this is done through Cameron.

Cameron is, clearly, much richer than Ferris. Whereas Ferris's house is a typical but very plush upper-middle-class suburban house, Cameron lives in what looks like a multi-million-dollar bunker for a Bond villain. His father's collection of vintage cars alone probably costs twice as much as the Bueller homestead. And Cameron is emphatically miserable. Hughes suggested that Cameron's parents simply don't love him (the reason there is a close-up on Mary Cassatt's painting, *Mother and Child*, in the museum montage is because, Hughes said, 'I thought it was very relevant to Cameron, the tenderness between a mother and a child which he didn't have'), and Cameron knows that his father loves his Ferrari more than he loves his family. Even in a film that ostensibly lightens up on wealthy kids, Hughes couldn't help but make the point, again, that being a rich teenager – despite how it might look from the outside – actually sucks. Even if you yourself are not a jerk, like Steff in *Pretty in Pink* or Hardy in *Some Kind of Wonderful*, chances are your parents will be.

'Class consciousness was very important to John, and you can see it as he wrote about it so much,' says Broderick. 'He didn't talk about things like that so much but as time has passed I've realised that although he was very conservative politically, I think, he had a real problem with wealth when it was too concentrated. He always writes about it, even in something like *Planes, Trains and Automobiles*.

There's very often somebody with money and somebody without. With Ferris, he tried to keep it on a fable level but those elements are definitely still in there.'

This issue of class consciousness became, thanks largely to Hughes, such a staple of eighties teen movies it is as much of a cliché as the climactic prom. But it is the one ingredient to the genre that has never been picked up by its many copyists. Plenty of films have come out in the past decade that pay explicit homage to eighties teen films, especially Hughes's teen films, from *Easy A* to *21 Jump Street*, which the film's star and producer, Jonah Hill, described as 'a mix of *Bad Boys* and a John Hughes film'. But none of these films ever deals with the class issues that Hughes depicted. Partly this is because the people who make these homages are remembering the films from when they saw them as kids and, by and very large, kids didn't notice all these arguments about social mobility, focusing instead on the power ballads and fights in the school canteen. But it is also because Hollywood – and by extension America – doesn't talk about class issues the way it used to.

'There is an avoidance of talk about class identification now. You'll hear talk of gender identification, sexuality identification, race identification, but never class,' says Eileen Jones, a lecturer in film and media at UC Berkeley, and a writer for the socialist-leaning magazine *Jacobin*. 'Class identification, in America at least, is going through what feminism went through in the eighties: it is completely passé.'

What is even more passé is to say that social mobility is impossible. This goes specifically against the American dream and therefore verges dangerously into the kind of talk that will get a filmmaker denounced by Fox News.

Mainstream Hollywood movies that have depicted social mobility in the past twenty years, such as *Erin Brockovich* or even *Pretty Woman*, have all suggested that it is possible to lift oneself out of one's class (even if one has to become a prostitute and – even worse – spend a week with Richard Gere in Beverly Hills to do so). Teen movies of the 1980s argue precisely the opposite. 'Eighties films were willing to deal with being poor and people's lives being screwed over by economic structures. You hardly see that at all in movies today,' says Dr James Russell, Principal Lecturer in film, De Montfort University.

The reason American teen movies specifically stopped featuring class issues after the eighties can be traced, again, back to one specific film: *Clueless*. *Clueless* was so big it inevitably changed everything about how teen films were framed, including the trend in teen pop culture of showing, not how middle-class American teenagers actually live, but how they didn't even know they would like to live. Already by the mid-1990s teen films such as *10 Things I Hate About You* and *American Pie* were depicting a world in which all teenagers came from the same upper-middle social class, in which everyone lived in big houses and drove big cars. Sure, there were still cliques and outcasts in the schools, but these had nothing to do with social class. Instead, the idea of a poor or even lower-middle-class kid appearing in a teen film today feels as outdated as a movie about workers unions.

But instead of looking at why American teen movies in particular don't deal with class any more, the question could be instead why so many of them did in the eighties.

'Never underestimate Hollywood's eagerness to copy something successful,' laughs *Dirty Dancing*'s Eleanor

Bergstein. 'The reason so many teen movies talked about class is because those movies were successful, so then more movies would come along just like them.'

Another factor is the demographic of the people who made the films. Hughes was from a lower-middle-class family, Bergstein grew up in a similar economic situation and *Dirty Dancing* was born out of memories of her child-hood, 'and these were subjects that we talked about,' she says. It is impossible to find precise statistics about the demographics of who works in Hollywood now but one thing is widely agreed on: 'Hollywood has never been culturally diverse, but it's getting narrower, and it's defi-nitely narrower than it was thirty years ago,' says Dr James Russell. 'It's much more male and more white and largely college-educated and middle-class. It doesn't draw from a particularly broad background, at least at the top end. It's hard to imagine Sam Peckinpah getting in today.'

But probably the most crucial factor of all is the fact that movies today are more dependent than ever on the interna-tional market.

'You can't sell a movie to Japan or China that is about specific American cultural issues. So while American movies are still set in America, they are much vaguer and certainly not about American social issues,' says Dr Russell. 'Also, it tended to be mid-budget films that dealt with social issues in the eighties, and Hollywood doesn't make films with those budgets any more. It makes big block-busters or low-budget independents.' Hollywood in the 1980s produced hundreds of films about American social issues. Four alone were produced about the 1980s farm crisis: *Field of Dreams, Places in the Heart, Country* and *The River*. These days, social engagement is left to the niche independents while the big-budget movies that are aimed at the masses take care to talk about nothing specific at all.

Ferris Bueller's Day Off isn't just a fantasy about wealth, it's about growing up. The best of Hughes's teen films – *The Breakfast Club*, *Pretty in Pink* and *Ferris Bueller's Day Off* – are ultimately about the dread of growing up, of moving away, of losing that sparkle you have as a teenager and becoming as dead inside as all the adults seem to be around you. Everyone who watches those films as teenagers grows up with that dread and, eventually, regret about it. And this is something Hughes struggled with as much as any of his fans. It is ironic that Hughes, who made such a sparkling film fantasising about what it would be like to be rich and popular, struggled when he attained that status for himself.

By the time he started shooting *Ferris Bueller's Day Off*, Hughes was already, as Broderick puts it, 'the god-like Spielberg figure of teen movies'. By the time it came out, and became his biggest success, he was one of the most sought-after directors and writers in Hollywood. Everyone wanted to meet and work with the former kid who used to lurk around museums on his own. 'And John, I think, really didn't like it,' says Howard Deutch. 'He always felt like an outsider, and that's how he was able to write those characters. When he became successful out in LA and everybody wanted him, from Spielberg to Katzenberg, and all the power elite all wanted to do business with him, he found himself as a member of the insiders boy club. I think he felt like it was actually an obstacle to writing these characters that he believed in because he no longer felt like himself.'

So Hughes and his family moved back to Chicago, Hughes's hometown where he always felt happiest, and he continued to write. But the films he wrote 'never had the emotional impact I recognised as John's real skill', says Molly Ringwald. Instead, particularly from 1990 onwards, he wrote his 'dopey-ass comedies': *Beethoven*, *101 Dalmatians* and, of course, *Home Alone*. He no longer wrote about soulful teenage outcasts, maybe because he knew he no longer was one.

He also cut himself off from almost all the friends he'd made on those teen films, leaving them behind when he left the genre. 'I went to John's funeral and I realised when I was there that I hadn't actually seen him in over a decade,' recalls Broderick. 'It was sad because it had been such a happy set when we were making the film, and even afterwards John would invite Jennifer [Grey] and me to his house and we'd hang out in the pool with his family.' He smiles at the memory, and then sighs: 'But then he just disappeared.'

Ferris had his one perfect day. It's what comes after that can be a drag.

THE TEN BEST LOVE SONGS ON AN EIGHTIES MOVIE SOUNDTRACK

10 'Almost Paradise', by Mike Reno and Ann Wilson, from *Footloose*
The song from when the kids are waiting for the prom to start. A classic eighties duet.

9 'It Might Be You', by Stephen Bishop, from *Tootsie*
One giant cheese mountain of a song, and that is no bad thing.

8 'Let's Hear it for the Boy', by Deniece Williams, from *Footloose*
Everything about this song, including the spelling of the singer's name, is adorable.

7 'I Melt With You', by Modern English, from *Valley Girl*
This song should be better known. The movie, on the other hand, should not.

6 'Hungry Eyes', by Eric Carmen, from *Dirty Dancing*
Quality keyboard intro, bonus points for use in the best montage of the decade.

5 'Take My Breath Away', by Berlin, from *Top Gun*
This song is so good it makes having sex with Tom Cruise seem almost sexy.

4 '(I've Had) The Time of My Life', by Bill Medley and Jennifer Warnes, from *Dirty Dancing*

It is a testament to the quality of love songs from eighties films that this classic is not at number one.

3 'Waiting for a Star to Fall', by Boy Meets Girl, from *Mannequin*

Terrible film, amazing song from the best one-hit-wonder band of all time.

2 'In Your Eyes', by Peter Gabriel, from *Say Anything*

The most beautiful song in the world, and that is a scientific fact.

1 'She's Like the Wind', by Patrick Swayze, from *Dirty Dancing*

Patrick Swayze sang AND wrote this little piece of genius. Obviously it's number one.

Steel Magnolias:
Women are Interesting

Of all the many extraordinary qualities that eighties Hollywood movies possess – the glorious hairstyles, their respect for power ballads, the endearing amount of confidence they had in the acting abilities of Steve Guttenberg – their depiction of women is not, strangely, generally cited as being among their strengths. Eighties movies, the theory has long gone, were absolutely awful when it came to women, and no one argued this more vociferously at the time than feminist critics. 'The backlash [against feminism] shaped much of Hollywood's portrayal of women in the eighties,' Susan Faludi writes in the 1990s *Backlash*, in her famous chapter looking specifically at eighties movies. 'Hollywood restated and reinforced the backlash thesis: women were unhappy because they were too free; their liberation had denied them marriage and motherhood . . . [whereas] in the 1970s, the film industry would have a brief infatuation with the feminist cause.'

Faludi is right about one thing: between the seventies and the eighties movies did change their attitude towards feminism. In the seventies there was a slew of overtly feminist films about independent women, such as *Private Benjamin*, *My Brilliant Career*, *Norma Rae* and *Alice Doesn't Live Here Anymore*. Marriage was shown to be a prison for women in films such as, most famously, *The Stepford Wives*. Of course, not all movies were so charmed with feminism: in 1979's bafflingly much lauded *Kramer vs. Kramer* feminism is portrayed as something kooky and selfish. It is explicitly blamed for the breakdown of Ted (Dustin Hoffman) and Joanna's (Meryl Streep) marriage[*1] and, the movie insinuates, will probably result in the couple's doe-eyed son spending the rest of his life hating women BECAUSE FEMINISM RUINS EVERYTHING. But it is fair to say that movies weren't as explicitly interested in feminism in the eighties as they were in the seventies – with the noted and glorious exception of 1980's *Nine to Five*. In this still very funny film, Dolly Parton, Jane Fonda and the glorious Lily Tomlin fight their sexist pig of a boss (Dabney Coleman) for equal pay, flexible working hours and an in-office nursery (come back, Dolly, Jane and Lily! We working women of the twenty-first century still need you!).

It is also certainly true that some 1980s movies were decidedly nervy about feminism – as nervy, in fact, as *Kramer vs. Kramer*. In 1988's *Die Hard*, for example, the whole reason John McClane (Bruce Willis) is visiting LA, where he is nearly killed by Alan Rickman's German accent, is because his wife Holly (the brilliantly named Bonnie

---

[*1] Faludi doesn't mention *Kramer vs. Kramer* in her discussion of 1970s films as a feminist utopia, but I of all people can hardly criticise her for providing a selective view of a decade's movies.

Bedelia) has SELFISHLY insisted on moving there for her career. And look what THAT gets her: a destroyed office, traumatised children and a beat-up husband. FEMINISM RUINS EVERYTHING. Thank heavens her husband happens to be in town to save her from her dreadful feminist mistake, right? Just to make the point even more clearly that this woman is a selfish feminist cow, she insists on going by her maiden name which is, like, totally outrageous, the film suggests, because her husband loves her so much. But by the end, she has learned her lesson and introduces herself as 'Holly McClane'. Her husband grins happily at his newly obedient wife. In the next scene, we see the McClane family happily eating cupcakes the wife has just baked, as they gaze happily out of their window at the pleasing view of 1952.

The popular argument that the eighties were terrible for women in movies is primarily based on one ridiculously OTT and all-dominating piece of evidence: *Fatal Attraction*. Directed by British former ad-man Adrian Lyne, *Fatal Attraction* was so clearly designed to needle women that it might well have been written by someone from the *Daily Mail*. The film's message is that women who work and aren't married by the decrepit age of thirty-six are pathetic, crazed with baby hunger and deserve to be shot by good and humble housewives (I am not exaggerating – this is literally the message of the movie). Along with S&M romcom *9½ Weeks*, which was also directed by Lyne, *Fatal Attraction* tends to skew all discussions about women in eighties movies, and that's a shame.

Sure, Lyne and his fantasies about how all women are masochistic bunny boilers are pretty attention-grabbing, but to let them grab all the attention is essentially doing Lyne's work for him.[1] Because, contrary to what Lyne seemed to think, there is a lot more to eighties women than stalkers and sadist shaggers. There were so many interesting female film characters in the eighties, and so many great movies about women. Not all of them were explicitly feminist, but the fact that these films were made at all, with largely female casts, featuring female stories, feels so feminist compared with today's movies they make Andrea Dworkin look a bit watered down. So much so, in fact, that feminist critics – ones who grew up reading Faludi – now look back to the eighties as the last highpoint for women in movies: 'The status of women in movies has gotten worse since the 1980s,' wrote journalist Amanda Hess, in a 2014 discussion about *Backlash* and eighties films.

'Just look at 1983, for example. I don't know what was going on but you had *Yentl*, *Terms of Endearment* and *Silkwood* – all big films for women. Then there were movies like *Frances*, *Places in the Heart*, *Gorillas in the Mist*, *Aliens* . . . But now, well, we know what's happened now,' says film writer Melissa Silverstein.

And this is all true. But when I think about women in eighties movies, I don't think of any of those perfectly fine examples (all of which are impossible to imagine being made now). Instead, I think about the classic women's movies.

---

*1 For a start, there were other movies around that were far smarter about male infidelity than *Fatal Attraction* such as, for example, *Moonstruck*. In this movie, Olympia Dukakis has to contend with her aged husband's compulsive womanising. But because this movie was sensible and not stupid like *Fatal Attraction* – or, more recently, the appalling *The Other Woman* (2014) – *Moonstruck* shows that marriage is about more than just point-scoring, infidelity is about more than just sex, and the betrayed wife is a smart woman in her own right. So don't watch *Fatal Attraction* – watch *Moonstruck*.

Most people know about the Bechdel test, which ascertains how feminist a film is by posing the following questions:

1. It has to have at least two women in it . . .
2. Who talk to each other . . .
3. About something besides a man.

Well, I'd like to coin the Magnolia test, named for a movie that is particularly close to my heart, which judges whether or not a movie is a proper women's movie:

1. The cast is largely, maybe even solely female . . .
2. And the female characters are kind to one another because they like one another, and they talk to each other about a million things other than men . . .
3. And the relationship between the women is far more important than any they have with a man.
(Bonus points if any of the following are in the film: Shirley MacLaine, Dolly Parton, Bette Midler, Olympia Dukakis. Triple for Sally Field.)

In an ideal world, these films would just be known as 'movies' as opposed to 'women's movies'. But as the ongoing success of Michael Bay proves, we do not live in an ideal world. And so, for too long, when it comes to leading roles in movies, women have been seen as the exception rather than the norm. Movies that focus on women's stories are – now more than ever – dismissed as 'niche', even though women make up more than half the human race and (arguably more to the point) cinema audiences. So the gendering is, gratingly, necessary, just as, apparently, Michael Bay is to Hollywood's current financial success.

Some people snark about women's movies and dismiss them as 'domestic', as though that were a negative thing. Home is a place most of us know and to write off 'domestic' as an embarrassment is to dismiss the lives millions and millions of women lead as worthless. I've also heard complaints that whereas men get action movies and Westerns, women 'only' get domestic dramas and big ol' weepies. Well, if I want to see movies set in jungles or outer space, I will, and thanks to eighties movies I can see those movies starring kickass women in the form of, respectively, *Romancing the Stone* and *Aliens*.

What I love about classic women's movies is that they tell women that their daily lives are interesting. Westerns and action movies and other genres considered to be the area of menfolk do not, because they do not depict lives led by most men, although heaven knows there are plenty of other movies out there that depict nothing but the daily lives of men. Women's movies show women living normal daily lives – raising their children, dealing with breast cancer, laughing with their friends, contending with unfaithful husbands, fighting sexist bosses: in other words, things that women around the world deal with every day. These movies also respect the value of women's emotional lives and show women talking to each other about things other than men. Men see this about themselves in pretty much any other movie. Women? Not so much. In women's movies, women exist in their own right, not as appendages, not as lonely spinsters, or idealised quarries, or someone's wife or someone's mother, but as funny, sad, angry, kind, supportive, independent human beings – and how many movies can claim that? So yeah, sure, men have their Westerns and their stoicism and tumbleweed. But women get to bond over cheesecake with Dolly Parton. If men make sneering comments about women's films, it's because they're jealous, and I really can't blame them.

Nine to Five amply passes the Magnolia test, as do those *ne plus ultra* eighties women's movies, *Terms of Endearment* and *Beaches*, two of the most classic women's weepies of all time. These movies starred women, were made for women, told distinctly women's stories involving breast cancer, straying husbands and motherhood, and the few men onscreen are repeatedly shown to be a disappointment, whereas the women are there for one another until death. *Beaches* comes with the obvious added bonus of being the last film to provide truly great hairbrush-microphone-in-front-of-the-mirror singing, thanks to Bette Midler's irresistible soundtrack, a quality frustratingly lacking from movies today, and it serves as some distraction from Barbara Hershey's lips seemingly inflating and deflating during the film. *Terms of Endearment* is probably not a film you've seen recently, but you should – it is as delightful as you'd expect a movie to be featuring Shirley MacLaine as a crotchety busybody and Jack Nicholson as her astronaut(!) lover. But the real heart of the film is the relationship between MacLaine and her charmingly daffy daughter (Debra Winger) who, while married to one useless man (Jeff Daniels) and being wooed by another (John Lithgow), develops breast cancer. These two films are both sad but, like the best weepies, they are also very funny, and this brings me to a quick defence of women's weepies.

American feminist film critic Mollie Haskell, writing a decade before the eighties, was very dismissive of women's movies and, in particular, women's weepies in her classic text *From Reverence to Rape: The Treatment of Women in the Movies*:[1] 'The woman's film,' she writes, 'fills a masturbatory need, it is soft-core emotional porn for the frustrated housewife. The weepies are founded on a mock-Aristotelian and politically conservative aesthetic whereby women spectators are moved, not by pity and fear but by self-pity and tears to accept, rather than reject, their lot. That there should be a need and an audience for such an opiate suggests an unholy amount of real misery.'

Well, first, unlike Haskell, I don't see too much wrong with providing fodder for masturbation, especially if that other person is frustrated. Seems like simple generosity to me. Second, the idea that crying at sad movies is a form of transference is, to be frank, grade A baloney. A movie that makes you both laugh and cry is as satisfying as a pop song that is both moving and ecstatic.[2] It's about the pleasure of experiencing the full gamut of emotions from a single piece of art, that feeling of standing up at the end, exhausted by the emotional pummelling but still giggling at some of the jokes. After all (cue stirring instrumental eighties women's movie theme song), isn't that what life itself is like? I can understand why some critics – and especially feminist critics – object to the trope of a woman dying in the women's movie (belated spoiler: someone dies in both *Terms of Endearment* and *Beaches*). But that is, in fact, only a tiny part of both of those films: they are really about

---

[1] One day I shall write a book about the mighty titles of feminist texts and studies. They are all reliably awesome.

[2] See: the oeuvre of The Cure and New Order – in the eighties, obviously.

female friendship and mothers and daughters. It's just that the deaths ramp up the tears and the tears are part of the way female audiences (by which I obviously mean 'me') bond with the movies and bond with each other while watching the movie. A movie that makes you cry is a movie you have to love, and crying while watching a movie with a female friend is as intimate as getting drunk with them.

But the really telling detail is that these movies make (the largely female) audiences cry over the death of a woman. So often, women who die in movies (and books) are either idealised or completely anonymous, and it's impossible to cry over such characters today (I have never, for example, cried over the death of tedious Miss Melanie in *Gone With the Wind*). Whereas with the women in *Terms of Endearment* and *Beaches*, we got to know them pretty well – their sexual desires, their flaws, their jealousies. That female audiences still cry at the end of these films is a testament to how hard the films work to make these female characters feel real.

This is why, of all the great eighties women's movies, my favourite one is *Steel Magnolias*. I watch this film at least twice a year (and always down tools if I happen to come across it on TV). It still makes me laugh out loud ('I'm not crazy, M'Lynn – I've just been in a very bad MOOD for forty years,' Shirley MacLaine's character Ouiser says to Sally Field's M'Lynn at one point, and that quote in particular has proven astonishingly useful in real life) and, yes, I still cry, every time, at the end. 'Laughter through tears is my favourite emotion,' says Dolly Parton's character, Truvy, in the film, which could be the motto of the film, and it's apparently everyone else's, too. Twenty-five years on, this film is still adored, so much so that it was remade (badly, sadly[1]) in 2012 with an all-black cast.

'People still talk to me about *Steel Magnolias* today – today!' says one of the film's stars, Olympia Dukakis. 'At benefits I ask women to put their hands up if they've seen the film five times, ten times, fifteen times. The other day I got up to twenty-seven times. These women had seen the movie twenty-seven times! What a draw that film has. It tells women that female friendship is profound, and women watch it together and cry together, still.'

But even more important than weeping and hooting is the way it teaches audiences to expect more from movies when it comes to the representation of women.

For a start, this movie stars six female characters and there is not a single bitch fight. Not once do they even fight over a man. Imagine that! What next, a movie suggesting women can work together without throwing tampons at one another? A movie suggesting women like and respect each other – get outta town! Each of the six female characters gets her own story, some more lightly sketched out than others: Truvy (Parton) has to deal with a deadbeat husband and son; Annelle (Daryl Hannah) is coming out of a bad marriage and making a new life for herself; Clairee (Olympia Dukakis) has just entered widowhood; Ouiser (MacLaine) is starting a new relationship; M'Lynn (Field) is facing the loss of her daughter; and Shelby (Julia Roberts) is risking her life to have a much longed-for baby. These are all typical women's stories, acted by six actresses who, between them, had an average age of fifty when the film came out.

---

[1] Says Hadley, madly.

It is impossible to imagine a studio film being made today featuring such everyday, even 'domestic' stories about women so unforgivably north of thirty-five. The only vaguely equivalent film that has been released in the past decade is *The Help*, in which the five leading actresses (Emma Stone, Octavia Spencer, Viola Davis, Jessica Chastain, Bryce Dallas Howard) had an average age of 34.8 between them when the film came out and instead of just focusing on real women's lives, it took as its plot one of Hollywood's most beloved storylines: white people solve racism. In fact, Hollywood hasn't made a classic women's movie since the nineties with *Fried Green Tomatoes* and *A League of Their Own*.

But if the telltale sign of a classic women's movie is that it illuminates the reality of women's lives, then it's no surprise that *Steel Magnolias* is so good because the reason it was written was to illuminate one particular woman's life. When paediatric nurse Susan Robinson, a sweet-faced brunette from Louisiana, died suddenly in 1985 from complications stemming from diabetes at the age of thirty-three, leaving behind a two-year-old son, her brother, Bob Harling, was distraught. But when his sister's widower, Pat, remarried a mere five months after Susan's death, he knew he had to do something. 'It was very, very hard. I mean, it was just five months which was a little, you know,' says Harling, from his house in Natchitoches, Louisiana, his and Susan's hometown. 'Susan had gone through all this out of devotion to her son and when I heard him call another woman "mama", I thought, No way, he needs to know the story of his mother and his grandmother.'

Harling had worked as an actor and had never written 'a

thing' before. But he became, he says, 'obsessed' with telling Susan's story. So, with the encouragement of some friends who were writers, he wrote it as a play about six women set in a beauty parlour, renaming his sister 'Shelby'. 'I wrote it very quickly because I wanted to capture how the women spoke. But I had no idea that anyone would do anything with it, I just wanted to make a document that celebrated Susan,' he says in his gentle Louisiana accent.

The first thing that someone did with it was to turn it into an off-Broadway play, and it opened to huge critical praise. To Harling's amazement, Hollywood studios then approached him, asking him to adapt it as a screenplay. This being the eighties, the fact that the play had an all-female cast did not dissuade producers from thinking this play could make a hit film and there was a bidding war. 'I think it spoiled me for the rest of my career, actually, because we had so many suitors for the film,' Harling says.

But one producer, Ray Stark, knew that for the movie to work, it had to feel real, and the best way to start that was to film it in the town where the story actually happened. And so, when Stark suggested making the movie in Natchitoches, Louisiana, among the places that Susan had known and the people who had known her, Harling signed with him.

Harling and his parents, Robert and Margaret, then had the extraordinary experience of watching their lives and the lives of their friends being played out in their hometown by some of the best known actors of their day: 'I had what was called "casting consultation", and they were very generous about that and let me hang around for all that.' He smiles. 'But when they come to you and say, Sally [Field] wants to play your mother and Shirley [MacLaine] wants to play Ouiser, and Olympia [Dukakis] – she just won the Oscar two or three weeks ago – she'll be Clairee, well, you're not going to say no.'

Being a Southern family, they were, understandably, especially excited at the prospect of Dolly Parton playing the beauty parlour owner, Truvy: 'Dolly was a little more glamorous than the original woman Truvy was based on, but that's just to be expected,' says Harling, with Southern sangfroid.

Meg Ryan was originally cast to play Shelby, but she dropped out when she got the lead in *When Harry Met Sally*. The near unknown Julia Roberts was cast in her stead 'and as soon as I saw that smile I said, "There's Susan,"' Harling recalls.

Roberts visited the Harlings frequently, looking through their family albums and hearing stories about Susan from people who knew her in the town. Field, on the other hand, kept more to herself, wanting to create her own character, 'and my mother, being a Southern belle, would never want to impose. Also, if you're a woman from a small Southern town and Sally Field is playing you in a movie, you go, OK, you go girl, whatever you do is fine by me.'

Although some things in the film were changed for dramatic effect – whereas Shelby collapses at home with her baby son, Susan in fact fell into a coma in hospital – the movie was remarkably true to the women and their stories, Harling says. His mother did in fact donate her kidney to her daughter, his sister did risk everything to have a baby and the women the characters were based on talked just as they do in the film, in 'bumper sticker slogans', as Harling puts it: 'Your husband is a boil on the butt of humanity'; 'If you can't say anything nice, come sit by me.'

'What I wanted to show was the strength of these women, and the strength they gave each other,' says Harling, who then went on to write *Soapdish*, also starring Sally Field, in the nineties. 'I enjoy writing women's emotional journeys, but it's hard today to get movies made that aren't based on comic books. Character-driven films are the domain of the independents which a studio is never going to attack because they're all corporations. It's getting harder and harder to [get films made] with human roles, and a part of that is that it's much harder to get films made with women's roles.'

'I don't think that *Steel Magnolias* would be considered "industry friendly" today,' says Dukakis with more than a touch of wryness.

Where once studios made women's movies, now they make 'the negative sisterhood movie' to use Wesley Morris's memorable phrase. This is what the women's movie has become today and it is a bafflingly popular genre, one that suggests the women hate each other and should be duly punished for their stupidity by having to spend their lives fighting over men and being humiliated onscreen as much as possible. You know these movies: they're 2009's *Bride Wars*, 2014's *The Other Woman*, the toxic glut of overly monikered films like *What to Expect When You're Expecting*, *He's Just Not That Into You*, *I Don't Know How She Does It*, pretty much anything starring Kate Hudson.

One could argue that this genre was kick-started in the eighties, with films like *Working Girl*, in which Melanie Griffith and Sigourney Weaver engage in a wearily

predictable catfight over their job, ostensibly, but boring
Harrison Ford, in actuality. This is one of the many
reasons why *Working Girl* is, to my mind, a far inferior
film to that other great eighties movie about women
working, *Baby Boom*.[1] *The Witches of Eastwick* could also
be described as an anti-sisterhood movie, but that film –
starring Michelle Pfeiffer, Susan Sarandon and Cher, all
obsessed with Jack Nicholson's penis – ultimately satirised
the genre.

Negative sisterhood movies are now the default style for
what were once romcoms and women's movies: movies
consisting of women hating each other and competing with
one another. What's strange is that these films are all less
successful than the traditional women's movies such as *Steel
Magnolias* ever were. So if you want to know how little
Hollywood cares about women today, watch a negative
sisterhood movie.

Everyone knows that the representation of women in
movies today is bad. Even Faludi, who raged so passionately against the representation of women in eighties
movies, had to admit that, in the early nineties, film roles
for women had dropped so far that male characters made
up two-thirds of people onscreen, and that number hasn't
changed since. When Faludi returned to *Backlash*, she
wrote in the new introduction to the 2005 edition: 'Back in
the 80s . . . were single women breaking courtship rules
and taking the sexual initiative? "You'll turn into a psycho-
killer and meet your maker in an overflowing bathtub!" the
Hollywood mullahs decreed. Ah, the good old days.' After

---

[1] Also, *Baby Boom* co-stars James Spader, which pretty much makes it an
automatic winner in my book.

all, she concluded, 'There are some things worse than a backlash.'

In 2013 women made up only 21.8 per cent of the crews of the 100 top grossing films in the US, and that number has remained pretty steady for the past twenty years. But people within the industry say it is far from the complete picture and what's actually changed is what studios will allow them to do. 'I love directing women but, for so long, it's just been a non-starter,' says Paul Feig, the director of female-led hits *Bridesmaids* and *The Heat*. 'You'd go into meetings and people would say, "Oh, a female lead? Can't you make her male?" A movie starring a male is normal but a movie starring a woman is a gimmick, and it just didn't make any sense to me.'

And this is as true of movies aimed at children as at adults. In 2006 Feig signed on to direct the children's film *Unaccompanied Minors*, about a boy and his little sister causing chaos in an airport.

'It wasn't until I got into the rewriting that I learned it was based on a real story that had happened to a girl and her sister. Again you go, "Gosh, they just changed the lead girl to a boy – that's really aggravating!" It was never entertained that it could have been a girl in the lead. It wasn't even an issue,' he recalls with a laugh of frustration. 'And this whole debate about whether female superheroes can open their own movie – just fucking do it! What is the big debate about it? Why does Wonder Woman have to be part of an ensemble? Why can't she come out of the gate in her own movie? Why are we so precious about it? To me it's not even an issue, but that's why it's so funny that it's an issue!'

The common argument in defence of the current low

representation of women in movies is that studios aren't sexist – they're simply looking after the economics. So while women will see movies starring men and women, men will only see movies starring men –in other words, it's the audiences who are sexist. This problem is hardly exclusive to the film world. The books website Goodreads recently surveyed 40,000 of its members and found that readers overwhelmingly preferred books written by authors of their own gender: 90 per cent of men's 50 most read books were by men and 45 of the 50 most read books by women were written by women. Currer Bell, George Sands, George Eliot and Robert Galbraith didn't need 40,000 people to confirm that readers judge authors by their gender.[*1]

Yet just as the Goodreads survey found that male and female readers alike both rated women authors more highly than male ones, so audiences – male and female – have repeatedly proven how much they like movies with female protagonists. Recent films featuring female protagonists including *Bridesmaids*, *Frozen*, *The Help*, *Gravity* and *The Heat* have all been enormous successes, while male-led ones like *The Lone Ranger* and *After Earth* have flopped. In fact, the biggest box office disasters of all time all featured male protagonists, including *47 Ronin* (Keanu Reeves), *The 13th Warrior* (Antonio Banderas), *The Lone Ranger* (Johnny Depp and Armie Hammer) and *Heaven's Gate* (Christopher

---

[*1] One of my favourite newspaper columns in the world is the *New York Times*'s By the Book series in which famous people discuss their favourite writers. Almost invariably, readers cleave to their own gender: Bruce Springsteen, for example, mentioned thirty-seven authors, only two of whom were women, which, to be fair, may well be an accurate reflection of Springsteen's own fanbase.

Walken and Kris Kristofferson). As yet, no one has taken the failure of these movies as proof that men aren't funny, men can't carry a movie or that maybe audiences just don't like to watch men.[1]

The fact is, women's movies – the few that still come out – are generally very profitable. They don't make as much money as many men's films, but that's because action movies (which now invariably star men) are bigger productions with bigger marketing pushes, but also with higher costs. In fact, Silverstein's blog Women and Hollywood found in 2013 that movies with a female protagonist that year earned 20 per cent more than movies with just a male protagonist, making $116 million compared to male-led ones making $97 million, even though, out of the 100 movies they sampled, only 16 had female protagonists. But as Amanda Hess pointed out: 'We still don't know whether gender equality in films would constitute a smart economic choice for Hollywood, because we've never gotten anywhere close to testing that assumption.'

And so one woman, who started acting in the eighties, decided to try to rectify that. 'Thelma & Louise [which came out in 1991] was my first experience with the difference between how media respond to something and how it

_____

[1] New York Times's Manohla Dargis pointed out that when Michael Mann's 2001 film Ali failed to make back its costs, his career was barely affected and he directed big-budget films for Paramount and Universal soon after. When Kathryn Bigelow's 2002 adventure film K-19: The Widowmaker didn't recoup its costs, she didn't make another film until 2007 and it was funded by a French company. 'Ms Bigelow is one of the greatest action directors working today, and it's hard not to wonder why failure at the box office doesn't translate the same for the two sexes,' Dargis writes ('Women in the Seats But Not Behind the Camera', Manohla Dargis, New York Times, 10 December 2009).

turns out in real life,' recalls Geena Davis. 'All of the press was about, "Get ready for many more female buddy pictures and road trip films." And then . . . nothing. Same thing happened with [1992's] *A League of Their Own*: "Proof that women's sports movies can make huge box office!" Name all of the female sports movies since then, right? This happens every few years, with the press anointing yet another female-starring film as the One That Will Change Everything, but nothing happens.'

Davis made her film debut as a rarely clothed starlet in 1982's *Tootsie*, sharing a dressing room with a somewhat embarrassed cross-dressing Dustin Hoffman. Her roles throughout that decade were remarkably, even hilariously, varied, including playing an insect's girlfriend in *The Fly*; a temptress of aliens in *Earth Girls Are Easy*; a rubber-faced ghost in *Beetlejuice*; and a mercurial dog trainer in *The Accidental Tourist*, for which she won an Oscar. She still acts occasionally today – she had a small part in 2013's *In a World*, about sexism in the movie trailer business – but, like many actresses before her, she found that studios stopped calling once she was over forty:

When I was starting out it was the era of Meryl Streep, Sally Field, Jessica Lange and Glenn Close getting nominated for movies with spectacular female roles in them. I had heard that great parts for women drop off at forty, but I thought, These women will change everything. It won't be a problem any more when I get there. But it didn't change. Before forty, I was averaging about one movie a year. During my forties, I only made one movie. That's a big change. But I look back on that decade when I was coming up and there were so many movies about interesting women: *Frances, Places in the Heart.* They were the anomaly then, which is why women were still in the minority then according to the statistics, but those movies were still made.

In 2004, while staying at home with her then toddler daughter, Davis noticed something odd about the movies and TV shows aimed at children: there were notably few female characters, and this 'absolutely floored' her: 'Then something else shocked me: NO one seemed to be seeing what I was seeing: not my friends (until I pointed it out), and not the decision-makers in Hollywood, either. Whenever I brought the subject up, if I happened to be meeting with a studio executive or director, to a person the response was, "Oh no, that's been fixed." And they would very often name a movie with one female character in it as proof that gender inequality had been fixed! That's when I knew I needed the data.'

Davis ended up sponsoring the largest amount of research ever done on gender depictions in entertainment media, covering over a twenty-year span at the Annenberg School for Communication at the University of Southern California. Inspired by this, she then launched the Geena Davis Institute on Gender in Media in 2007. The data the research and institute uncovered appalled her: 'In family-rated films, crowd and group scenes contain only 17 per cent female characters. Seventeen per cent! In animation and live-action. That means the fictitious worlds that are being created for kids have only about a 17 per cent female population. Why, in the twenty-first century, would we be training kids to see women as taking up far less space in the world than men?' she asks.

Nor is it just the numbers of women who are being represented: it's how they're represented, full-stop, says Davis. 'Female characters in animated G-rated movies [US equivalent of a U], made for the youngest of kids, wear the same amount of sexually revealing clothing as the female characters in R-rated [US equivalent of 18] movies. Astounding, isn't it? And in research, there are no fuzzy definitions; this is not sexy appearance in a generalised way. It's specifically revealing clothing. These findings highlight how seemingly innocuous children's fare can be sending a damaging message to kids: it's teaching kids to see women and girls as less important than men and boys, and that girls should be judged on their sex appeal,' she says.

The sexualisation of young women onscreen is – as will surprise precisely no one – getting more extreme. In a study of the top 500 films of 2012, 31.6 per cent of female characters were featured in sexy clothes (compared to 7 per cent of male ones) and 31 per cent were at least partially naked (compared to 9.4 per cent of male ones). Even more creepily, actresses aged between thirteen and twenty are more likely to be sexualised than those between twenty-one and thirty-nine (ugh – twenty-one! Who would want to see such a hag naked, amirite??), and the number of near-naked female teenagers increased onscreen between 2007 and 2012 by 32.5 per cent.

In 2011 women accounted for 33 per cent of all characters, but only 11 per cent of protagonists. In 2013 one journalist calculated that 90 per cent of the film screenings showing near her in Washington DC were stories about men, and the ratio would have been even worse if she didn't live in a major city. That year, women made up only

15 per cent of protagonists in the biggest movies from the US. And as *New York* magazine pointed out, it has been thus for the past twenty-five years.

Statistics don't necessarily tell the full story, of course. For a start, the figures from 1980–89 don't look much better: according to the Annenberg Public Policy Center in Pennsylvania, only 29 per cent of the 'main characters' in a movie were women. But as Amy Bleakley, who conducted the more recent study, points out, they did not take into consideration the context of the women's roles, such as whether they were the protagonists or near nameless girl-friends.

'We can see that women are not onscreen any more,' says Melissa Silverstein, founder and editor of the blog Women and Hollywood. 'They are not protagonists in films and they're not leaders, and this says a lot about how women are valued in our culture.'

'Women have advanced, while much of the movie industry has not,' writes the *New York Times*'s film critic Manohla Dargis.

The theory that women are being pushed out of movies in order to appeal to the Chinese market doesn't necessarily stand up, Davis says. After all, according to the latest report from the institute, China has a pretty good record in featuring women in its own films: in films made by China aimed at children and young people released between 1 January 2010 and 1 May 2013, 30 per cent featured casts with a gender balance. In equivalent films from the US, precisely 0 films featured a gender balance. In fact, according to the study, it's not China that's the problem, but America. When looking at, again, equivalent films made by the UK, 38 per cent featured a female character, 30 per cent featured a female lead and 20 per cent featured casts with a gender balance. In US/UK co-productions, these figures plummeted to, respectively, 23.6 per cent, 0 and 0.

But Davis stops short of suggesting that any kind of nefariousness lies behind this. Instead, she puts it down to something that is, in fact, worse: blitheness. 'There is no plot against women in my industry; creators are simply not aware of how many female characters they're leaving out!' she says.

Amy Bleakley suggests that the increasing reliance on violence in movies also plays a part: 'Some of the more profitable movies (including PG-13) feature a lot of violence content, which historically has primarily involved male characters,' she says. '[Also], most successful writers and directors are men, and they may be drawn toward telling stories through perspectives and characters they are most familiar or comfortable with – i.e., other men.'

Kathleen Turner, Davis's cast-mate in *The Accidental Tourist*, also played an extraordinarily wide range of roles in the eighties, and this was a conscious decision on her part: 'Once I have explored and created a character, I have no desire to repeat it so I automatically look for the thing that's the opposite,' she says, in that voice that's only gotten more impressive with age. 'So from playing a femme fatale in *Body Heat* I went to *The Man with Two Brains* which is a take-off on the femme fatale, to *Romancing the Stone*, which is a woman who doesn't know anything about her sexual power, then to *Crimes of Passion* which is a woman who sells herself on Sunset Boulevard for $50. Pretty much each role is a contrast to the one before.'

These days, she says, not only does she see fewer studio

films for women ('and that's just fucking unbelievable"[1]) but less variety in the roles: 'For years I have been rather disgusted by the studio films coming out of Hollywood because the women are such clichés. Women in particular today are encouraged to build on their successes, by which they mean to play the character that sells, and I don't know if audiences really want to see that. That poor woman, Jennifer Aniston, has been playing the same role for twenty years. I'm like, come on, honey, aren't you bored?"[2]

Paul Feig agrees with Geena Davis up to a point: yes, he says, there's no nefarious plot against women in Hollywood, but women are being deliberately excluded from movies. 'Right after I did *Bridesmaids*, a very successful producer said to me, "You're going to have to be careful because you're going to be put in this niche of directing women and that's a problem."' He continues: 'You know, Hollywood is not an altruistic town. We are in business and if someone gives you a compelling business reason [for not having women in a movie], then you have to actively change that because the idea of going, "Well, OK, I guess we can't do it!" – that's a non-starter for me. You say, how do we solve this?'

The answer, he decided, was to make big commercial movies that starred women that would be so successful that 'there would no longer be an argument'. But he had to wait a while until he had enough power in the industry to do this. In 2007 his friend and frequent colleague Judd

---

[1] An interview with Kathleen Turner is pretty much all that you want it to be. Sadly I can't print everything she told me as I'd be sued for libel by half of Hollywood. But if you ever have the opportunity to spend an afternoon with her, I highly recommend you take it.

[2] Told you.

Apatow, who by then had quite a lot of power, gave him the script for *Bridesmaids* 'and I fell in love with it – the idea that all these women have roles in it, it seemed like a dream to me,' he says.

Bridesmaids was, fortunately, a huge success ('And thank God. I was in a terrible panic half the time making the movie thinking, If we fuck this up . . . But how terrible that there was such pressure!' Feig recalls), and on the back of that, he was able to make *The Heat*, a female buddy cop movie. When we talk, he has just finished making a female spy movie ('I'm a huge fan of James Bond and I just thought – Why not make it with a woman? That's interesting!') and he has just been confirmed to write and direct an all-female version of *Ghostbusters* 'because that sounds really fun to me!'.

'You know, if Hollywood thought monkeys starring in movies were the highest grossing thing, then all you'd see is monkeys starring in movies. You can't look to Hollywood to fight a cause, you have to look to individual filmmakers to care and to do it well enough so that it makes money,' he says. 'And the success of [female-led international hit] movies like *The Hunger Games* and *Lucy* starts to open the door. Why just sit there with the door closed?'

Feig's films are probably the closest Hollywood will come today to making classic women's movies. In *Bridesmaids* and especially *The Heat*, what's at stake isn't whether a woman will Get a Man but rather the maintenance of a female friendship. *Bridesmaids* has plenty of rom with its com, and it does end with the obligatory closing-scene kiss, but the film takes pains to emphasise that the real happy ending comes from the two main female characters becoming friends again and the rest of the bridesmaids becoming friends with each other. Neither of these films has the gentle domesticity of *Terms of Endearment* or *Steel Magnolias*, but they were clearly made by someone who likes women, respects them and finds them interesting. Feig might have to front-load his films with some gross-out gags (*Bridesmaids*) and action (*The Heat*) and a few too many self-deprecating gags from Melissa McCarthy, but if that means good movies are being made that star women and get proper distribution, that feels like a trade-off worth making.

So does he think things are going to get better for women in movies?

'Oh yeah. It's so obvious that [women starring in movies] draws people to theatre and makes money. Things just have to change. They have to. People won't accept it any more.'

TOP FIVE BREAKAGES OF THE FOURTH WALL

5 Eriq La Salle, *Coming to America*
Before he was punching the air in the credits to *ER*, La Salle was Darryl, the evil greasy-haired boyfriend in *Coming to America*. At the end of the movie his ex-girl-friend's little sister wants to get her paws into that greasy hair, and La Salle can only look to the audience for help.

4 Jon Cryer, *Pretty in Pink*
When Duckie finally gets his happy ending at the prom, and shares it with the audience, it almost makes up for the fact that the ending doesn't make any sense at all.

3 Rick Moranis, *Spaceballs*
Moranis talking directly to the audience? That's an eighties peak for me right there.

2 Matthew Broderick, *Ferris Bueller's Day Off*
Nobody has yet bettered Ferris's skill at talking to the camera, and that includes Matthew Broderick.

1 Eddie Murphy, *Trading Places*
The moment when the evil Duke brothers are patronising Billy Ray Valentine about commodities, and he looks dead at the camera. Total Murphy perfection.

Back to the Future:
Parents are Important

Even today, thirty-five years later, screenwriter Bob Gale can still remember the moment 'vividly'. It was a hot day in August 1980, and he was in the middle of promoting his latest film, *Used Cars*, a very funny satire about car salesmen starring Kurt Russell and directed by Robert Zemeckis. The promotion tour had taken Gale back to his hometown of St Louis, Missouri, and he was at his parents' house, in a suburb a little way out of the city. 'One afternoon, I was digging around in my parents' basement – I don't exactly recall why – and I discovered my father's high school yearbook,' he says.

Gale thumbed through it and discovered, to his surprise, that his father had been the president of his high school class. He'd never mentioned that. This made Gale think about the kids who had been involved in student government when he'd been at school, and how much he sneered at them. In fact, he'd been on the committee to abolish student government.

'I wondered, would I have liked my dad if I'd been at school with him?' he says. 'Would I have even been friends with him?'

When he got back to Los Angeles, he called Zemeckis: 'Bob, I think I got an idea . . .'

Despite what most teenagers would like to admit, parents are an essential part of their life, for better or worse. But only smart teen films appreciate that and the bone-deep complications this entails: 'I rag on you a lot about your family, but it's only because I'm jealous – it must feel good to have someone looking out for you like that,' says the parent-less Watts (Mary Stuart Masterson) to her best friend Keith (Eric Stoltz) in 1987's *Some Kind of Wonderful*.

'Uh, sometimes,' replies Keith with a pronounced lack of enthusiasm.

It is nice to have someone care about you when you're a teenager – it's just a shame it has to be your parents.

You can always tell whether a teen film is good or not by how smart it is about the parents. Sure, there are some decent teen films that don't feature parents at all: *The Breakfast Club* is obviously great, *The Outsiders* is OK in a pretentious, overly styled way. But in the main, a teen film that doesn't have any well-written parental figures feels like a movie that was made by a studio trying to anticipate what teenage audiences want as opposed to a film capturing what teenagers are actually like.

Parents in teen films have gone through more growing pains than any adolescent. In the 1940s, when the word 'teenager' was first coined, parents were the helpful patriarchs who the teenagers aspired to become, meaning the teenaged characters (often played by young Mickey Rooney or Judy Garland) would say realistic dialogue like 'Oh Dad, I hope I grow up to be just like you one day.' In teen films of the 1950s and 1960s, when studios realised that all these baby boom teenagers preferred films that wholly validated them as opposed to patronised the hell out of them, parents became the representatives of conventional morality that the teenagers were rebelling against with their sexy modernity. By the 1970s, when teen films were being made by filmmakers who were young enough to have once been dubbed teenagers themselves but were now old enough to feel fondly about their youth, parents were either sentimentalised to the point of blandness (*Grease*, *American Graffiti*), or as doomed as the kids (*The Last Picture Show*, *Carrie*).

It wasn't until the 1980s that parents really came into their own. In the best eighties teen films they are invariably among the most fun characters in the movie, given many of the best lines and played by supremely talented actors momentarily slumming it in a kids' movie and having a ball with it, such as Harry Dean Stanton all sad-eyed and sweet-voiced in *Pretty in Pink*, John Lithgow enjoyably preaching fire and brimstone in *Footloose*, and John Mahoney playing a very different kind of paternal figure years before he became Frasier's dad in *Say Anything*.[*1] Partly this is because they assumed an entirely new kind of role in these movies, and partly it's because of the social attitudes of the time, and no other film made before or since encapsulates these changes more enjoyably than *Back to the Future*.

It is, arguably, a bit of a fudge to describe *Back to the Future* as a teen film, at least according to those who made it. '*Teen Wolf* was a teen film, but I always thought of *Back*

[*1] Weirdly, Bebe Neuwirth is also in *Say Anything*, playing the school's careers counsellor, meaning that both Frasier's dad and Frasier's wife were in the same film together, yet without Frasier. Kelsey Grammer should call his agent.

to the Future more as a time-travelling adventure comedy sci-fi love story,' says its star, Michael J. Fox.

'By the time I was cast in *Back to the Future*, I'd done a lot of eighties teen movies, like *The Wild Life*,*1 *Red Dawn**2 and *All the Right Moves*,*3 and this didn't feel like that to me,' says Lea Thompson. 'This felt more like a science-fiction blockbuster.'

But despite what those who made it thought, people who watched it at the time very much saw it as a teen film. By the time it was released in 1985, the teen film craze was well in swing and audiences were now very used to increasingly ridiculous genre movies structured around teenagers. Teenagers could now be karate aces (*The Karate Kid*, of course), fighters of communism (the aforementioned *Red Dawn*) or even detectives at Eton College (the completely brilliant *Young Sherlock Holmes*). So the idea of a time-travelling teenager seemed par for the teen genre course – as, in fact, it would soon become. The following year, Francis Ford Coppola's underrated *Peggy Sue Got Married*, also set in the fifties,*4 was released. Four years later the utterly

---

*1 Cameron Crowe's fratty follow-up to *Fast Times at Ridgemont High*, featuring Christopher Penn, Eric Stoltz and – pleasingly – Rick Moranis.

*2 TEENS FIGHT EVIL COMMIES! America's fate lies in the hands of Charlie Sheen and Patrick Swayze, God help us all.

*3 Tom Cruise fights to get a football scholarship to college instead of having to work in a mine with his father. If you like the mining scenes from *Zoolander*, you'll probably enjoy seeing the inspiration.

*4 When looking at other eras, teen movies in the 1980s invariably celebrate the innocence of the 1950s, such as *BTTF* and *Peggy Sue Got Married*, and invariably mock the hippy revolution of the 1960s. The optimism and consumerism of the 1950s would have been easier for eighties Reaganite and Thatcherite teen audiences to grasp than the hippy rebellion of the 1960s, which would just have looked hilariously out of step with their own time, such as in 1982's *Valley Girl*, where the female lead sneers at her hippy parents' restaurant where 'everything tastes of nothing'.

delightful *Bill and Ted's Excellent Adventure* arrived to cause parents of teenagers untold torment with its catchphrases and dudespeak.

'Teenage tastes now dominate mainstream moviemaking, and that's where Gale and Zemeckis are working. Marty is . . . a teen idol . . . *Back to the Future* makes you feel like you're at a kiddies' matinee,' Pauline Kael wrote somewhat sniffily in her review of *Back to the Future* in the *New Yorker*. (She also wrote: 'I'm not crazy about movies with kids as the heroes,' which must have made reviewing films in the eighties a bit of a drag for her.)

But Kael was right about one thing: Michael J. Fox, she wrote, was 'exactly what the moviemakers wanted' for their star. After Gale pitched the film idea to an excited Zemeckis, it took years for the two of them to get the film made, and it wasn't until Zemeckis finally had a hit with *Romancing the Stone* that they got the go-ahead.[*1] Zemeckis knew from the start that he wanted Fox to play Marty as Fox has the kind of boyish energy that the character needs to carry the film. Unfortunately, the actor was busy starring in the hugely popular sitcom *Family Ties* and the producers wouldn't release him for the movie. So, a little warily, Zemeckis cast Eric Stoltz. You can still find photos on the web of Stoltz shooting *Back to the Future*, standing with Doc Brown in the Twin Pines shopping mall parking lot, wearing that now iconic sleeveless puffa – and it just looks wrong. Stoltz is many things – ginger, soulful, eccentric – but he is neither energetic nor funny.

[*1] The reason Marty is given two older siblings is because Zemeckis and Gale had to keep throwing in more kids to make it seem credible that George and Lorraine got together in 1955 but didn't have Marty until – given he's a senior in high school in 1985 – 1967.

'Eric was more of an internal actor and he simply didn't have the extroverted comedic "thing" that we wanted in the character,' Gale recalls. And so, after six weeks on set, Zemeckis fired him. He then went back to the *Family Ties* producers to beg them to let him use their star.

'Bob Zemeckis pointed out to Gary [Goldberg, *Family Ties*' producer] that a lot of the scenes in the movie take place at night, so we could shoot the movie then and the TV show during the day, if I was up for it,' Michael J. Fox remembers. 'And I was.' Goldberg reluctantly agreed and Fox agreed 'with a big grin'.

With his naturally energetic comedy style, heightened by his manic exhaustion from filming both the show and film simultaneously, Fox holds the disparate timelines and characters of *Back to the Future* together, bouncing in his hi-tops. But he does more than that: he creates the illusion that Marty is an interesting character, one worthy of the audience's emotional investment, which, in truth, he isn't. He's barely a character at all. He doesn't have any defined personality traits besides wishing he owned a car and wanting to be back in good ol' 1985. His only role is to move the plot along and explain things to the characters and the audience.

'Marty takes the role of what's known in story theory as "the mysterious stranger". He comes out of nowhere and helps the characters sort out their lives. It's a construct that's been used in countless Westerns,' says Gale.

Which is fine, but mysterious strangers tend not to have much in the way of personality, and therefore don't make for good protagonists. But the reason the role was so under-written is not because the script failed – because it definitely didn't – but because *Back to the Future* is not about Marty at all: it's about his parents.

Gale was inspired to write this, the most successful of all eighties teen films, when he was looking at his dad's yearbook. So it makes sense that, he says, 'the pivotal character in the film is actually George McFly – he's the one who grows.' To emphasise this, he and Zemeckis cast one of the weirdest and most scene-stealing actors of all time as George: Crispin Glover. 'When we auditioned him, we recognised that he had an unusual quality that we thought would make the character particularly memorable. He made the part so much his own that I can't even recall what we were thinking when we wrote him, other than having some endearing awkwardness and charm like a young Jimmy Stewart,' remembers Gale.

But Crispin Hellion Glover, to give him his full name, is a far stranger proposition than good ol' boy Jimmy Stewart ever was.

All the performances in *Back to the Future* are great, but they are great teen movie performances. Glover, by contrast, seems to be method acting in his own very different, very funny movie. When we first meet middle-aged George at the beginning of the movie, cackling like a cricket chirping at Jackie Gleason on TV, his family stare at him as though he's from another planet, and it's an understandable reaction from those other actors.

'Crispin's always been interested in being an iconoclast, whereas I'm way more mainstream,' says Lea Thompson. 'He worked so hard on *Back to the Future* and he approached it really differently from me, more like something out of the seventies, like De Niro and Pacino and all that kind of character work.'

Only Glover (and possibly Nicolas Cage[*1]) would ever think of method acting in an eighties teen film. These days, Glover devotes himself to veganism and making films 'that reflect my psychological interests' in a chateau he bought in the Czech Republic. Not even Gale and Zemeckis envisioned a future that bizarre for George McFly in their movie's sequel.

Back to the Future is extremely funny and sweet, but the real jokes come, not from the culture clashes between 1955 and 1985, but the way the lies George and Lorraine spun in 1985 about their teenage years are unspooled when their son travels back to 1955. At the beginning of the film Lorraine insists that, as a teenager, she would 'never call a boy on the phone', but in fact as a teenager she throws herself at Marty, drinks alcohol and enthusiastically 'goes parking' with him, whatever that means. The reason George gets hit by Lorraine's father's car – which then leads to the two of them meeting one another – is because he fell out of the tree outside her house while spying on her putting on her bra. When Marty takes his leave of his parents in 1955, his parting message is resoundingly aimed more at the parents in the audience than the kids. Instead of telling George and Lorraine to give their third child a car, as a more teenager-focused film might (and as *Ferris Bueller* definitely would), he says, 'If you guys ever have kids and one of them when he's eight years old accidentally sets fire to the living room rug, go easy on him.'

'Bob Z and I concluded that there's probably one horrific punishment seared into every child's memory that he – or

---

[*1] According to Molly Ringwald, Judd Nelson was, hilariously, 'doing this method thing' when they made *The Breakfast Club*. This both explains a lot and excuses nothing.

she – can never forget. Besides, Marty would have seemed like a jerk if he asked his parents for a car, especially knowing that – in his timeline – they couldn't afford it,' says Gale.

But when did looking like a jerk ever stop a teenager – at least in a teen film – grousing about how car-deprived they were? Here, more clearly than anywhere else in the film, Gale and Zemeckis were talking at least as much to the parents in the audience as the kids.[*1]

This also explains the film's attitude to sex. With the exception of John Hughes's films, eighties teen films were remarkably open-minded about teen sexuality. But it's difficult to think of a film not directed by David Cronenberg that works as hard at making sex seem as unappealingly perverse as *Back to the Future*. The only vaguely sexual scenes in this film are when Lorraine unwittingly tries to seduce her own son in the car followed by Biff attempting to rape her in the same cursed vehicle. Zemeckis has said how nervous he was while writing and rewriting the script with Gale in the early eighties because at that time the nation's youth was besotted with the *Porky's* franchise: 'Gosh, we're in a high school in this movie and we never went into the girls' shower!' Whereas in *Porky's* sex is the only ambition, in *Back to the Future*, sex is something to be fearfully avoided, which makes sense as the film is about

---

*1 And in the case of at least one parent, it worked. On the day *Back to the Future* came out in the US, I, age seven, decided to paint my nails in the living room. My mother told me three times to do it in the bathroom but I ignored her and duly spilt nail polish all over the rug, and I got a good spanking for it. That evening, to calm my mother down, my father took her out to see this new film, and when Marty uttered that line to his parents about setting the living room rug on fire, my mother promptly burst into tears.

parents, not teenagers, and if there's anything more horrifying than a parent's suspicion that their teenage child
might be having sex, it's a teenager's realisation that their
parents ever had sex. And yet, the film tricks teenage audiences into hoping desperately that the parents get together,
because without the parents getting it on, there is no teenager. When George beats up Biff, and then when he and
Lorraine finally kiss in the dance – those are the romantic
points of the film, the emotional lodestars.

Actually, there is one thing more horrifying to teenagers
and parents alike and that's the idea of a mother 'having
the hots', as Marty puts it, for her son.

'The average teen films in the eighties were drinking,
drugging sex comedies, and these were the films that made
a lot of money. So the studios all thought our film was too
soft, except for Disney who thought that because of the
relationship between the son and the mother it was too
dirty,' Zemeckis said.

And to be honest, Disney had a point. This plot could
easily have sunk the movie into gross-out freakiness, and
would have done so without Lea Thompson's sweetness: 'I
remember Bob Zemeckis was so freaked out when we shot
the scene when I kiss Marty because the whole movie had
to change in that. The whole plot had to twist on that,' says
Thompson.

Of course, the real problem with this plotline, never
mind the incest, is, come 1985, George would surely have
been a bit worried by his youngest child's strong resem-
blance to that guy his wife had a crush on in high school,
especially as she names their son after him. But
complaining about credibility issues in a movie about time
travel is surely the definition of carping, particularly a film

about time travel in which a DeLorean works at all, never mind at 1.21 gigawatts.

The most popular image of parents in an eighties teen film is that of the blithe couple walking through the living room door in the final scene of the film just as their son replaces the last piece of furniture that was moved out of place during his shenanigans while they were away (see: *Weird Science*, *Risky Business*, *Ferris Bueller's Day Off* and, more recently and less filmically, Yellow Pages adverts for French polishers). This was certainly part of their purpose. But the real role for parents in eighties teen movies is to be fixed by their kids.

In *Sixteen Candles*, Sam has to teach her father how to be a good dad again after he forgets her birthday; in *Pretty in Pink*, Andie gets her father out of his depression after his wife leaves him; in *Say Anything*, Diane Court and Lloyd Dobler teach Mr Court about good morals; in *Dirty Dancing*, Baby teaches her father about good values; in *Footloose*, Ariel teaches her father not to be a deranged religious wingnut; in *Some Kind of Wonderful*, Keith teaches his father that teen romance is more important than going to college (not all these lessons exactly stand up to analysis by anyone over the age of eighteen). These kids are parents to their parents. Sometimes there is nothing to teach the parents: they are simply deeply flawed and the kids learn to be the grown-ups in the relationship, as in *The Breakfast Club*. In *Heathers*, which brilliantly satirises all eighties teen film tropes, J.D. (Christian Slater) calls his father 'son' and his father calls J.D. 'Dad', and the result of this screwy lack of parental guidance is that J.D. blows himself and his groovy trench coat up on the school steps.

In *Back to the Future*, it is emphasised from the beginning how mortified Marty is by his weak father and drunken mother, and how disappointing they are as parents. It is only when he goes back to 1955 that he is able to teach his parents how to be the people they always wanted to be and, by extension, the parents he wants them to be. The ultimate message of all these movies is, your parents are idiots and you are right.

'It's in the eighties that you really start to see what I call the Tyranny of the Teen, with that repeated message: your family is mixed up, and you know everything,' says Steven Gaydos, editor of *Variety*. 'Also, a lot of people from the world of TV commercials and family TV were starting to make movies in Hollywood, like Jeffrey Katzenberg and Michael Eisner, who knew how to sell things to young people. They realised that people over forty weren't seeing movies, so they created films that valorised young people's experience. There was less finger wagging and more "Why are adults so weird?"'

But because these movies were asking 'Why are adults so weird?', this meant adults were made more of a central feature of teen films than ever before.

Teenagers are supposed to be rebellious: that's what movies had been saying ever since the 1950s. Teenagers in eighties films, however, had a very different kind of rebellion. Not for them did biking across the country high on cocaine appeal. Ferris Bueller skives off school to go to a fancy restaurant, the stock exchange, a museum and a parade. Ren (Kevin Bacon) in *Footloose* wants to have a prom. Daniel (Ralph Macchio) in *The Karate Kid* wants his mother to have a nice house. Sam in *Sixteen Candles* wants to have a birthday cake. As rebellion goes, these kids make Milhouse from *The Simpsons* look like Johnny Rotten. Far from rebelling against middle-class capitalism, they are striving to be more stolidly average and middle class. Even Joel (Tom Cruise) in *Risky Business*, who would seem to be the most rebellious teenager of all when he runs a brothel out of his parents' suburban house when they go away, is actually living by his parents' ideals, as the film makes clear, because he is taking the money-making capitalistic lifestyle that his friends aspire to (and his parents subscribe to) to the extreme. He is rewarded for doing so when he gets offered a place at Princeton precisely because the admissions tutor is so impressed by his pimping skills (in the pantheon of films about prostitution, *Risky Business* makes *Pretty Woman* look grittily realistic). In *Back to the Future*, Marty's meddling in the past results in his parents living in a nicer house, with chicer furnishings, posher breakfast dishes and even domestic help in the form of Biff Tannen in 1985. Marty's triumph is to lift his family up to middle-class status.

As much as teen films railed against the importance of social class in America, the teen protagonists themselves all aimed very much to be part of the mainstream middle-class world. This is part of the reason why eighties teen films still hold so much appeal to middle-class kids today: the forms of rebellion depicted in them feel eminently accessible and familiar. When life is as comfortable as it largely is today for middle-class white kids in the western world, there's nothing, really, to rebel against without hurting themselves, so they may as well help their parents buy a bigger house. This is anti-rebellion as a form of rebellion, and its popularity in the eighties reflects this cosiness and the conservatism of the decade.

Back to the Future proved to teen filmmakers that they needn't be scared of making parents part of their story. In fact, teen audiences rather liked seeing their parents humanised. Even if there has been no teen film since in which the parents are quite as centre stage as they are in *Back to the Future*, many of the funniest, smartest and sweetest depictions of parents in teen films have come in *Back to the Future*'s wake: Dan Hedaya as the terrifying litigator father in *Clueless* (so much more fun than his nineteenth-century counterpart, the profoundly irritating Mr Woodhouse in Jane Austen's *Emma*); Larry Miller as the neurotically protective Mr Stratford in *10 Things I Hate About You*; Eugene Levy showing those whippersnappers how comedy is done in *American Pie*; the mighty Amy Poehler as 'the cool Mom' in Juicy Couture in *Mean Girls*, doing her usual thing of being at once hilariously exaggerated and wholly credible.

Back to the Future is one eighties film that would definitely be made now – plenty of spectacle, guaranteed franchise material – and it's not too hard to imagine a studio remaking it, maybe starring Channing Tatum or some such. But it would be a completely different film because Lorraine and George would not be at the heart of it. As much as movie marketers want to reach as many quadrants of an audience as possible, teen movies today are just about teenagers and not adults, so as to keep the focus on the most important audience members: teenagers. A teen movie in which the love story is the one between the parents would be unthinkable. More obviously, the idea of a mom trying to seduce her son in a mainstream teen movie would just never fly today because that would be too risky, too ick, too dependent on subtle acting and storytelling. Stiffler's mom seducing her son's friends in *American Pie*? Raunchy good fun. Stiffler's mom unwittingly seducing her son? No.

Hollywood is far too risk-averse for such things now.

Teen films in the 1980s taught kids three things about their parents: if they are divorced, they'll get back together for you; they will never notice when you've had a party; and they are deeply, deeply square. But George McFly and Lorraine Baines taught them something else, as well: parents are weird, but they're weird just like you're weird, and no matter what the kids in *The Breakfast Club* say, some day you will be them, too, and that's why parents in smart teen films are so fun. Because while you might be able to change destiny and become a sci-fi writer instead of a bullied wimp, George McFly-style, you can't ever change that.

TOP FIVE EIGHTIES STEVE GUTTENBERG MOMENTS

Plenty of eighties stars saw their careers die out in the nineties: Molly Ringwald, Andrew McCarthy, Judd Nelson. But no one vanished quite as spectacularly as Guttenberg, the man who was ubiquitous in the eighties only to disappear entirely in the nineties. These are his greatest moments.

5 *Short Circuit*
How much you accept Guttenberg could be a scientist for the military depends on how much you rate his acting skills.

4 *Three Men and a Baby*
The beginning of the end for Guttenberg, I suspect, as he is totally out-charisma-ed by Tom Selleck and Ted Danson. Still, it's one of his best films.

3 *Cocoon*
Why doesn't anyone watch *Cocoon* these days? It's such a lovely film full of such cool older people. Guttenberg doesn't get to do much here and is acted off the screen by Don Ameche, but that's fair enough, really.

2 *Diner*
Mickey Rourke – and Steve Guttenberg. Truly, a natural pairing! Guttenberg is sweet in this, playing the virginal bridegroom. You'd almost think watching it that he might become an actual actor one day.

1 *Police Academy*

No, I would not claim that *Police Academy 7: Mission to Moscow* is the greatest contribution to the world of film since *Citizen Kane*. But I would strongly argue that Mahoney, the cheeky police recruit, is Guttenberg at his finest.

Batman:
Superheroes Don't Have
to be Such a Drag

Along with every other over-sensitive kid of the eighties, it was love at first sight for me and the films of Tim Burton. Which was something of a surprise because the first film I saw of his – which was also the first feature film he made – was *Pee-Wee's Big Adventure*. Now, despite being very much an American child of the eighties, I did not like Pee-Wee Herman. In fact, it would be fair to say that I actively disliked Pee-Wee Herman. As I was seven when the film came out, I didn't quite have the ability to articulate what it was I didn't like about him, but now that I'm thirty-six I very much do: I thought he was creepy.[*1] I

---

*1 Some snarky types out there might be encouraged to remark that later events in the life of Pee-Wee's creator, Paul Reubens, who was arrested in 1991 for indecent exposure when he was caught masturbating in a porn cinema, validated my initial impression. But I would disagree most vehemently with this. For a start, now that we live in an era where a person is turned into a celebrity by appearing in a sex tape, the idea of a celebrity's career being destroyed by masturbation seems downright quaint – as quaint as the idea of porn cinemas, really. For heaven's sake, what are people supposed to do in a porn cinema if not masturbate – eat popcorn? (Public health announcement: do not eat in a porn cinema.) In fact, I'd go so far as to claim that masturbating in a porn cinema was the least creepy thing Paul Reubens did in the entertainment industry by 1991.

might have been only a kid, but I wasn't stupid and I could see that Pee-Wee was not so pee-wee – he was an adult. And yet, he was an adult pretending to be a kid. That's creepy. On *Sesame Street* (my children's TV show *du choix*), the adults acted like adults, the children acted like children and the muppets acted like muppets, just as God intended. There was no confusion between the ages or species, and that was how my hardened little conservative heart liked it.

But a girl in my first grade class, Alison Schnayerson,[*1] was having a birthday party, which involved going to see *Pee-Wee's Big Adventure*. Obviously, you can't turn down an invite to a seventh birthday party without incurring social death so, with a heart as heavy as when my mother dragged me to my weekly swimming lessons, I set out to meet my school friends at the 86th Street and Lexington Avenue cinema. Reader, I loved him. No, that's not right – I never loved Pee-Wee Herman. But I loved it, the film, with its cartoonish over-exaggerations (Pee-Wee's dreams about his bike are so theatrical they are like the fantasy dance sequence, 'Broadway Melody', in *Singin' in the Rain*), the heightened colours (the rich green wooden postboxes especially appealed to me, probably because they were so far from the anonymous metallic pigeonholes we had in our apartment building) and the depiction of suburbia as a place with all sorts of nefariousness simmering beneath the manicured lawns, and worse was beyond its rose bush borders. I still thought Pee-Wee himself was weird, but somehow, getting him out across America on a task, as happens in the film, made him seem slightly less creepy than he did on his TV show, *Pee-Wee's*

---

*1 Not actually her real name, but all middle-class New York girls in the eighties had names like Alison Schnayerson.

Playhouse, where he just sat inside and talked to the window.'[1] Also, he spoke less in that blaring horn-like tone in the movie than he did in the show, and that helped A LOT.'[2]

So I liked *Pee-Wee's Big Adventure*, in other words, for many of the qualities I would later recognise in all Burton's films. Burton himself said about the movie, 'I could add, but I wasn't imposing my own thing on it completely. I got to take the stuff that was there and embellish it.' It wasn't until he made *Beetlejuice* three years later that he got to impose a lot of himself on a film, and my initial spark of love turned into a lifelong burning affair.

Beetlejuice, which is about a couple (Geena Davis and a bizarrely miscast and visibly uncomfortable Alec Baldwin) who die and try to scare a family out of their home with the aid of the eponymous Beetlejuice (Michael Keaton), is such a weird and interesting film that I'm not even going to try to discuss it here as it deserves its own chapter. So I'll limit myself to noting just that so many of the qualities and tropes that are now seen to define a Burton film have their roots in *Beetlejuice*: the misunderstood male loner; the

---

*1 I am not exaggerating: that is literally what *Pee-Wee's Playhouse* was. I think to enjoy that show you have to have an already existing or incipient love of psychedelics.

*2 A separate sentimental part of me also fancies that part of the movie's appeal comes from the fact that the wonderful and sadly now late Canadian comedian Phil Hartman co-wrote it. Hartman appeared occasionally on *Pee-Wee's Playhouse* and was a much beloved cast member on *Saturday Night Live* in the 1990s, but he is best known in the UK as the voice of shady lawyer Lionel Hutz and cheesy infomercial host Troy McClure in *The Simpsons*. Hartman, by all accounts one of the sweetest and lowest key guys in show business, was shot and killed by his wife in his sleep in 1998. Sorry, I know this is a terribly distracting and pretty unnecessary footnote, but some people should be commemorated at any possible opportunity.

soulful female outsider; the permanent black sky; the raggedy rooftops; the black and white stripes; the model village. *Beetlejuice* also has the look and tone of what would become Burton's distinctive style: cartoonish artifice coupled with noirish comedy, plus a character with whom the movie seems to feel such a strong sense of emotional affinity that it's hard not to suspect there's some autobiography going on. In *Beetlejuice*, this character is Lydia (Winona Ryder), the angry, gothy teenager who is filled with such righteous disgust towards her boring bourgeois father (Jeffrey Jones) and stepmother (Catherine O'Hara) and their obsession with interior decoration that she rejects them to live in the Underworld – and what teenager has not fantasised about doing that at some point? Lydia's predicament is one that Burton repeats throughout his work: the freak stuck in an artificially beautiful world, echoing the frustration he felt when growing up in Burbank, California – Lydia even has Burton's skew-whiff hair and his all-black uniform. 'I know people say [my work] is slightly autobiographical but if I think about it too closely I get freaked out. It's weird; I need to feel connected but also distanced,' Burton said.

Kids and teenagers are pretty good at spotting phoneys, especially people who pretend they're in touch with their younger selves when they're really just putting on a baby voice. Burton, for better or worse, was no phoney. Despite being in his early thirties by the time the eighties ended, his films of that era expressed the mentality of a disaffected kid, one who felt ostracised from his school friends and family and told himself that this proved he was morally superior. And yet, he had the maturity to construct this mentality into wonderful and strange stories. I loved to read about his early, miserable years working as an illustrator at Disney, which he joined when he was twenty-one: 'I was very strange back then. I could see I had a lot of problems. I was always perceived as weird. I would sit in a closet a lot of the time and not come out, or I would sit on top of my desk, or under my desk, or do weird things like get my wisdom teeth out and bleed all over the hallways . . . I was having emotional problems at that stage. I didn't know who I was,' he said.

Already by the age of ten, I was starting to cultivate my own sense of estrangement from my peers, holding it close to my chest and stroking it jealously, like Blofeld petting his white cat. I had neither the emotional problems nor, arguably, the courage of Burton to externalise my sense of inner weirdness as much as he did, but it thrilled me to know I could watch things made by someone who, I felt sure, understood my own increasingly lonely confusion. What nineties teenagers felt about Kurt Cobain, I felt about Tim Burton in the late eighties.

I think part of the reason I and so many other former eighties kids feel such a strong affinity with Burton is because, in many ways, he grew up alongside us. Although he is about two decades older than my generation, having been born in 1958, his films seemed to go through the same life-stages as us in real time: there were his childlike playful years when he started, with *Pee-Wee's Big Adventure*, *Beetlejuice* and *Batman*;[1] his step into teenagehood in the

---

[1] 'I really liked [*Pee-Wee's Playhouse*] because it really tapped into the permanent adolescence thing, and I completely connected with that,' Burton said (*Burton on Burton*). When Burton made *Pee-Wee's Big Adventure*, he was twenty-seven.

nineties with his more self-consciously gothy films that celebrated outsiders and loners, such as *Edward Scissorhands*, as well as *Ed Wood* and *Mars Attacks!*; his stumble into adulthood in the 2000s, with sentimental films about the impact of the death of one's parents (*Big Fish*, *Charlie and the Chocolate Factory*[1]), half-hearted attempts at big-budget films for grown-ups (*Planet of the Apes*) and kids (*Alice in Wonderland*), and a creative stasis with films apparently made on sleepy autopilot (*Sweeney Todd*, *Sleepy Hollow*); his eventual happy maturity, with films that featured his familiar interests (*Frankenweenie*) but without the narcissistic tendency of his youth to make films only about himself (*Big Eyes*).

As the subtitle of this book might have suggested, I'm interested in why so many movies made in the eighties could not be made today, and that is true of Burton's films – but not necessarily because of changes in the studio system and what have you (although that, too: it's hard to imagine a director with such relatively little experience getting to work on *Pee-Wee's Big Adventure*, to say nothing of *Batman*). Rather, it's because Burton himself changed. He grew up, and watching the films of his I loved from the eighties onwards is a little like watching the progress of my own inner life from childhood to adulthood, noting the changes but also the consistencies: 'Certain images and feelings stay inside of you all your life,' he said. 'You think you've worked through them, but you don't, really. You just keep drawing something for a long time and it becomes

---

[1] 'Even though I wasn't that close to them, [losing your parents] obviously has a huge effect on your life. I was shocked at how much I was affected,' he said ('Dark Arts', *Guardian*).

part of you. Just when you've reached a new plateau in your life, it mysteriously comes again.'

Burton has said that the repetition of imagery in his films merely reflects his own 'limitations'. But to ten-year-old me, who had never before encountered a modern-day American director with such a strongly recognisable vision, this coherence was something else: it was art. With his films of the eighties and, later, the nineties, Burton taught me about visual style, and how the way something looks can be exciting in itself. He also taught me that a movie can capture the spiralling unhappiness I often felt inside, but still be funny about it, and the eighties film that taught me these lessons most clearly was Burton's blockbuster, 1989's *Batman*.

Like me, Burton was not a comic book fan (another personal affinity that pleased me), but we both learned to love comic book movies with *Batman*. Burton snobs (who are very distinct from Burton fans, which is what I am) sometimes dismiss *Batman*, saying it is the least Burton-esque of his films due to studio control over the film. But I've never understood that, and have often suspected that what these snobs actually dislike is that the film was so ridiculously successful in the mainstream. Burton's supporters generally come from the same demographic as the director: that is, current or former school misfits, and it's hard when one nerd sees their fellow nerd friend suddenly elevated to being the coolest kid in the playground. What a sell-out, right? And I got that, I really did. I refused to buy any of the *Batman* memorabilia that flooded the world the way *Star Wars* toys did ten years earlier, because I knew Burton would never have been involved in such bland, corporate, identikit junk. But the movie itself was different.

No one, really, can argue that *Batman* doesn't feel like a

Tim Burton film. All the familiar Burton motifs are there, bigger and – therefore to my eleven-year-old mind – more exciting than ever. Gotham City – always a stand-in for New York City – thrilled me, with its mix of looming architecture and rickety buildings, the worst of art deco mixed with a circus from hell. Gotham is chaotic, jumbled and un-navigable, and everything is absolutely HUGE, from the buildings to the crime waves. It's a far cry from the idealised and sparkling New York of, say, *Breakfast at Tiffany's*, and it looked, to be honest, a lot like how New York looked to me as a kid: big and scary and confusing and exciting.

Burton's Gotham encapsulates not just Burton's style but also an attitude towards modern-day cities that runs through eighties movies. For an era that was ostensibly so upbeat about capitalism and all the possibilities it offered, eighties movies were remarkably negative about modern-day cities. Even besides the obvious examples, like *Blade Runner* and *Escape from New York*, think of the poverty and the squalor in Hill Valley 1985 in *Back to the Future* and the filth and crime in eighties New York in *Ghostbusters*. With Gotham, Burton took that trend to its climactic extreme at the end of the decade and, in doing so, established the template for how cities would be depicted in superhero films for the next thirty years.

It is a real testament to comic book artist and writer Bob Kane and Bill Finger that two of the most influential movies of the 1980s and the twenty-first century feature the same protagonist, one they created back in 1939. But it's also quite something to look back now at the early coverage of Burton's *Batman* and see how fretful critics and fans were that it would be 'too dark' and 'too scary' for kids. Instead, he changed the way Hollywood depicted superheroes for ever, rescuing them from the bright and cheerful campness of the *Superman* movies (and Adam West's kitschy TV show) and turning them into phenomenally lucrative brooding men of mystery. Burton's influence has only deepened over the past few decades, now that superhero films are so ubiquitous and form the spine of the US film industry, and compared to superhero films made in the twenty-first century, the 1989 *Batman* looks like *Sesame Street*: there are colours, there is relatively little violence and the characters don't all look absolutely miserable. There were huge protests at the time against Burton's casting of Michael Keaton as Batman, with fans suggesting he was too weird and too weedy to play an all-American superhero. But next to creepily intense (and Welsh! Scandal!) Christian Bale, Keaton, with his crazy eyes, looks perfectly bat-like.

Christopher Nolan picked up this baton again in 2005 with *Batman Begins*, saving the franchise from the camp mess Joel Schumacher made of it in the 1990s,[1] and he restored the dark look of the movie franchise to something more in line with its comic book origins. The impact of this shift has been enormous in Hollywood, arguably even more so than it was when Burton did it in 1989, simply because there are so many more superhero films being made now than there were two decades ago, thanks in part to the nigh-on superhero-like rise of Marvel Studios. All superhero films after 2005 became much darker as a result

---

[1] I don't think we need to talk about Schumacher's *Batman* films too much for two simple reasons: they were made in the nineties and are therefore fairly irrelevant to our purpose here, and they are absolute garbage. When the best performance in a movie comes from Elle Macpherson, as is the case in *Batman and Robin*, you know you are in the presence of a Thanksgiving-sized turkey.

of *Batman Begins*'s success, from the *X-Men* to the *Avengers* to *Spiderman*.

But I'm going to lay it on the line here and just say it: I don't like the Christopher Nolan *Batman* films. Not out of loyalty to Burton – although I admit I did think that would be why when I first went to see *Batman Begins* with a sceptically cocked eyebrow – but because they're boring. God, they're so boring, full of endless speechifying from the characters about how good and evil are two sides of the same coin, and we all wear masks, and true power is a terrible burden, and it's always darkest before dawn[1] and the rain in Spain stays mainly on the plain and blah blah di freaking blah. I suspect Nolan knows this, which is why he sticks in about seventeen action sequences per minute in his films. But the scene in the museum in *Batman*, in which Jack Nicholson serenades Kim Basinger to Prince while poison-gassing everyone else sticks in my mind far more than any of the 10,781 action scenes from Nolan's series, because contrary to what superhero filmmakers think today, the more action scenes you include, the more diluted they become.

The only interesting thing about Bruce Wayne – a rich playboy whose power resides in his access to jazzy toys invented by others – is how he became Batman, and Burton knew this, which is why he focused on it in *Batman* and it's why his sequel, *Batman Returns* (1992), stumbles a little, because he no longer had that storyline to mine. Nolan knows it, too, and so the first part of his trilogy, *Batman Begins*, takes that as its main plotline – and

---

[1] Which, by the way, isn't even true. Of COURSE it isn't darkest before the dawn – it's darkest in the middle of the night, not at 5 a.m. Sheesh!

stretches it out to an insomnia-curing length of two hours and twenty minutes, padded out with seemingly endless scenes involving Christian Bale training to be a ninja in the snow. Hey, Nolan, I came here to see *Batman* – not *Kung Fu Panda*.

Burton is a much punchier storyteller, conveying what needs to be said (Bruce Wayne's a rich loner! He was really messed up over the murder of his parents!) with a single scene. His action scenes are also far, far easier to follow than Nolan's, which are a jumbled mess because too much is going on in them with too many characters. After *Batman Returns* (starring Keaton, Christopher Walken, Danny DeVito and Michelle Pfeiffer), all superhero films became overstuffed with famous actors in the belief that audiences would be so distracted by the celebrities they wouldn't notice that the plots don't make a jot of sense. The problem with this is that it then increases the chances of the heroes themselves – always the dullest characters in a superhero film – being overshadowed by all the villains. This is not a problem in Burton's film, because Burton revels in the weirdness of Batman,[*1] and Keaton's eyes are always fascinating to watch, even when they're near hidden beneath a mask.

But Bale, while a brilliant actor, doesn't have Keaton's deranged magnetism – if anything, the mask makes him look weirdly pouchy – and giving him a stupid vocoder voice when he's Batman simply obscures Bale's charisma even more. Thus, *Batman* becomes a boring, opaque drag

---

[*1] 'Part of what interested me was that it's a human character who dresses up in extremely vulgar costumes . . . [it's] the freakish nature of it, and I found it the most frightening thing' (*Burton on Burton*).

and it often feels like the heart of Nolan's *Batman* films is not with Batman, but with Jim Gordon (Gary Oldman), the good police officer, and this is especially true in the second part of Nolan's trilogy, *The Dark Knight*. This is by some measure the best of the modern *Batman* series because it features *Batman*'s best villain – the Joker – who is played by Heath Ledger, giving the most mesmerising performance in the whole trilogy. But even here, I have to admit that I still think of Burton: with his cracked white face-paint, skew-whiff hair, brightly coloured suit and self-description as an 'agent of chaos', Ledger's take on the Joker looks an awful lot like Beetlejuice.

There is no point in debating who did the Joker better, Ledger or Nicholson, because they're both, clearly magnificent: Nicholson's feels iconic from the moment he steps on the screen whereas Ledger's performance snarls and burrows its way beneath your skin with its creepiness. But Nicholson's Joker is ultimately more satisfying because he gets a backstory (the snappy tale of Jack the lad ending up in a vat of acid because he slept with his boss's girlfriend, played respectively by Jack Palance and Jerry Hall[*1]) and he gets a death, when Batman's trickery makes him plummet hundreds of feet down to the pavement, landing with a smile on his face and a mechanical toy laughing in his coat pocket.

In truth, it's fortunate that Nolan doesn't bother with his Joker's backstory because he'd probably have taken four hours to establish it. But the lack of a death, well . . . Nolan is oddly averse to showy dramatics, as if slightly embarrassed that he's making a film about, you know,

---

[*1] Another major point in Burton's *Batman*'s favour: it has a STELLAR cast.

SUPERHEROES. Compare, for example, the thrilling opening scene in which Batman is introduced in Burton's film ('I want you to tell all your friends about me.' 'What are you?!?!?!' 'I'M BATMAN.') with Nolan's decidedly less exciting version in which he makes banter with a homeless man ('Nice coat'). So it is perhaps not surprising that in *The Dark Knight* he doesn't even kill the Joker – he just leaves him hanging upside down somewhere. But it is also less satisfying.

Nolan fans say they prefer the 'realism' of Nolan's films compared to Burton's, and critics frequently cite the 'gritty reality' of the movies admiringly; but, if these films were 'realistic', they would consist of crowds of people standing around and pointing at Batman and saying, 'Oh look! It's one of those Fathers4Justice morons! What a DICK.' Also, take it from a reformed fashion writer: no man can wear a full-length cape in the real world without sparking serious mockery. But the real point is, who comes looking for realism when they watch a movie about some dude who flies through the air dressed as a freaking bat? I'll tell you who: people who are trying to pretend that they're not watching a superhero film, and they're trying to convince themselves that this film is Saying Something Important.

Many of the differences between Burton's and Nolan's *Batman* films can be ascribed to the different style of the directors. But that's not the full story and many of the reasons I find Nolan's *Batman* films often next to unendurable has to do with the time in which they were made.

All disaster films set in New York now look like responses to 9/11, even if they were made years before (I find 1996's *Independence Day* almost unwatchable now for that reason, not that I try to watch it too often). But it is pretty obvious that the wild rise of superhero films in Hollywood since the beginning of the twenty-first century is as much a response to 9/11 as it is to the growing importance of international audiences. Superhero films provide escapism, and they also create a self-validating narrative for an America that feels under attack by an enemy it doesn't understand.

People have been writing about how superheroes reflect American self-identity pretty much since the day after Superman first appeared in 1938. Whole Ph.D.s are written on this subject today, with titles such as 'Rethinking the American Man: Clark Kent, Superman and Consumer Masculinity' and 'Nationalism and Power: Captain America, Governmental Policy and the Problem of American Nationalism'.[*1] You can easily widen this argument out to movie heroes in general: from the 1920s to the 1960s, American film heroes were masculine, dominant, even swashbuckling, reflecting America's self-pride after the two World Wars. This attitude crumbled during the Vietnam War, and so enter stage left – the flawed hero! This pretty much started with Arthur Penn's 1967 film, *Bonnie and Clyde*, and today, in the twenty-first century, even the superheroes are riddled with self-doubt and inner conflict. You don't need to have written an essay with a colon-laden title about Clark Kent and heteronormative masculinity to see the glut of superhero movies post 9/11, featuring tortured superheroes who

---

[*1] I did not make those titles up (how could I?). They come from *Ages of Heroes, Eras of Men – Superheroes and the American Experience*, ed. Julian Chambliss, William Svitavsky and Thomas Donaldson. Knock yourself out with that tome.

are tasked with saving the world but are often misunderstood by the dull-witted masses as destructive vigilantes, as a reflection of how America sees its position in the world today.

When Alfred (Michael Caine), the loyal voice of caution, asks Bruce Wayne in *Batman Begins* whether he needs to cause quite so much destruction while trying to save Gotham, Bruce smirks, 'Damn good television . . . Didn't have time to observe the rules of the road, Alfred.' The year this film came out, 2005, was also the year when US public opinion about President Bush really began to tank. Nearly half of Americans in 2005, according to a survey by Pew Research, believed the war in Iraq ultimately caused more damage than good. Did we need to cause so much destruction? Bush scoffed at this, saying in a speech on 7 October that such concerns were ridiculous because he was dealing with a terrorist movement that wanted to 'intimidate the whole world'. Who has time to observe the rules of the road when dealing with 'the enemy'? Certainly America's right-wing media had been echoing this sentiment for years. David Brooks wrote approvingly in 2001: 'We will destroy innocent villages by accident, shrug our shoulders, and continue fighting.'

The parallels between Batman and Bush post 9/11 are even more obvious with *The Dark Knight*: there's the bad guy who sends his minions out on suicide missions and blows up random buildings just to prove he can; a villain who is so unlike any others that the good guys need to break their own rules to get him, such as Batman's use of sonar to tap civilians' cell phones to fight crime (v Patriot Act, that); the fact that most people wrongly see Bruce Wayne as a screw-up blessed with a wealthy daddy, and

Batman as a terrorist. Indeed, even the previously road safety-aware Alfred has come round to Bush's razed-earth point of view in this film, and he counsels Bruce that the way to destroy a villain who 'just wants to watch the world burn' is to 'burn the forest down'. In an article in the *Wall Street Journal* entitled 'What Batman and Bush Have in Common', Andrew Klavan describes *The Dark Knight* as 'a conservative movie about the war on terror, making a fortune depicting the values and necessities that the Bush administration cannot seem to articulate for beans'. The *Washington Independent* went further, suggesting that *The Dark Knight* was, in fact, a specific endorsement of Dick Cheney, particularly in regard to its attitudes towards security, justified law-breaking and references to 'the dark side' (a favourite Cheney coinage).

At the end of the film, Batman tells the police commissioner that their acts must be hidden in a massive cover-up because the general public can't deal with the truth. The Bush administration also hid plenty of things from the American public, from the cost of the war to the use of torture. It was only in 1992's *A Few Good Men* Colonel Jessup's (Jack Nicholson) claim that people 'can't handle the truth!' was taken as proof of his dangerous megalomania; in *The Dark Knight* hiding the truth is seen as part of Batman's wise and self-sacrificing nature. As one journalist wrote in *Mother Jones*, '[The Dark Knight says] we need dark knights to do the dirty work to keep us safe while we can sit back and self-righteously dismiss them as going too far . . . This film seems to laud rule-exempt leaders as the only effective weapons against our evil enemies, a message I thought Americans had finally decided to reject.'

Unsurprisingly, the film's cast tried to distance themselves from such political readings of the film. Aaron Eckhart, who plays district attorney Harvey Dent, insisted 'certainly that wasn't the intention' and that it 'is simply good drama for good movies'. But he admitted, 'I agree [with the analogy] in a way. Of course [it has analogies]. When I read *The Dark Knight* for the first time, I saw a lot of political issues. You know, obviously today's culture seeped in. It's a mirror of our times.'

Whether or, more likely, not Nolan meant his Batman to represent Bush and Cheney, the American media and government had been paving the way for this analogy to be made for years in their desperate search for heroes after 9/11, the more cartoonish the better. A month after the attacks, Marvel published *Heroes*, an oversize comic book featuring drawings of firemen rescuing women from the rubble, and it sold out in one day. Susan Faludi writes in *The Terror Dream*, her study of how 9/11 affected the American psyche: 'The president's vows to get the "evildoers" won him media praise BECAUSE it sounded cartoonish.' One especially ridiculous American columnist compared Bush giving the 2003 State of the Union address to the moment when Clark Kent moves 'to tear open his shirt and reveal the big "S" on his chest'. Another commentator, Peter Roff, wrote: 'Bush punctuates his rhetoric with verbal "Whams," "Pows," "Biffs," and "Whaps" to make clear who are the good guys and who are the bad guys.' Roff also compared the President to the superhero the Shadow, 'a man of mystery who strikes terror into the very souls of evildoers everywhere'. 'That,' Roff writes, 'is just the kind of hero America needs right now.' These columns, remember, were written – not for comic book-consuming teenagers – but broadsheet-reading adults.

Nolan's *Batman* movies are aimed far more at adults than Burton's ever were. They are far more violent with huge body counts, because who has time to observe the rules of the road nowadays, Alfred? But perhaps the most obvious difference between the two franchises is the tone. Despite Burton's reputation as a messy-haired gloom-meister, his films are funny, and *Batman* is no exception. From Jack Nicholson's larkishness ('Where DOES he get those wonderful toys?' 'This town needs an enema!') to Michael Keaton's dry irony ('You know, I don't think I've ever been in this room before . . .'), *Batman* is definitely a funny movie. Even when Keaton seems at his most lonely in *Batman* he's amusing, such as when he sneaks up behind people in his house making fun of his possessions. But he's still alone: Keaton's Bruce Wayne wanders around unseen at his parties, unrecognised by his own guests and therefore always alone. Bale, by contrast, plays Bruce Wayne as a rich asshole who turns up late to his own parties with a girl on each arm and immediately dominates proceedings by making snarky speeches.

All superhero films take themselves ridiculously seriously nowadays, and this is especially true of Nolan's *Batman* films, which are portentous and pretentious and po-faced. Superhero movies now affect to provide some kind of socially and politically relevant narrative, and the political narrative in America these days is pretty demoralising (I discussed the bizarre anti-Occupy message of the final part of Nolan's trilogy, *The Dark Knight Rises*, in the chapter 'Ferris Bueller's Day Off: The Impact of Social Class'). Also, studios themselves take these films so seriously because they are the tentpoles to a studio's financial year. But as Burton's *Batman* proves, you don't need to keep telling the audience how SERIOUS and IMPORTANT a movie is for it to feel like a big deal, and you don't have to act like the film is as significant as the cure for cancer for it to become a world-wide smash. Because at a certain point, someone is going to stand up and say, 'Do we really want to spend our adult lives the way we spent our teenage years – looking to superheroes to make sense of our world for us? And if we do, couldn't we make these movies a bit more, I don't know, FUN?'

After *Batman*, Tim Burton made his masterpiece in 1990 – *Edward Scissorhands*, the most beautiful and most explicitly autobiographical of all his feature films (Burton wrote it as well as directing it), and when I saw it, it left me so breathless I couldn't even get out of the cinema seat at the end of the film. So I stayed and watched the next screening. It combined everything I loved about his eighties films – the surreal suburbia of *Pee-Wee's Big Adventure*, the desire for escape from this world of *Beetlejuice* and the loneliness of Batman – but more so in this story of a miserable loner with blades for hands. I was only twelve when I went to see it and I don't know if I subconsciously recognised in it the deeply depressed teenager I would become – one who felt so alone and longed to be hugged but hurt anyone who tried – or if I just fancied Johnny Depp. But I probably watched that film more than any other as a teenager. Today, though, I can hardly bear to look at it. To watch *Edward Scissorhands* now is like pushing on a scar that covers some still sparking nerve endings.

But just as I grew up with Tim Burton, for a while I grew out of him. Along with other childish things, I put his films away in my twenties, and it embarrassed me that I once thought of all that Hollywood gothicism as art. God, what a dork. And look! Burton was right! His films all DID look the same, mainly because they all starred the same damn actors. Was Burton perhaps unaware there are other actors in the world besides Johnny Depp? Should I track him down and whisper when he steps out of his house, 'Psst! Hey, Tim! Two words: James Spader.'

But thankfully, I grew out of the childish self-loathing that I mistook in my twenties for mature self-awareness, and I came back to Burton in my thirties when I went to see *Frankenweenie* (2012). It was like coming back home after a long and difficult trip away: everything felt familiar but a little different and it was comfortable but also exciting to be back in a place that, still, spoke to a small and dark corner inside me. (It also helped that *Frankenweenie* marked the beginning of Burton heaving himself out of the creative rut in which he'd laboured for the past decade. Neither of us had the greatest starts to this century.) I no longer queue up to see the first performance whenever a new Burton film opens – to be honest, I don't even see every film Burton makes at the cinema these days (I still haven't ever made it through the whole of *Planet of the Apes*, and I reckon we're both fine about that). But I'll always feel extreme fondness for him for waking me up to the excitement of movies in the 1980s, and for holding my hand through the 1990s. Burton's *Batman* doesn't try to make a comment about socio-political power-playing – it's about loneliness, but done in Burton's sweet, stylish and surprisingly subtle way. I, personally, find that a lot more moving than a two-and-a-half-hour defence of the Bush presidency. We Burton fans are weird like that.

PS For the record here is the official order of the *Batman* films from the past thirty years, from best to worst.

1. *Batman* (1989, Burton):

'Simply the best! Two thumbs up!' Tina Turner.[1] The best cast of any *Batman* film of all time. Jack Palance, for God's sake! Jack freaking Palance!

2. *Batman Returns* (1992, Burton):

So much better than you remember. Christopher Walken is completely wasted but Danny DeVito as the Penguin is brilliant. His penguin funeral haunts my dreams.

3. *The Dark Knight* (2008, Nolan):

There are too many climaxes, too many characters, and too much Bush-ness, but unquestionably this is a good film. Aaron Eckhart and Gary Oldman are good, Heath Ledger is great.

4. *The Dark Knight Rises* (2012, Nolan):

I can make out about 25 per cent of the dialogue in this film, and the anti-Occupy Wall Street plot is insane. Still, it's better than Nolan's first one. Which is . . .

5. *Batman Begins* (2005, Nolan):

The film that reminded us all that Katie Holmes cannot act and Liam Neeson and Morgan Freeman stopped even bothering to try long ago.

6. *Batman Forever* (1995, Schumacher):

Sort of how I imagine a gay club on cocaine in the 1980s would look. But not in a good way.

---

[1] Possibly not an entirely true quote.

7. *Batman and Robin* (1997, Schumacher):

The movie that proved George Clooney is actually a super-hero because he alone among the entire cast was able to rise like a phoenix out of the ashes of this unspeakable dreck.

THE TEN BEST ROCK SONGS ON AN EIGHTIES MOVIE SOUNDTRACK

10 'When the Going Gets Tough, the Tough Get Going', by Billy Ocean, from *The Jewel of the Nile*
Not, strictly speaking, a rock song. But if you have never seen the video for this song, starring Michael Douglas, Kathleen Turner and Danny DeVito as backing singers, well, your life is just about to get a whole lot better.

9 'Eye of the Tiger', by Survivor, from *Rocky III*
The only acceptable song to play when you're beating up Mr T.

8 'Stir It Up', by Patti LaBelle, from *Beverly Hills Cop*
I love Patti LaBelle, I love this song and, most of all, I love the moment Eddie Murphy gurns to this song at the end of *Beverly Hills Cop*.

7 'You're the Best', by Joe Esposito, from *The Karate Kid*
Play this song before leaving the house and you will win every karate tournament that day, and that's a fact.

6 'Footloose', by Kenny Loggins, from *Footloose*
Seriously, how awesome must it be to be Kenny Loggins? The man's an eighties movie soundtrack legend.

5 'The Heat is On', by Glenn Frey, from *Beverly Hills Cop*
Like the Big Lebowski, I cannot stand the Eagles. But such is the power of *Beverly Hills Cop* that I cannot resist this song by head Eagle Glenn Frey.

4 'Power of Love', by Huey Lewis and the News, from
Back to the Future
MARTYMCFLY4EVA.

3 'Into the Groove', by Madonna, from *Desperately
Seeking Susan*
I totally agree with you – there is not enough Madonna in
this book. For the moment in *Desperately Seeking Susan*
when she dances to herself on a jukebox, she deserves her
own chapter.

2 'Danger Zone', by Kenny Loggins, from *Top Gun*
Just listening to this makes me want to ride Val Kilmer's tail.

1 'Don't You Forget About Me', by Simple Minds, from *The
Breakfast Club*
Come on, there is just no competition. Not just the best
eighties movie rock song but the best musical moment in an
eighties movie. Punch the air, Judd Nelson! Punch it hard!

TOP TEN WEIRDEST SONGS ON AN EIGHTIES MOVIE SOUNDTRACK

10 'The Goonies R Good Enough', by Cyndi Lauper, from *The Goonies*

Why 'R' and not 'are'? And why are the Goonies only 'good enough' for Cyndi – is that not damningly faint praise? And was Cyndi good enough for them? So many questions.

9 'We Built This City', by Starship, from *Mannequin*

Why IS Marconi playing the mamba?

8 Queen's songs for *Highlander* soundtrack

All credit to the group for getting references to the movie's plot in each of their songs, even if they make no sense now. 'A rage that lasts a thousand years', indeed.

7 'Please, Please, Please Let Me Get What I Want', by the Dream Academy, from *Ferris Bueller's Day Off*

I feel rather guilty putting this in because it's not weird. I love it. But there is still something very amusing about a self-pitying song by the Smiths getting turned into an instrumental piece by an Australian band and rendered into a love song.

6 'Daddy's Girl', by Peter Cetera, from *Three Men and a Baby*

This song is about the love a daughter feels for her father. Sweet, right? Wrong! Here's the chorus: 'Little baby wanna hold you tight / She don't ever wanna say good night / She's a lover, she wanna be Daddy's Girl.' I love *Three Men and a Baby* but someone needs to call CPS, stat.

5 'Ghostbusters', by Ray Parker Jr, from *Ghostbusters*
A classic. Also: weird.

4 'Peace in Our Life', by Frank Stallone, from *Rambo: First Blood Part II*
Sylvester Stallone's brother singing about peace in a movie in which his brother bombs the world. God bless you, Stallone family.

3 'Magic Dance', by David Bowie, from *Labyrinth*
David Bowie, in a mullet, singing about a magic dance to a bunch of muppets and a baby. I love the eighties.

2 'Oh Yeah', by Yello, from *Ferris Bueller's Day Off*, etc.
I feel like this song was in every eighties movie, but it was actually only in two: *Ferris Bueller's Day Off* and *The Secret of My Success*. It just feels that way because it was so weird. And bonus: the band were Swiss.

1 'The Dragnet' rap, by Dan Aykroyd and Tom Hanks, from *Dragnet*
And people say white people can't rap.

Eddie Murphy's Eighties Movies: Race can be Transcended

Time has not been kind to 1980s comedy superstars. John Belushi is long dead, Harold Ramis is recently dead, Martin Short has largely faded from view, Dan Aykroyd is only spotted these days flogging vodka, the brilliantly gifted Steve Martin moved over to romantic leads with somewhat mixed results,[*1] Chevy Chase appears to be engaged in a full-time job of generating negative publicity about himself,[*2] and Steve Guttenberg was last spotted doing

---

[*1] *LA Story*: brilliant. *Shopgirl*: kill me.
[*2] Choice Chevy Chase anecdotes from over the years: in 1996 he made a guest appearance on *Saturday Night Live* and, among other things, told a female writer 'Maybe you can give me a handjob later' (*Live from New York*, Tom Shales and James Andrew Miller); no one who works with him has a good word to say about him ('Chevy has a reputation for being a dick, and that reputation is earned,' said Dino Stamatopoulos, who co-starred with Chase on the sitcom *Community*); even Will Ferrell, who is widely agreed to be one of the nicest men in comedy, described Chase, who he reveres, as 'the worst host [of *Saturday Night Live*]... maybe he took too many back pills that day' (*Live from New York*, Shales and Miller).

panto in Bromley.[*1] Out of all the comedy legends who emerged in that decade, the only one still standing with any real current critical credibility is Bill Murray.

And that's great – I love Murray. Murray is my favourite thing (Venkman) in my favourite movie (*Ghostbusters*, as I might have already mentioned) of all time. He's also my very favourite thing (Jeff the flatmate) in one of my most watched films (*Tootsie*) of all time. *Caddyshack, Tootsie, Stripes, Ghostbusters, Scrooged*: there is no doubt, Murray had a very good eighties. But back in 1989, if you'd asked anyone on any street in any western country which American comedy star they reckoned would still be revered in twenty-five years' time, you would have got one universal answer, and that answer would not have been Bill Murray. It would, instead, and quite rightly, have been the man who remains the biggest comedy star of all time, and the one to whom time has been comparatively the most cruel: Eddie Murphy.[*2]

Public attitudes towards Murray and Murphy exemplify how short people's memories are. No matter how good Murray's eighties were, the reason he is still adored today is because he has made some very smart career moves in the past fifteen years. With the noted exception of *Groundhog Day* (which is really just a mystical update of *Scrooged*, for the record), Murray, like most eighties comedians, had a pretty meh 1990s.[*3] He made films like the laughably miscast *Mad Dog and Glory*[*4] and *The Man Who Knew Too*

---

*1 Well, Guttenberg was a comedy superstar in MY world, OK?

*2 '. . . and Steve Guttenberg!' nine-year-old Hadley.

*3 Suggested essay: 'The nineties were to eighties comedians what the eighties were to seventies musicians. Discuss.'

*4 In which Murray plays a mafioso and Robert De Niro plays an everyman nebbish. Sure, that makes sense, right?

Little in which he starred alongside such unlikely co-stars as Richard Wilson and, er, Dexter Fletcher. Someone presumably thought this might be Murray's *A Fish Called Wanda*. It was not.

Things would very likely have continued in this vein had he not been rescued by Wes Anderson who, with *Rushmore* (1998) and *The Royal Tenenbaums* (2001) reminded the world that Murray is, in fact, a wonderful dramatic actor.[1] Anderson's friend Sofia Coppola took note and cast him in 2003's *Lost in Translation* as the jaded celebrity bored by money and Japanese people, and lo, suddenly, it became a truth universally acknowledged that there is not a person on the planet who does not worship at Murray's altar. Murphy, on the other hand, is a different story.

Most people born before 1980 think of Murphy with the kind of bemused, embarrassed disappointment one feels about a cousin who once seemed so cool only then to grow up and become a tedious old fart who works in PR and gets drunk every Christmas and makes homophobic jokes.[2] Murphy, it is widely agreed, hasn't made a decent comedy in almost twenty years, having opted for the grim career of a sell-out consisting of fat suits, kiddie franchises and movies so bad you can only hope he was paid $30 million for his time.

And this is really not fair. Sure, Murphy's wasted a lot of

---

[1] Although some of us are getting a little tired of Murray playing the same role of the cuckolded husband in Anderson's films, and miss the manic Murray of the eighties and wish he didn't always have to play a jaded cynic now. But that's a subject for another day.

[2] Although, ironically, when Murphy made homophobic jokes in the eighties – which he did A LOT, and later apologised for – the only people who protested were gay people.

years in unwatchable dross like *Holy Man* and *The Adventures of Pluto Nash*, one of the biggest box office disasters of all time. But he has also made some excellent movies in (relatively) recent years: in the very funny Steve Martin 1999 comedy *Bowfinger* he is completely brilliant playing both a Hollywood superstar and the superstar's dopey brother, and he absolutely should have been nominated for an Oscar for it. But the Oscars, of course, don't do comedy so instead, in classic Oscars style, Murphy got nominated for a later and less deserving but still good performance in the otherwise pretty mediocre *Dreamgirls* (2006). As Jimmy Early, the heroin-addicted, washed-up soul singer, Murphy proved to audiences that he can do dramatic acting, but he also reminded them how spectacularly lazy he has otherwise been in his later career, which presumably wasn't quite his intention.

Having said all that, don't, for heaven's sake, underestimate *Shrek*. Without Murphy's charming voiceover work as Donkey, that film would have just consisted of Mike Myers grunting about in a Scottish accent, and no child (or parent) wants to sit through that. *Shrek* would have barely been a movie were it not for Murphy, let alone three movies. Moreover, for all the sneers (mine included) lobbed at Murphy for making franchise movies for kids, like *The Nutty Professor*, *Daddy Day Care* and *Doctor Doolittle*, no one has done it as successfully as him: altogether, those films, including their sequels, made $3.5 billion worldwide, which can't be described as a career failure.

But not even I fancy expending too much time and energy defending Murphy's post-1989 career, particularly compared to Murray's. As I said, the man has been pig-ass lazy.'[1] What I will do, though, is argue to the death that Murphy's eighties career more than compensates for a million Pluto Nashes. Eddie Murphy deserves so much more respect than he is accorded, first, because he was once the most exciting person to watch onscreen in the world. Just thinking of his grinning face in his eighties movies makes me smile. And second, because he made America believe, for the first and maybe only time in history, that race can be transcended.

In order to understand just how incredible it is that a black man became the biggest movie star of the eighties, we need to look at just how much racism eighties mainstream movies felt was A-OK. As chance would have it, I have watched a lot of eighties mainstream movies and here, in a handy list form, are some examples of the typical kind of racism to be found in eighties movies:

1 Wacky Asians

Sixteen Candles (1984): Despite *Sixteen Candles* being a John Hughes teen movie, he was more in his slapstick *National Lampoon* mode as opposed to his soulful *Breakfast Club* gear. An exchange student from an unidentified Asian country called Long Duk Dong (ha ha! Asian people have funny names!) comes to stay with Molly Ringwald's family. He is obsessed with sex ('No more yanky my wanky!') and, of

---

[1] And he knows it, and what's more, he doesn't care. Murphy: 'I'm never gonna go, "I want to do this role because it's a challenge. I might not be able to pull it off, that's why I'm excited about doing it." For someone to sit on the outside, talking about, "They need to push themselves," it's so ridiculous. Push myself? I've had a whole fucking career already, these are the gravy years. I have more than distinguished myself in the movie business' ('Eddie Murphy Speaks', Brian Hiatt, *Rolling Stone*, November 2011).

course, embarrassingly nerdy (Asians – amirite?!). His every entrance onscreen is announced by a background gong, like something out of an old Tintin comic now banned by school libraries. Twenty-four years later, America's National Public Radio described Long Duk Dong as 'one of the most offensive Asian stereotypes Hollywood ever gave America'.

2 Scary black people who teach white kids about real life

Adventures in Babysitting (1987): This film is adorable. It exemplifies so many of the best things about eighties teen films – the sweetness, the silliness, the innocence. However, it also exemplifies one of the worst things, which is using black people as a signifier for danger. Here, for reasons that need not be overly elucidated, babysitter Elisabeth Shue must leave the safety of the white suburbs and travel into the ghettoised city where she encounters all sorts of dangerous black people, ranging from car thieves to gangs to fans of blues music who force her and her youthful charges to sing some bee bop. See also: *Risky Business* and *Weird Science*.[*1]

3 Blacking up

Soul Man (1986): When I tell people today that my sister

---

*1 John Hughes was especially bad at portraying ethnic minorities. Aside from *Sixteen Candles* and *Weird Science*, there was 1983's *National Lampoon's Vacation*, which he wrote. In this film, the Griswold family get lost in the ghetto, which is populated by scary profane black people, and they promptly have their hubcaps stolen, because that's what black people are like.

'I wonder if these guys know the Commodores,' the Griswold son (Anthony Michael Hall) muses.

'I'm not going to pretend I know the black experience,' Hughes said in an interview with the *New York Times* in 1991, and that is fair enough. Unfortunately, he did seem to think he knew the black experience, and it was an experience consisting of thieving and jive talk.

and I actually rented this film from the local video shop back in 1987, I can see them looking at me the way I used to look at my grandfather when he talked about growing up in a time of segregated public bathrooms. Seriously, who knew people were still alive today who lived in such racist times! In this career-killer of a film, C. Thomas Howell plays Mark, a spoilt white guy whose father, for no obvious reason other than to serve as a handy plot device, tells him he has to pay his own way through Harvard Law School. Mark hits upon the idea of posing as a black student in order to blag a scholarship – because everyone knows it's super-easy to get a scholarship to Harvard if you're black. They basically give them out to 'the brothers', as Mark would say. So Mark takes a load of tanning pills and carries out this foolproof plan and stupid ethnic stereotypes ensue, all with a white actor in blackface for an entire movie. Perhaps the weirdest thing about *Soul Man* isn't that it was made at all, but that the black female lead, Rae Dawn Chong, ended up marrying Howell. At least one person wasn't totally repulsed by his blackface make-up.

4 Black people as comedy slaves

The Toy (1982): Again, a movie I am amazed was made in my lifetime. In this film, Richard Pryor plays a poor black dude who is bought by a rich white dude to act as a toy for his spoilt brat of a kid. That's right: a black man as a white kid's toy. We can all only hope that Pryor was smoking a freak tonne of crack when he signed up to make this one.

5 Scary Asians

Indiana Jones and the Temple of Doom (1984): We've looked

at wacky Asians, now let's look at scary Asians. Eighties movies are full of menacing, mystical and, yes, inscrutable Asians: *The Golden Child*, *Big Trouble in Little China* and, on TV, pretty much every episode of *The A-Team*. Until George Lucas decided in 2008 that, after trashing the legacy of *Star Wars* with his utterly pointless prequel trilogy, he would now decimate people's memories of Indiana Jones with the appalling *Indiana Jones and the Kingdom of the Crystal Skull* in 2008, the worst Indiana Jones film was undoubtedly *Temple of Doom* (1984). Here, Spielberg bravely but unwisely decided to swap his usual villains, Nazis, for a blood-drinking Indian cult. Now, this is weird enough, but even worse is the portrayal of what wealthy Indians eat, which is living snakes, giant beetles, eyeball soup and monkey brains. Ha ha ha, Asian people are GROSS. Happily, Spielberg returned to the Nazis in the next *Indiana Jones*, and that's probably the only circumstance in which I would use 'happily' and 'returned to the Nazis' in a single sentence.

6 Wise Asians

The Karate Kid (1984): I imagine Mr Miyagi (so wise! So inscrutable! So asexual!) isn't on the Japan Society's Board of Noted Cultural Figureheads, but at least he isn't played for laughs. Well, except for when he fails to catch a fly with his chopsticks – how all Japanese people spend their evenings, you know. What a LOSER.

7 'LIBYAAAAAAANS!!!!!!!'[1]

In fact, we can just look at Murphy's own early movies to

---

[1] *Back to the Future*, as you well know.

see what he was up against in this decade. In *48 Hours*, Murphy's first film, he plays Reggie, a convict who is teamed up with Jack, played by Nick Nolte, a charmingly gruff cop, and by 'charmingly gruff' I mean 'totally racist'. Here are just some of the names Jack calls Reggie TO HIS FACE:[1]

'Watermelon.'

'Spearchucker.'

The n-word.

Truly, nothing makes a film's protagonist more adorable than some good ol' racism. It is worth noting that Jack is the lead in the movie and Reggie is his sidekick – it's just because Murphy is so charismatic that the movie seems like it belongs to both of them. It's Jack who has the personal life, and it's Jack who has the emotional journey in the film; Reggie is just there to serve the plot. So here we have a movie protagonist, who we're supposed to like, being openly racist, in 1982. When Jack later apologises to Reggie for saying those things 'I shouldn't have said', this is depicted as proof of his inner sensitivity beneath his gruff (read: 'racist') shell, and how he is actually more perceptive than the other cops who just see Reggie as a 'con' – although no one in the film other than Jack uses racist slurs about him. *48 Hours* is one of the most influential cop movies ever made, and its pairing of unlikely guys, one white, one black, was copied so extensively in the eighties (*Lethal Weapon*, *Die Hard*, *Miami Vice*) and later (*Men in Black*), it's easy to forget just how original it once was. But not one of the movie's many copies took

---

[1] Obviously, calling him these names behind his back wouldn't be great either, but watching him say them to Murphy's face is physically painful.

inspiration from Jack's racist language, and for a goddamn reason.

Decades later, Murphy spoke about the racist language in *48 Hours*:

> You know why it worked then and the reason why it wouldn't now? My significance in film – and again I'm not going to be delusional – was that I'm the first black actor to take charge in a white world onscreen. That's why I became as popular as I became. People had never seen that before. Black-exploitation movies, even if you dealt with the Man, it was in your neighbourhood, never in their world. In *48 Hours*, that's why it worked, because I'm running it, making the story go forward. If I was just chained to the steering wheel sitting there being called 'watermelon', even back then they would have been like, 'This is wrong, wrong, wrong, wrong!'

And he's right, to a certain extent: Murphy positively chews up the screen in this movie, which is no easy thing to do when you're acting alongside a certified ham like Nolte doing his usual gruff-old-goat Nolte thing. He absolutely dominates the film, and this in turn renders the abuse, according to Murphy, less appalling. But he's slightly mixing up cause and effect. Murphy is making the movie go forward, but no one thought that would be the case when he was cast. In fact, Richard Pryor was originally envisaged for the role and, for all Pryor's undoubted gifts, he was never able to break out of the limited (read: racist) boxes in which he was put in films (see the aforementioned *The Toy*). So the fact remains Murphy's first big film was one in

which the sympathetic protagonist is a big ol' racist – and
he triumphs over him. Readers who like metaphors are
encouraged to make their own connections here.

In Murphy's next film, the still completely delightful
Trading Places, he plays Billy Ray Valentine, a poor black
con artist who switches places with a wealthy white dude
called Louis Winthorpe III (Dan Aykroyd). Here, when
Mortimer Duke (Don Ameche) uses the n-word about
Valentine, this is depicted as proof of his evilness, and it's
what motivates Valentine to take revenge. However, the
other good male protagonist in the film, Louis, does have a
tendency to refer to Valentine as a 'negro', much to
Valentine's understandable irritation. Strangely, though,
Valentine seems totally fine when Louis later blacks up
when he adopts the disguise of a Jamaican stoner in order
to trick the guy who played the evil principal in *The
Breakfast Club* and the stupid police chief in *Die Hard*[1] (do
try to keep up).

'That was very controversial, even back then, and [the
studio heads] Barry Diller and Ned Tannen hated that we
did that,' says *Trading Places*' director, John Landis. 'But the
point is, that it's supposed to be ridiculous and pathetic,
and it is. Danny can do a very good Jamaican accent, but
he's doing a terrible one here.' And this is true – but again,
it does mean that we have a mainstream movie featuring a
protagonist employing an offensive black stereotype that
would not even be used by villains in movies today. But I
do have some sympathy with Landis when he adds, referring to the ending of *Trading Places* in which the bad guy
is trapped in a cage with a gorilla, 'I was fascinated that

---

[1] Paul Gleason, the go-to man in the eighties for stupid villains.

[studio heads] were outraged by [the black face] but not some guy being fucked in the ass by a gorilla."[1]

Murphy's career began when he was turned down at the age of nineteen by *Saturday Night Live* in 1980. Even though *Saturday Night Live* prided itself on being ever so cutting edge, the show had yet to be convinced that its audience could handle more than one black cast member at a time, and when Murphy turned up he was told that Robert Townsend had already been cast and so the role of 'the black guy' was filled. Instead, Murphy was half-heartedly assigned as a featured player, as opposed to a regular cast member. After a year and a change of boss, Murphy's talent and popularity were simply impossible to ignore and so he was promoted – and he promptly saved the TV sketch show.

'If not for Eddie's talent and popularity, *SNL* would probably have died in the early 80s,' Tom Shales and James Andrew Miller write. And if that had happened, comedians who got their start on *SNL* after Murphy's era, including Chris Farley, Chris Rock, Mike Myers, Will Ferrell, Tina Fey and Amy Poehler, might well have never been launched. Many, many comedians today stand on Murphy's shoulders.

Being 'the black guy' was pretty much par for the course for black actors in America in the early 1980s. 'The status of the black person in pop culture in the early eighties reflected a kind of tokenism on some levels,' says Mark Anthony Neal, a Professor of Black Popular Culture in the Department of African and African-American Studies at

---

[1] I should probably stress again at this point that I completely adore this film and watch it at least three times a year.

Duke University. 'You look at TV shows that started up then, such as *The Facts of Life* [in which one black girl is at a posh all-white girls boarding school] or *Diff'rent Strokes* [in which two poor black boys are adopted by a rich old white man], and you have token black bodies in strange, white situations. I think many black audiences appreciated the move away from the blaxploitation images that were very popular in the seventies, but I think there was also concern that a lot of the characters you saw were not fully rounded at all.'

Being 'the black guy' on *SNL* was about as thankless a job as it sounds. Garrett Morris, the first black cast member, was, according to original cast member Jane Curtin, 'treated horribly, horribly – by the writers, by some of the performers, and by Lorne [Michaels, the show's creator]', which is demonstrably true. During his *SNL* tenure Morris was repeatedly humiliated in sketches that did more than border on racist: he was made to wear a monkey suit and one time the writers wrote a parody commercial for him in which he advertised a toothpaste called Tarbrush to darken black people's teeth (Lorne Michaels cut it from the show after seeing it in rehearsal although, according to Morris, two black technicians walked out in protest that it was even considered). For his part, Morris said he built 'the only non-white chair in that whole thing, and I shed blood for that'. It cost him more than blood. The comedian became so depressed about his situation, and so bored from being under-used by the writers, that he started freebasing.

Even after Murphy proved that 'the black guy' could be a real asset to the show, *Saturday Night Live* continued to

treat black cast members as mere tokens, there to imper-
sonate black celebrities and little else. Damon Wayans (on
the show from 1985 to 1986) got so annoyed with the
programme he started wearing sunglasses inside and
telling people, 'It's too white in here, it hurts my eyes.'
Eventually, he sabotaged a skit while on air and was duly
fired and soon after established *In Living Color*, a comedy
sketch show featuring mainly black comedians. Chris
Rock (*Saturday Night Live* cast member from 1990 to
1993) also got frustrated with 'this weird, Waspy world of
a show' – and that was in 1993, thirteen years after
Murphy arrived.

This was the world in which Murphy got his start. And
yet, despite all these seemingly insurmountable hurdles,
he became *SNL*'s biggest breakout star of all time. But as
Bill Simmons points out, 'Eddie never catered to *SNL*'s
white audience, that's for sure.' His jokes were about
specific African-American tropes and icons, from the
ghetto to James Brown to, most famously, his imitations of
Stevie Wonder. He broke through *SNL*'s white ceiling, and
the lagging racism of America in the eighties, not by
being reductive or offensive about black people, but
simply by being so incandescent that no one could resist
him.

'He was young and he was tuned into what was
happening in young black America, and he wasn't Cosby,
but he wasn't Richard Pryor,' says Professor Neal. 'You
never got the sense that he was whitewashing who he was,
or what his experience was.'

Murphy looked up to both Cosby and Pryor as mentors,
and a large part of his success came from synthesising the
lessons he learned from them: he wasn't quite as dangerous

as Pryor, but nor was he as conservative as Cosby. In his stand-up, he talked about working-class black experiences, like Pryor did, but not in a way that would alienate white audiences, as Cosby feared. His mentors, perhaps unsurprisingly, had some reservations about his tactics. Cosby, according to Murphy's very credible account in his 1989 live show, *Raw*, thought Murphy used too much dirty language. Pryor wrote: 'I never connected with Eddie. People talked about how much my work influenced Eddie, and perhaps it did. But I always thought Eddie's comedy was mean. I used to say, "Eddie, be a little nice," and that would piss him off.'

But despite his predecessors' reservations, he was more successful than they ever dreamed of being. 'Eddie was making jokes in high school when he was sixteen, he was playing in comedy clubs at eighteen, he was on *SNL* at nineteen, he was a movie star at twenty and he was a superstar by twenty-two. He was just an unbelievable meteorite,' says John Landis.

He is also, as Bill Simmons points out, the only cast member of *SNL* to break into movies properly while still on the show. Even before *48 Hours* had been released, he was cast in *Trading Places*, a film that had originally been envisioned for Richard Pryor and Gene Wilder but, as the film's director John Landis delicately puts it, 'Richard unfortunately set himself on fire, so the project went on hold.' When the studio previewed *48 Hours*, test audiences went completely nuts for Murphy. Studio boss Jeffrey Katzenberg called up Landis, best known then for directing *Animal House* and *The Blues Brothers*, the movies that launched former *Saturday Night* comedian John Belushi, and asked him to repeat this trick with Murphy, and Landis agreed.

So, for the second time, Murphy was cast in a role that had been Pryor's, and, unlike Pryor, Murphy was smart enough to know that his success depended on him staying clean.[*1] In Hollywood's eyes, Murphy was taking over from Pryor as 'the black guy'.[*2]

Unfortunately, Paramount 'hated everyone' else Landis cast. They didn't want Aykroyd because Belushi had just died and Aykroyd's last film, *Doctor Detroit*, had flopped. 'So conventional wisdom was that it was over for Danny. It was like when Dean Martin and Jerry Lewis broke up, everyone was like, "Poor Dean Martin, we'll never see him again." But I cast him anyway and the studio was furious but I said, "I'm sorry, you gave me final cut and that's who I want,"' recalls Landis. 'People forget what a good actor Danny is. Winthorpe has nothing to do with Elwood [his character in *The Blues Brothers*], they're on a different planet from one another. If you give Danny direction he's great; if you leave him to his own resources, you get this strange Danny thing. But such a brilliant guy, really smart and funny.'

---

*1 Murphy: 'I've never actually even physically had cocaine. When I was 18, I was down in the Blues Bar with Belushi and Robin Williams, everybody was partying, I was like "No." Every now and then, I'd think about that moment, too, because I was around those guys, it was easy to party, and how everything would have changed. I know if I fucked around with that, I would have been all the way in. I'd have made a million headlines. There would have been no success, the story would have stopped in the Eighties' ('Eddie Murphy Speaks', Brian Hiatt, *Rolling Stone*, 19 November 2011).

*2 Murphy later said in an interview with Spike Lee: 'Richard doesn't like me . . . There's this thing where Richard feels that the reason his shit is the way it is, is because I came along and fucked his shit up. He really believes that . . . It's really weird to find out that your idol hates you and shit' ('Eddie', Spike Lee, *Spin* magazine, 1990). On the one hand, Pryor is right, Murphy did take his place. There was room for only one black man at the table back then. But on the other, it wouldn't have been so easy for him to do so if Pryor hadn't been setting himself on fire while freebasing crack.

The studio was even more outraged when he cast Jamie Lee Curtis, then known only for horror movies, as Ophelia, the kindly prostitute. 'The script is wonderful but the big flaw in it is Ophelia, the hooker with the heart of gold, which is a total Hollywood cliché and a false character. So I knew I needed someone special to play her and when I met Jamie I could immediately see how funny and smart she is, and very sexy in a totally unorthodox way,' says Landis.

Paramount, though, was so unimpressed by Landis's choice to hire 'a B-picture actress', as studio boss Barry Diller put it, that they docked $2 million from the film's budget.

For the role of Coleman the butler, Landis desperately wanted to hire Ronnie Barker, as he was 'a huge fan' of *The Two Ronnies*. However, Barker told Landis that he never worked 'more than twenty-five miles from home', so Denholm Elliott was hired instead. Finally, Landis wanted to include some old Hollywood in the cast, so he hired Don Ameche and Ralph Bellamy as the wicked Duke brothers. 'And they were so supportive of Eddie, so good to him, who, you gotta remember, was still only about twenty when we made this, and the two of them were huge Hollywood legends who had been working for fifty years,' says Landis. 'I remember one day we were shooting the scene when Eddie's in the back of the Rolls-Royce with Don and Ralph and I have headphones on outside to hear them. Don says, "You know, this is my ninety-ninth motion picture." And Ralph says, "That's funny, this is my hundredth feature film," and Eddie shouts, "Hey, Landis! Between the three of us we've made 201 movies!"' Murphy was, Landis recalls, 'so happy when we were making

Trading Places, just bouncing off the walls and so, so gifted. He just popped on screen.'

Murphy has said that the reason his eighties movie characters feel so real is because 'From the very beginning, I always tried to make dialogue flow comfortably, I always did that to make it seem more authentic.' However, he barely improvised in *Trading Places*. Even the scene when he pretends to be a blind Vietnam vet, which feels so much like a Murphy riff, was 'all on paper': '*Trading Places*, John Landis movies, period – it looks like a bunch of improvisation, but John Landis is on you more than any other director I've ever worked with. He'll tell you how to read the line, and if he wants you to do a physical stunt, he'll show you. He really gets in there and you're like, "This motherfucker,"' Murphy said.

Landis laughs at this: 'Well that's not exactly true, Eddie does improvise. I'm pretty specific, but there were times when we did improvise. One of my favourite lines in the movie was improvised. In the script [in that scene] when he's hassling the woman he says, "Once you've had a man with no legs there's no going back. We can make it, baby, me and you." But I just let the camera keep rolling and he then shouts out, "Ain't you never seen *Porgy and Bess*? Bitch!" That was Eddie.'

During all this, Murphy was still making *SNL*. 'I only had Eddie three days a week, because of *Saturday Night Live*, just like I'd only had Belushi two days a week when we were making *Animal House*,' says Landis. But this would soon not be the case. *48 Hours* came out when they were still shooting *Trading Places* and audiences went insane for Murphy. When *Trading Places* came out in the summer of 1983, it was clear that Murphy was a star, and about five minutes after it arrived in cinemas, he quit *Saturday Night Live*, and it was at this point that Murphy began to transcend race.

Mickey Rourke was the first prospective Axel Foley, but he dropped out. He was then followed by (good Lord) Sylvester Stallone, who rewrote the script as a straight action movie, but he left the project two weeks before filming and made *Cobra* instead. So Jerry Bruckheimer and Don Simpson quickly hired Eddie Murphy for the role, and, in doing so, made the film the biggest hit of 1984 and one of the biggest hits of all time. Murphy is at his absolute comic prime in the film: in the scene in which he bluffs his way into getting a room at a swish Beverly Hills hotel, he goes from sweet to exaggeratedly angry to deadpan in the space of two minutes without even moving his body, and his reaction to being told the price of a room at the hotel remains one of the coolest double-takes ever committed to film. Few actors – comic or otherwise – can convey so subtly so many conflicting emotions on their face, in this case, shock, trying not to look shocked and a growing hysteria about being in Beverly Hills.

He stuck in one or two jokes about his race in the movie, including in the hotel scene, but otherwise there is hardly any reference to it whatsoever, which seems both sweetly innocent and frankly incredible considering this is a movie about a black guy running around Los Angeles in the eighties with a gun. Yes, Foley is supposed to be an outsider in Beverly Hills but, according to the script, it's the fact that he's from Detroit that signifies his interloper status, not his race, although Murphy's race does compound that impression (it's notable that the only other black person in the movie is Foley's boss back in Detroit. Is everyone in Beverly Hills white?[*1]). For the first time in his career, Murphy's race did not define his character, and that this was allowed to happen is a testament to Murphy's superstardom, and Bruckheimer and Simpson's forward thinking.[*2]

Whereas in *48 Hours* the black character is very much second-in-command to the white cop, in *Beverly Hills Cop* Axel is the leader of the pack of white cops, who don't just rely on him to catch the bad guys, they need him to show them how to behave in a bar. This wasn't just the first time a black cop was depicted as being both professionally and socially superior to his white colleagues – it is the only time, until *Training Day* (2001), in which Denzel Washington is in charge of Ethan Hawke, and even in that film Hawke eventually triumphs over Washington. 'There's this little box that African-American actors have to work in, in the first place,' said Murphy. 'And I was able to rise above it.'

But even in *Beverly Hills Cop*, there was a notable restriction placed on Murphy: his onscreen romance. The only woman in the film is Jenny (Lisa Eilbacher), who is white. When Stallone rewrote the script, Axel and Jenny are romantically involved, which completely makes sense in the universe of the film. But in the version shot with Murphy, Axel seems utterly oblivious to Lisa, even though the character keeps throwing herself at him, reclining on

---

*1 Yes.

*2 A decade later, they would, again, recast a film written with white actors in mind with black stars. *Bad Boys* was originally supposed to star Dana Carvey and Jon Lovitz, of all the dweebs in the world. But they were then wisely swapped for Will Smith and Martin Lawrence.

his bed, following him on stake-outs for no reason what-soever other than to be annoying in that way only women in male-led action films ever are. There is no need for Lisa to be in this movie – she serves less than zero func-tion – and while I don't mean to suggest that if a woman is in an action movie then the least she can do is sleep with the male lead, that is nonetheless very clearly why she was in the story in the first place. But because Murphy is black and Lisa is white (to have cast a black actress as well as a black lead would have made this main-stream action movie 'too black', presumably), no romance can happen between them.

Instead, in both *Beverly Hills Cop* and its 1987 sequel, Axel is rendered completely asexual, and deliberately obliv-ious to white women, even when one of those white women is Brigitte Nielsen, for God's sake. This is to makes him seem 'safe' to white audiences, especially white male audiences: 'See, this isn't one of THOSE kind of black guys – this is a good black guy! Sure, he's fun and knows where all the strip clubs in town are, but he's also the kind you can trust not to touch a white woman, even if she's lolling across a bed when alone in a hotel room with him!' the movies say.

In this regard, Axel is pretty much the opposite of the image Murphy went out of his way to portray in the hugely successful films of his stand-up that sandwich the decade, *Delirious* (1983) and *Raw* (1987), in which he prowls around the stage in head-to-toe leather: 'If I took Brooke Shields to the Grammy's, y'all would lose your mind', he riffs in *Raw*. 'Because y'all know Brooke would get fucked that night.'

The few love interests Murphy is allowed onscreen are

black women,[*1] and audiences are never allowed to see
them actually having sex, from *48 Hours* to *Coming to
America*. In Murphy's film after *Beverly Hills Cop*, *The
Golden Child*, he is allowed to kiss a 'Tibetan' woman
onscreen (actually played by the Chilean-Iraqi-Irish actress
Charlotte Lewis, but not strictly Caucasian, and that's all
that matters here), but no more. Even in the last scene of
Trading Places, when Billy Ray, Louis, Ophelia and
Coleman have escaped to an unidentified paradise island,
Coleman's girlfriend appears to be Tahitian and an island
native, which makes sense, but Billy Ray's girlfriend is definitely, pointedly black. It's not that I'm so desperate to see
Murphy have sex onscreen (and as anyone who has seen
1992's *Boomerang* knows, Murphy's enthusiasm in a sex
scene can make a little go a very long way), or to see him
hook up with a white woman. But it's pretty extraordinary
to see how nervy eighties filmmakers were about letting a
young, attractive black man onscreen seem in any way
sexual to mainstream white audiences. Tom Cruise, Tom
Hanks, hell, even Dan Aykroyd were allowed to have
onscreen sex lives in the eighties – but not Murphy.

The Golden Child is the second film in which Murphy's
race is irrelevant to the character. There is absolutely no
reason why Chandler Jarrell, private investigator for lost
children, should be black, and there is no reference to it in
the film. Murphy proved by now he had transcended race,
an achievement that would feel a little more triumphant if
Murphy didn't look quite so bored onscreen during the
whole of this movie. Although, to be fair, this is a ridicu-

[*1] And notably much lighter skinned than him, to boot, particularly in *48
Hours* and *Coming to America*, reflecting yet another racial stereotype.

lous movie, a shameless rip-off of *Raiders of the Lost Ark* and one that makes so little sense it's like watching a film that was dubbed into a foreign language and then redubbed into English. Although it's not quite as ridiculous as the hat Murphy wears for the whole film.

Murphy was by now one of the biggest superstars alive. He was so popular, in fact, he was able to release the delightfully stupid single 'Party All the Time' in 1985, with an extraordinarily be-weaved Rick James – and it still reached number two in the Billboard chart, denied the top spot by Lionel Ritchie's 'Say You, Say Me'. (Britain, rather commendably, was a bit harder to impress and Murphy only got to eighty-five in the UK charts. Well done, Britain.) The man believed he could do anything, and American audiences agreed. But times were about to change, again.

Murphy's feelings about having a social responsibility as a black actor have never been that hard to fathom: he's resented it. 'I know because of the level of my celebrity I have been forced – I am being forced – to be a politician in a manner of speaking. And what happens, although I know I have a responsibility politically, ultimately I am an entertainer, I am an artist first and foremost. And you accept the responsibility, but the artist part of you resents the fact they don't just give you the freedom to just be an artist,' he said in 1990. Murphy was very aware that he was the successful 'black guy' in Hollywood, and with that came the awareness that in order to maintain his position, and to keep transcending race, he had – to a certain extent – to play along.

Which is not to say he didn't occasionally speak up – but, unlike Richard Pryor or, later, Spike Lee, he would do so with a smile on his face so some people might miss the punch. In 1988 he presented the Best Film Award at the Oscars and when he got up onstage he told a palpably confused audience that he initially declined the offer to present because the Academy 'haven't recognised black people in the motion pictures . . . Throughout sixty years Hattie McDaniel won the first [Oscar], Sidney Poitier won one and Lou Gossett won one.'

He paused a little at this point, as though going off script: 'I'll probably never win an Oscar for saying this but, hey, what the hey I gotta say it!' He shrugged with a laugh. 'Actually, that might not be any trouble because the way it's going we only get one every twenty years so we ain't due until 2004 so by this time this will have all blown over.'[1]

But, he said onstage, his agent said, 'You can't snub the Academy.' So he went, even though he believed that 'black people [were still made] to bring up the rear of society'. If he hadn't come, then he simply would have been absent, but this way at least they noticed his speech.

'I don't think you can beat the system,' Murphy said two years later. 'I think you can be successful within the system.'

He argued with Spike Lee, who criticised him for not insisting on having more black actors and crew members in his movies. Murphy felt, probably rightly, that if he took this stand his career in the studio system would be jeopardised and then there would be no black actors in the mainstream A-list in Hollywood at all. 'The scariest thing about you to me,' he said to Lee, 'is that every black person who really stood up and said, "Fuck it, I'm about this," got dissed, filled, fucked over – everybody from Dr King to Ali, you know?'

But things were shifting in African-American film with

---

*1 Murphy was almost right: the next African-American actors to win an Oscar were Denzel Washington and Halle Berry, both in 2001.

the rise of the independent industry. By the late 1980s, Spike Lee had released *She's Gotta Have It* and was making *School Daze*, two independent movies emphatically about African-Americans and African-American experiences. Murphy, however, felt, 'I am very black and I have a very strong black consciousness, but I am about gradual change and dialogue that is much more civil.' What this meant was not making an assertively black film, but a big glossy Hollywood movie that happened to feature African-Americans. Succeeding within the system, in other words.

'Eddie called me up and had this idea about an African prince who has an arranged marriage, but didn't want it. So he comes to the United States to find a liberated woman of his equal,' says Landis. 'He really had no story other than that, and so I went home and told my wife, and she got incredibly excited. She said, "John, don't you understand? It's Cinderella! It's Sleeping Beauty! It's a fucking fairy tale – from Africa!"'[1]

Landis started to plan the story about an African prince, Akeem (Murphy), who, along with his best friend Semmi (Arsenio Hall), comes to America to find his bride. He heads to – where else? – Queens, where he works in a fast food restaurant, McDowell's, and falls in love with the owner's daughter while pretending to be a pauper. The film includes still hysterically funny and knowing references to African-American culture, including the advertisements for 'Soul-Glo', a horrible product that makes Afro hair shimmer, and god-awful black soul singers fronting bands

---

[1] Landis's wife, costume designer Deborah Nadoolman Landis, was right to be excited: she ended up getting nominated for an Oscar for her work on *Coming to America*.

with names like 'Sexual Chocolate'. It also gave roles to established African-American actors, such as James Earl Jones, and launched a then totally unknown Samuel L. Jackson.

'As I planned the story, I got very excited, but for reasons I wouldn't discuss for twenty years,' says Landis. 'I suddenly realised, "The plot will have nothing to do with their colour!" So it was essentially a black movie but it's not – it's not about their colour, it's a fairy tale. It's a romantic comedy, and the storytelling itself is very conservative and traditional, and it looks like a traditional Hollywood movie – these were all my intentions. It's the movie of mine that made the most money. Around the world, it's made almost $1billion. It was a huge hit, and, importantly, a huge international hit. But the great success of that movie is that it's an African-American movie and people don't really notice, and that's very satisfying to me.'

This, though, was precisely the sort of thing that Spike Lee objected to: he didn't want covert success, or success within a white framework, and he certainly didn't see the point in making an African-American film if no one knew it was one. Whereas Murphy believed his success was the statement, Lee argued there was no statement without a specified message. This is the trade-off that all minorities face in the search for success: in order to achieve mainstream success, how much are you willing to risk leaving behind your core audience?

According to Professor Neal:

In the early days black audiences appreciated Murphy's presence onscreen. But when you start to see some of the tensions in the late 1980s, particularly

around films and the tension between him and Spike
Lee, and folks that were looking for quote unquote
more authentic and even political black filmmaking
that resonated especially for a hip hop generation,
Eddie Murphy got left behind. He was doing something else. It's really not until the nineties that he did
Boomerang that he begins to reclaim some of what he
had lost in terms of a black following. But this was
something that befell that whole 1980s crossover
generation. Michael Jackson struggled with that,
losing a core black audience because he had crossed
over so much, Whitney Houston got booed at the
1989 Soul Train Music Awards; obviously what Eddie
Murphy was doing was in there, too.

Murphy knew this and struggled with it, uncertain what to
do and horrified that the people he thought he was repre-
senting were turning against him. 'You get these black people,
it seems like they turn on you,' he said to Spike Lee. Coupled
with that, he was increasingly bogged down in the weird
claustrophobia that comes with extreme fame, cut off from
the real world and surrounded only by his tight adoring
coterie, and simultaneously filled with resentment towards his
critics with whom he felt he could do no right. 'If I was
rubbing you the wrong way, at the core of it was some racist
shit: "Look at this arrogant nigger, two thumbs wayyyyy
down!"' he said with a laugh in a 2011 interview, recalling the
late eighties. 'Then I wasn't helping either. I wasn't giving no
humble pie: "Fuck y'all, suck my dick motherfucker!"'
      He is utterly wonderful in *Coming to America* but,
Landis recalls, 'he was less joyful, much less joyful, than the
person I made *Trading Places* with five years before.' So

much less joyful, in fact, that he tried to beat Landis up one day on set and grabbed him by the throat. 'To this day, I don't know what happened,' says Landis. 'We were shooting in McDowell's on Queen's Boulevard, and it was snowing heavily outside. I was talking to someone and Eddie grabbed me from the back and put me in a headlock, and I was like "What the fuck was that?!" I was furious! And he was furious with me! And I grabbed the script girl's notebook and I shouted at Eddie, "Here, shove this up your ass!" and I stormed off the set.'

Eventually, Landis angrily returned to the movie set and went to see Murphy in his trailer. 'I go in and it wasn't even a confrontation, it was just Eddie venting. He was very angry at his family, I don't know what was going on, and he was very angry at me, saying I was treating him the same as everyone else. He said, "I'm the star, you're not giving me enough." I don't know what the hell . . . Eddie said, "I'm going to have you fired," and I said, "OK, but let's finish the day."'

So they finished shooting the scene in which Murphy's character, Prince Akeem, meets Patrice (Allison Dean) at McDowell's, and she invites him to a basketball game – no one watching this sweet, funny scene would guess that Murphy was raging inside, or that the director was furious at him. Murphy went home that night and, usually teetotal, had some alcohol: 'I went back to the house and Arsenio got me drunk . . . I can't drink,' he said.

Landis went home that evening, similarly enraged, because he fully expected to be fired from the movie. 'So [studio boss] Ned Tannen calls me and says, "Listen, John, Eddie called and is very, very upset. But we told him he has no power to fire you, we've seen the dailies, this is his best work, he's an idiot so we said, Eddie, here's the choice: we fire John and shut down the movie and sue you for the production costs, or we continue." I was really shocked!' Landis recalls.

The next day, he returned to the set and went to talk with Murphy.

'So I go see him and – this is a terrible story but it's true – and he said, "All right, we're going to finish the movie but we are no longer friends." And I said, "Deal!" So we did the movie, but we didn't talk offset at all.'

Despite his anger about the film, Murphy later said that he did his best acting in *Coming to America*. The scene he specifically cited as being his biggest source of pride is the famous barbershop scene, in which he, along with Arsenio Hall, played multiple characters, including an old white Jewish man ('Like a boid!').

Landis remembers:

Those characters were never supposed to be played by Eddie and Arsenio. In fact, we'd already hired actors to play them. But one night I saw a black filmmaker – I won't say who – on television talking about his new movie, and he said something really shocking to me. He was talking about minstrel shows, and he said blackface was created by 'Old Jews who wanted to play young black men.' Obviously he was referring to Eddie Cantor and Al Jolson – but does he know anything about the history of blackface? So the next day I came into work and said, 'Eddie, can you do a Yiddish accent?' And he said, 'I don't know.' And I said, 'Well I know you can, you can do anything.' And he said, 'Well how will I look?' So I had Rick [Baker, the make-up artist, who was nominated for an Oscar for his work here] make him up and Eddie was so thrilled.

Landis then shot the barbershop scene using cutaways, using Murphy's comedian brother Charlie as a double in some scenes.

'From that point on, as soon as Eddie saw what Rick Baker could do, he was like, I want to play the barber! And Arsenio said, "I want to play the preacher!" And we had to pay off all the actors we hired.'

This use of disguise in movies, which Murphy would then employ repeatedly for the next two decades, was a means for him to escape the pressures and demands he felt from critics and audiences, both black and white.

'From then on, whenever you look at Eddie's greatest performances, they're always in disguise, and it's interesting. If you look at the *Nutty Professor* remake, when he's in the fat suit, he's brilliant, when he's the other guy, he's not that interesting. And in *Bowfinger*, when he plays the movie star he's not that interesting, but as the brother he's dazzling. It's strange, but it somehow frees him and he's brilliant at it,' says Landis.

Coming to America marked the end of Murphy's triumphant movie run, and a large part of this is because it was around this time that Murphy got tired of being funny: 'I think you got tremendous pressure on you, Eddie. Because every time you open your mouth, people want to laugh. And that's crazy,' Spike Lee said to him in 1990.

'And they want it to be as funny as the last time I said something,' Murphy replied, almost certainly with an eye-roll.

Maybe Murphy was sick of the pressure to be funny. Maybe it got too easy. Or maybe to be funny requires being aware of what life is like in the real world, and Murphy was now lost in the orbit of a superstar, cloistered up in his big homes. Whatever the reason, it wasn't a bad idea of Murphy's to try to break into drama; for the few comedy actors who made it into the nineties, moving into drama was the way they achieved this: Tom Hanks, most obviously, and, later, Bill Murray. Unfortunately, Murphy's talent for picking stinkers in drama was almost as refined as his skill at picking successful comedies. He wrote, starred in and directed 1989's *Harlem Nights*, which he admitted soon after was an absolute mess, and thereafter began his fallow run in the nineties, with only *Boomerang* alleviating the dreariness.

In 1993 John Landis got an unexpected call: Sherry Lansing, who then ran Paramount, told him that Murphy was going to make *Beverly Hills Cop 3*, and he had asked for Landis to direct it. Landis was astonished: he and Murphy hadn't spoken since their fight on the set of *Coming to America*, five years earlier. But a bigger surprise was in store for him.

'Eddie didn't want to be funny, so that made it a strange experience,' he says. 'He was very jealous of Denzel Washington and Samuel Jackson, and he wanted to be an action star so he would go out of his way to avoid a joke, and I gave him so many opportunities. That became a very demoralising movie to make. Luckily it made a lot of money, but it's a weird movie, because it isn't funny.'

By now, Murphy was looking extremely out of step with the times. Although he increasingly made movies with largely African-American casts (*Harlem Nights*, *The Distinguished Gentleman*, *Boomerang*), they were not the kind of movies about African-Americans that were in vogue. Spike Lee's *Do the Right Thing* came out in 1989, followed by John Singleton's *Boyz in the Hood* and Mario van Peebles's *New Jack City*, both in 1991, and these films were a far bigger part of the zeitgeist than anything Murphy was making then. He was still making glossy Hollywood products, but audiences and critics were more interested in politically aware films. Murphy's run – one unparalleled by any comedian, white or black, ever since – was done.

In terms of the representation of African-Americans in movies, no other decade saw as much progress, and as quickly, as the eighties. Going from Nick Nolte calling Murphy a 'spearchucker' in 1982 to Spike Lee's *Do the Right Thing* getting nominated for Oscars in 1989 is an incredible leap, and the person who made this happen was Murphy.

'Hollywood had to be convinced that black stars could be bankable,' says Professor Neal. 'Pryor started that a little bit in the seventies but it really went full tilt in the eighties with Murphy. He was the necessary step in getting stories featuring black people to the mainstream. Now folks like Denzel Washington and Halle Berry can open movies, and it was Eddie Murphy who allowed for that to occur.'

The irony for Murphy, though, was that in carving this path for others, he made himself look redundant. He was no longer 'the black guy'. There were other black guys, from Samuel L. Jackson to Laurence Fishburne to Denzel Washington, and he's the one who made the space for them.

'His films introduced or featured many black stars who later became stars, such as Arsenio Hall, Chris Rock, Halle Berry, Damon Wayans, Cuba Gooding Jr, and others. He did not "pull up the ladder" after himself,' adds Anna Everett, Professor of Film and Media Studies at the University of California Santa Barbara.

What Murphy achieved in the eighties is more than any

black actor had done before him or has done since, and the proof of that is that no one has been able to move the representation of African-Americans in Hollywood pictures significantly further forward since Murphy's era and the immediate years after.

'We haven't fully realised the promise that was hinted at with *Do the Right Thing* in 1989 and *Boyz in the Hood*,' says Professor Neal. 'Then we saw black films by black independent auteurs getting nominated for Hollywood awards. But that kind of promise has not been sustained.'

In Hollywood movies nowadays, black actors are still largely cast as the convict, the slave, the outsider, or shunted into secondary roles, like a judge or a police chief.'[1] No movie with an all-black cast, from 1993's *What's Love Got to Do with It* to 1995's *Waiting to Exhale* to 1998's *How Stella Got Her Groove Back*, has ever achieved the kind of mainstream and commercial success that *Coming to America* did.

Most tellingly of all, no black actor since has come even close to Murphy's success: 'Eddie's movies have grossed over $6.5 billion worldwide before adjusting them for inflation. Will Smith's total: $5.735 billion. Denzel Washington's total: $2.788 billion,' Bill Simmons writes. 'I'm just sayin'.'

Eighties comedies are, for me, the height of comedy, in that they're silly without being stupid, they're sweet without being slushy, they're funny without being mean and they understand the importance of a good script above all, and

---

*1 And depictions of Asian men have hardly improved since the eighties either. The screaming Asian gangster in *The Hangover*, played by Ken Jeong, is a direct descendant of Long Duk Dong.

Murphy's eighties films, especially *Trading Places*, *Beverly Hills Cop* and *Coming to America*, exemplify all those qualities. No one was funnier in the eighties than Eddie Murphy. Goddamn, that man was funny. He could swear like opera singers can sing and he would say more with his eyes in two seconds than other comedians manage with their voices in a year. No comedian before or since was more charismatic onscreen than him. Murphy is the case in point that for a black man to be on a par with his white contemporaries, he has to be ten times better than them. Murphy was a million times better than anyone else so he succeeded above everyone. Maybe he just made it all look so easy in the eighties and that's why he doesn't get the credit he deserves today.

'No matter what you do, that shit is all getting turned into gobbledygook. In 200 years, it's all dust, and in 300 years, it ain't nothing, and in 1,000 years, it's like you wasn't even fucking here. But if you're really, really lucky, if you really did something special, you could hang around a little longer,' Murphy said recently.

Murphy's achievements will hang around longer.

TOP EIGHTIES QUOTES

I've been so restrained – so far. Cut a lady some slack now, OK? These are the top twenty, and I quote them all, aloud or in my head, on a weekly basis. I've also made separate categories for the three most important movies of the decade in terms of quotes and, quite possibly, in terms of everything, ever.

20 'I'm too old for this shit.' (*Lethal Weapon*)

19 'You are evil, and you must be destroyed.' (*Steel Magnolias*)

18 'Any girl that did that to me I would not be too JAZZED to hold on to.' (*Pretty in Pink*)

17 'You think what you want about me – I'm not changing. I like me.' (*Planes, Trains and Automobiles*)

16 'You have chosen . . . wisely.' (*Indiana Jones and the Last Crusade*)

15 'I love you.' **slap** 'Snap out of it!' (*Moonstruck*)[*1]

14 'Fuck me gently with a chainsaw, do I look like Mother Teresa?' (*Heathers*)

13 'Looking good, Billy Ray!' 'Feeling good, Louis!' (*Trading Places*)

[*1] Also from *Moonstruck*, I would like to give special mention to 'Chrissie, over on the wall – bring me the big knife', because I love that scene so.

12 'You know what I am? I'm your worst fuckin' nightmare – I'm a nigger with a badge.' (*48 Hours*)

11 'Shame on you, you macho shithead!' (*Tootsie*)[*1]

10 'The royal penis is clean, your highness.' (*Coming to America*)

9 'If you build it, he will come.' (*Field of Dreams*)

8 'Strange things are afoot at the Circle K.' (*Bill and Ted's Excellent Adventure*)

7 'If Jesus came back and saw what's going on in his name, he'd never stop throwing up.' (*Hannah and Her Sisters*)

6 'When you grow up, your heart dies.' (*The Breakfast Club*)

5 'Roads? Where we're going we don't need roads.' (*Back to the Future*)

4 'Your ego is writing cheques that your body can't cash.' (*Top Gun*)

[*1] Also, special credit to 'Dr Brewster has tried to seduce several nurses in this unit, claiming to be in the throes of an uncontrollable impulse. Do you know what? I'm going to give every nurse on this floor an electric cattle prod and instruct them to zap them in his badoobies. Ruby? Hi, you wanna open the Yellow Pages under the section, Farm Equipment Retail . . .'

3 'I gave her my heart and she gave me a pen.' (*Say Anything*)

2 'Human sacrifice! Dogs and cats living together! Mass hysteria!' (*Ghostbusters*)

1 'Nobody puts Baby in the corner.' (*Dirty Dancing*)

TOP *FERRIS BUELLER'S DAY OFF* QUOTES

5 'You heartless wench!'

4 'The sportos, the motorheads, geeks, sluts, bloods, wastoids, dweebies, dickheads – they all adore him. They think he's a righteous dude.'

3 'I weep for the future.'

2 'Bueller . . . Bueller . . . Bueller . . .'

1 'Life moves pretty fast. If you don't stop and look around once in a while, you could miss it.'

TOP *THE PRINCESS BRIDE* QUOTES

5 'Never go in against a Sicilian when death is on the line! Hahahahahaha!' **dies**

4 'No more rhymes now, I mean it!' 'Anybody want a peanut?'

3 'Inconceivable!' 'You keep using that word. I do not think it means what you think it means.'

1 = 'As you wish.'

1 = 'Hello. My name is Inigo Montoya. You killed my father. Prepare to die.'

TOP *WHEN HARRY MET SALLY* QUOTES
(no, I did not include 'I'll have what she's having.' It is the most famous but there are too many better quotes)

5 'Someone is staring at you in Personal Growth.'

4 'I'm going to be forty!' 'When?' 'Some day!'

3 'It's amazing. You look like a normal person but you are actually the Angel of Death.'

2 'Thin. Pretty. Big tits. Your basic nightmare.'

1 'You're right, you're right, I know you're right.'

Epilogue

On 27 April 2013 director Steven Soderbergh walked up on stage and gave a speech at the San Francisco International Film Festival about what he saw as the state of cinema. Now, as he was the leading force behind the rise of independent filmmaking in the late eighties with the release of *Sex, Lies and Videotape*, Soderbergh focused largely on the crushing of the independent film sector. But as he is also the man who has proven studios can make stylish and interesting commercial films, such as *Out of Sight* and *Ocean's Eleven*, he also had some thoughts about how studios are crushing the movie business as a whole:

'Speaking of meetings [at Hollywood studios], the meetings have gotten pretty weird. There are fewer and fewer executives who are in the business because they love movies. There are fewer and fewer executives that know movies. So it can become a very strange situation. I mean, I know how to drive a car, but I wouldn't presume to sit in a meeting with an engineer and tell him how to build one, and that's kind of what you feel like when you're in these meetings. You've got people who don't know movies and don't watch movies for pleasure deciding what movie you're going to be allowed to make. That's one reason studio movies aren't better than they are . . .

Well, how does a studio decide what movies get made? One thing they take into consideration is the foreign market, obviously. It's become very big. So that means, you know, things that travel best are going to be action-adventure, science-fiction, fantasy, spectacle, some animation thrown in there. Obviously the bigger the budget, the more people this thing is going to have to appeal to, the more homogenised it's got to be, the more simplified it's got to be. So things like cultural specificity and narrative complexity, and, God forbid, ambiguity, those become real obstacles to the success of the film here and abroad . . .

If you've ever wondered why every poster and every trailer and every TV spot looks exactly the same, it's because of testing. It's because anything interesting scores poorly and gets kicked out. Now I've tried to argue that the methodology of this testing doesn't work. If you take a poster or a trailer and you show it to somebody in isolation, that's not really an accurate reflection of whether it's working because we don't see them in isolation, we see them in groups. We see a trailer in the middle of five other trailers, we see a poster in the middle of eight other posters, and I've tried to argue that maybe the thing that's making it distinctive and score poorly actually would stick out if you presented it to these people the way the real world presents it. And I've never won that argument . . .

Now, I'm going to attempt to show how a certain kind of rodent might be smarter than a studio when it comes to picking projects. If you give a certain kind of rodent the option of hitting two buttons, and one of the buttons, when you touch it, dispenses food 40 per cent of the time, and one of the buttons when you touch it dispenses food 60 per cent of the time, this certain kind of rodent very quickly figures out never to touch the 40 per cent button ever again. So when a studio is attempting to determine on a project-by-project basis what will work, instead of backing a talented filmmaker over the long haul, they're actually increasing their chances of choosing wrong. Because in my view, in this business, which is totally talent-driven, it's about horses, not races . . .

The most profitable movies for the studios are going to be the big movies, the home runs. They don't look at the singles or the doubles as being worth the money or the man hours. Psychologically, it's more comforting to spend $60 million promoting a movie that costs $100 million, than it does to spend $60 million for a movie that costs $10 million. I know what you're thinking: If it costs 10 you're going to be in profit sooner. Maybe not. Here's why: OK, $10 million movie, $60 million to promote it, that's $70 million, so you've got to gross $140 million to get out.[1] Now you've got a $100 million movie, you're going to spend $60 million to

---

[1] Soderbergh explained earlier in his speech that exhibitors take half the gross, therefore a movie needs to make twice what it cost in order to break even.

promote it. You've got to get $320 million to get out. How many $10 million movies make $140 million? Not many. How many $100 million movies make $320 million? A pretty good number, and there's this sort of domino effect that happens too. Bigger home video sales, bigger TV sales . . .

The sort of executive ecosystem is distorted, because executives don't get punished for making bombs the way that filmmakers do, and the result is there's no turnover of new ideas, there's no new ideas about how to approach the business or how to deal with talent or material. But, again, economically, it's a pretty straightforward business. Hell, it's the third biggest export that we have. It's one of the few things that we do that the world actually likes . . .

Taking the 30,000-foot view, maybe nothing's wrong, and maybe my feeling that the studios are kind of like Detroit before the bailout is totally insupportable. I mean, I'm wrong a lot. I'm wrong so much, it doesn't even raise my blood pressure any more. Maybe everything is just fine. But . . . admissions. This is the number of bodies that go through the turnstile, ten years ago [in America]: 1.52 billion. Last year: 1.36 billion. That's a 10½ per cent drop. Why are admissions dropping? Nobody knows.'

Movies are filled with clichés, and so are books about movies. Probably the biggest cliché of all in a film book is to bemoan that movies aren't as good as they used to be. Well, I love eighties movies so it seems apt that I should run to the cliché.

I quoted Soderbergh's speech at some length because it

seems to me that when you have a phenomenally successful studio director – as opposed to, say, a thirty-something woman in her bathrobe writing a book about her *Ghostbusters* obsession – saying that movies are getting worse, and for specific, very real reasons, he probably has a point. At the risk of sounding like Mad Ol' Granny Time, sitting in my rocking chair and reminiscing about the glory days of art when people made PROPER movies like *Twins* and *Weekend at Bernie's*, clearly the movie business is very, very different from what it was thirty years ago, and that is reflected in the movies it makes. It is simply impractical now for studios to make movies that aren't (seemingly) guaranteed bankers. No longer is there the model that a studio would make one, maybe two big blockbusters a year and that would support smaller, weirder projects like *Field of Dreams*; now the whole business model is predicated on tentpoles. In 2013 George Lucas predicted that cinemas would soon be reserved for the special and few block-busters, and they would be seen as a luxury pastime, like the theatre: 'You're going to end up with fewer theatres, bigger theatres with a lot of nice things,' he said. 'Going to the movies will cost 50 bucks or 100 or 150 bucks – like what Broadway costs today, or a football game.'

To a small degree, this is already happening, with big blockbusters going to Imax theatres. Studio movies have become too expensive to make, market and distribute, and too dependent on foreign markets, and so they increasingly feel like monolithic identikit juggernauts, because that's what they are. The formula is safely conservative.

Ah, but what about the independent sector? you cry. Indeed, many of the best films of the past twenty-five years have come from the independent sector, from 1994's *Pulp*

Fiction to 2001's *Mulholland Drive* to 2014's *Boyhood*. In fact, some of my favourite movies from the eighties were produced independently, from *Dirty Dancing* (obviously) to Spike Lee's wonderful *Do the Right Thing*, which still looks extraordinarily modern almost thirty years after it was made.

However, it has never been harder to get an independent movie released, despite all the advances in technology that have rendered them, ostensibly, cheaper to make. Soderbergh said:

> In 2003, 455 films were released. Two hundred and seventy-five of those were independent, 180 were studio films. Last year 677 films were released. So you're not imagining things, there are a lot of movies that open every weekend. Five hundred and forty-nine of those were independent, 128 were studio films. So, a 100 per cent increase in independent films, and a 28 per cent drop in studio films, and yet, ten years ago: studio market share 69 per cent, last year 76 per cent. You've got fewer studio movies now taking up a bigger piece of the pie and you've got twice as many independent films scrambling for a smaller piece of the pie. That's hard. That's really hard.

But this doesn't mean that good storytelling is dying. Far from it.

No one is sitting around now and claiming this is 'the Golden Age of American Movies'. Instead it is roundly agreed to the point of cliché to be the Golden Age of American TV, illustrated by the success of prestige box set shows such as *The Sopranos, Sex and the City, The Wire,*

Mad Men, Breaking Bad, Orange is the New Black and *Transparent.* All these shows were made by cable networks such as HBO and AMC, and streaming platforms like Netflix and Amazon Prime. This is where filmmakers and screenwriters can experience the luxury of making stories that aren't intended to appeal to everybody, and where they can write stories about women, abortions, sex and older people. Shortly before Soderbergh made the above speech, he released his film about Liberace, *Beyond the Candelabra,* on HBO because 'the feeling amongst the studios was that this material was too "special" [i.e., gay] to gross [the necessary] $70 million'.

Filmmaker Jill Soloway has worked in theatre, TV (she was the co-executive producer of *Six Feet Under*) and had made well-regarded independent films, including *Afternoon Delight* (2013), for which she won the Directing Award at the Sundance Festival. But when she got that award, instead of celebrating it, she immediately started worrying how she could make another film. 'I was with all these other filmmakers and we were asking the question "What's next?" Everyone there was so focused on distribution, and when you make a movie you have to beg and scrabble. And then this turned up.'

'This' was Amazon Prime, Amazon's streaming service which makes original films, and, through them, Soloway made the critical smash hit series *Transparent,* starring Jeffrey Tambor as a transgender father. 'They don't need everybody to watch something, so I can make something that's very niche-specific, something for women, Jews, intellectuals, queers, not necessarily heterosexual white middle-class men,' says Soloway.

The way Soloway sees it, the American entertainment business is now divided in two: 'There's old Hollywood, that's owned by traditional corporations. There are your Time Warners and your Viacoms, and all of these organisations where you have the feeling that the people in charge of the decisions are being made on the golf course by old, white golf-y men. Then you look up to the north in Silicon Valley and you think the people in charge of these companies have probably all been to Burning Man and maybe aren't so good at golf, but are people of a different generation and are able to see without waiting for their ratings and testing results, because they use their instincts.'

Whether or not people at HBO have been to Burning Man, it is clear that TV has become the place for filmmakers and actors who want to tell interesting stories. It is also far more welcoming to women than movies. So many of the actresses who triumphed in film in the eighties, after finding that forty years old was still considered the sell-by date for women by Hollywood studios, have increasingly moved over to TV: Jessica Lange, Kathy Bates, Glenn Close, Sally Field.

'I remember I was in bed, online, watching Twitter and Facebook blow up when *Orange is the New Black* started, and watching the critical reviews come in,' says Soloway. 'Here was a show featuring ten women in prison and the only guy was the villain. There was nobody mediating the experience of whether the women were pleasing to men. That felt like such a change.'

'Actors are running now to content,' says Jeffrey Tambor, the star of *Transparent*. 'Amazon Prime has Malcolm McDowell, Gael Garcia Bernal, John Goodman – they're running over there because an actor will always go to a good script. The revolution is here now and those not paying attention will go to the dinosaur area. It used to be the agent saying, "If everything goes well [in TV] you'll get a movie," and they don't say that any more – it's flipped. And that's the big surprise.'

This is great, of course. Maybe kids in two generations' time will dress up for Halloween like Walt and Jesse the way adults today still don proton packs for fancy dress parties. But as great as those shows can be at giving depths to characters and layers to plot, there is also an argument to be made for concision over flabbiness, punchiness over pretension. My test of a great movie is to ask myself two questions:

1. Do I want to see this movie again right now?
2. Does it make me view the world a little bit differently?

The eighties movies I've mentioned in this book fulfil both those criteria and then some. I've watched every one so many times they have become part of my mental landscape. But it takes a person with more stamina than me to watch a fifty-hour drama as many times as my generation has watched *Back to the Future*, getting to know its every nook and cranny.

There is something to be said, too, for the collective experience of seeing a movie in a theatre with others, as opposed to watching it on your own on a tablet, tweeting to others, like a vision of dislocative solitude from a dystopian sci-fi novel. It is easy to get sentimental about the excitement of a movie (and alarmist about modern technology), and I'm afraid I'm a total sucker for stories about that.

'I remember going to see *Ghostbusters* on opening night and it was like a rock concert on Long Island – the line went down the whole street!' Judd Apatow recalls.

'One of the great movie experiences of my life [was *48 Hours*],' Bill Simmons writes.

> We went on opening weekend in December (me, my mother, my stepfather and a friend) to the old Avon Theater in Stamford, Connecticut. The crowd couldn't have been more jacked up – it was about 70 percent black and 100 percent pro-Eddie. If you remember, Eddie didn't appear on-screen for the first 15 minutes. When he finally showed up (the scene when Nick Nolte's character visits him in jail), there was an electricity within the theater unlike anything I can remember. People were hanging on every line, every joke, everything. At the end of the scene, when Nolte storms off and Eddie screams, 'Jack! Jack! (Defiant pause.) FUCK YOU!,' someone who had already caught a few showings stood up on cue and screamed 'FUCK YOU!' with Eddie. And it went from there. The scene when Eddie rousts the redneck bar practically caused a riot. Bullshit, you're too fucking stupid to have a job. People were doubled over. People were cheering. I've never seen anything like it.

'There's that gag in *Coming to America* about the [black characters'] hair leaving a [grease] mark on the sofa,' says John Landis. 'If you saw the movie with a white audience, that scene got a little laugh – a scandalised laugh, but a laugh. But if you saw it with a black audience, they went crazy! It was terrific!'

These are collective experiences future generations simply won't have because the kinds of movies that will make it to cinemas won't inspire that same kind of love and excitement. It's fun to talk about box set series on social media with friends and fellow fans, follow critics who live tweet the shows. But it's not quite the same. What we've gained in fifty-hour dramas on prestige cable channels, we've lost in ninety minutes of pure pleasure in local cinemas.

But if there's one thing I've learned from eighties movies, it's that you should never end on a downer. And there is nothing to be down about! Even if there is never a Hollywood studio movie that affects people the way *Ghostbusters* or *Back to the Future* did, we still have all these wonderful, hilarious and deeply formative movies they made in the eighties that we can watch for ever. A friend asked when I started writing this book if I was worried that writing about eighties movies would make me sick of the subject. This was a fair question: after all, this friend had been to university with me and saw first-hand how studying for a degree in English Literature made me incapable of reading a novel if it wasn't written by Jilly Cooper for three years after graduation. With apologies to my university tutors, the same has not happened with this book, which conclusively proves that *Coming to America* has more depths than *To the Lighthouse*. Indeed, writing this book has achieved what I heretofore would have thought was impossible: it has made me love these movies even more.

The man who is lucky enough to share a home with me spent nine months dwelling with a strange creature who lived in a tracksuit and was incapable of fitting conversation with him (or washing herself) into her busy schedule of watching about six hours of eighties films a day, only emerging to bark out some catchphrase from *Three Amigos!* at him (like I said, he is a lucky, lucky man). In fact, just typing 'Three Amigos!' has made me need to watch that movie again, so excuse me for a few minutes. (This, actually, was a very common problem in writing this book: every time I typed out a film's title, I had to go watch the movie again, which explains why it ended up taking so long to write. Sorry, editor people, but such are the obvious risks when you commission me to write a book that entails the typing of words like 'Tootsie', 'Ghostbusters' and 'Moonstruck' repeatedly.)

In August 2014 I emerged from my tracksuited pit of unwashed eighties movie-watching long enough to get on a train to east London and go to an outdoor screening of *Back to the Future*, held by the company Secret Cinema. It was easy enough to find my way there from the station: I followed the hundreds and hundreds of groovy-looking twenty- and thirty-somethings all dressed like Marty McFly, Lorraine Baines, Biff Tannen and Dr Emmett Brown. The venue was mocked up to look like 1955 Hill Valley, replete with the Baines' house, Hill Valley School and Lou's Café. The wide-eyed adults wandered around delightedly, their faces split with excited smiles, thrilled by this Disneyland for sentimental adults. Actors played the parts of Doc and Marty, and spectators followed them around as excitedly as if they were, not just Christopher Lloyd and Michael J. Fox, but actually Doc and Marty. People happily braved a spot of London summer rain for the joy of watching this movie, which they'd all seen at least a hundred times before, outside and with other fans.

My boyfriend and I went inside Hill Valley School, got yelled at by 'Mr Strickland', the school principal, and danced to the band at the Enchantment Under the Sea dance, who started playing 'Earth Angel' just as we arrived.

I had come partly to observe the event for this book (and partly because, duh, of course I was going to go to this), and ended up being completely swept away by it. I looked around at all the other thirty-somethings around us, dancing on a drizzly London night, under the looming Westfield shopping mall building, with the same faraway look in their eyes that I had as we all imagined that we were Lorraine and George and would now be happy for ever and ever and I thought, Aha. Here you are, my people. You were around me all along.

The reason I – sorry, WE – love movies such as *Back to the Future*, *Ferris Bueller's Day Off*, *Trading Places* and *Ghostbusters* is because they are sweetly specific in their references and completely universal in their humour and stories, whether it be about parents, friendship or money, and that's a key combination and one that won't ever change. One question I did get asked a lot when writing this was why I like eighties movies so freaking much. The simplest answer is also the most honest: because they make me happy. I think – hell, I KNOW – they make other people happy, too. I hope this book has captured some of that.

Obviously, the only way to end this is with an eighties film quote and, when it comes to eighties films, you're spoilt for choice for quotes. Originally I thought I might go for 'I guess you guys aren't ready for that yet – but your kids are gonna love it.' But it didn't really make sense (not that that has ever stopped me from using an eighties quote before). Then I considered some timeless life advice: 'If someone asks if you're a god you say YES!' But then I thought, The hell with it, let's go for the obvious jugular here and use the quote that sums up the message of this book, which is that movies are changing and it's easy not to notice it – with added Ferris: 'Life moves pretty fast. If you don't stop and look around once in a while, you could miss it.'

THE END

EIGHTIES MOVIES I DIDN'T LOOK AT PROPERLY IN THIS BOOK THAT YOU REALLY NEED IN YOUR LIFE

20 *Weekend at Bernie's*
The second greatest Andrew McCarthy film, and that is high praise.

19 *Little Shop of Horrors*
Rick Moranis singing! Of course you want to see this.

18 *The Blues Brothers*
You probably haven't seen this for a while. You should rectify that.

17 *Spaceballs*
Lone Star, Dark Helmet, Pizza the Hut – it's a rare day that I don't make some reference to *Spaceballs*, and it's an even rarer day that someone recognises it.

16 *Young Sherlock Holmes*
A truly great teen adventure film and that it isn't better known is definitive proof there is no God.

15 *Desperately Seeking Susan*
Feminism, fashion and Madonna.

14 *Three Amigos!*
The Singing Bush! The Invisible Horseman! This film has what its director John Landis calls 'a real commitment to silliness', and songs by Randy Newman to boot.

13 *A Christmas Story*

A Christmas film staple in every American home, and it should be in everyone's home. Like *Radio Days*, but without the sentiment.

12 *Parenthood*

Cheesy? Yes. Conservative? Damn right. But it's also really funny, really sweet and it's got Jason Robards, Tom Hulce, Dianne Wiest, Martha Plimpton, Keanu Reeves, Rick Moranis, Steve Martin, Mary Steenburgen and Joaquin (then Leaf) Phoenix all being brilliant in it. Come on.

11 *St Elmo's Fire*

It causes me physical pain that I haven't written about *St Elmo's Fire* in this book. Please ease that pain for me by promising to go and watch the film, OK?

10 *The Flamingo Kid*

A too little known Matt Dillon film, featuring Hector Elizondo as his father, and a truly classic 1960s soundtrack.

9 *The Accidental Tourist*

Not as good as the book, no – but how could it be? William Hurt was made for the part of Macon Leary, the sad, repressed writer.

8 *The 'Burbs*

Crazy and dark, in a great way. I miss funny Tom Hanks.

7 *Stand By Me*

It would be too sad to watch poor River Phoenix as a sweet little boy if this film wasn't as great as it is.

6 *Bull Durham*
Yeah, I love eighties Costner, but he is acted off the screen here by a young Tim Robbins. A great funny and sexy sports film.

5 *Troop Beverly Hills*
A movie about Girl Scouts, shopping and the importance of shoulder pads. Shelley Long at her best.

4 *Planes, Trains and Automobiles*
After Molly Ringwald, John Candy became John Hughes's film muse, and this is the pair at their finest.

3 *Bill and Ted's Excellent Adventure*
Another movie to be discussed in depth in this book's inevitable sequel.

2 *Field of Dreams*
Best film ever about dead people playing baseball in a cornfield, and the filmmakers are welcome to put that quote on the DVD.

1 *Lucas*
One of my favourite films of all time, albeit starring one of the most cursed casts ever. Go watch it now, it's wonderful.

Notes

Introduction

We're massive fans of John Hughes: 'The 1975 Takes Cues From John Hughes for Debut', radio.com, 12 July 2013.

Some of the people who come up to me: Interview with the author.

I still get stopped in the street: Interview with the author.

There are a million reasons: Interview with the author.

The studios had been individually held entities: Interview with the author.

The world has changed: *Sleepless in Hollywood*, Lynda Obst.

But it's less brilliant: 'How Transformers 4 Became the No 1 Film in Chinese History', P. Nash Jenkins, *Time* magazine, 8 July 2014.

I doubt very much: Interview with the author.

Half of my movies: Interview with the author.

would rather spend $250m: *Variety*, 12 June 2013.

It's very much like when television: Interview with the author.

Teen actors: As noted by Charlie Lyme, producer of *Beyond Clueless*.

Without a film: Interview with the author.

Field of Dreams: Interview with the author.
What happens in movies: Interview with the author.

Dirty Dancing

to present in a pleasurable way: Interview with the author.
Vincent Canby: 'Dirty Dancing: Panned as a Dud but Dynamite', Carrie Rickey, *Philadelphia Inquirer*, 19 August 2012.
You can have a movie: Interview with the author.
The subway scene: Interview with the author.
What makes the movie industry's: US Views on Overturning Roe Versus Wade: Gallup poll, January 2013.
The indie film *Obvious Child*: Source: boxofficemojo.com; thanks also to Amanda Hess on medium.com for the comparison.
The entertainment industry has elected: 'Knocked Up Bans Abortion From Script', Sandra Kobrin, womensenews.org, 20 June 2007.
Anyway, I'm as pro-choice: 'Judd Apatow: I Still Feel like a Nerd', Hadley Freeman, *Guardian*, 27 August 2009.
Any feminist out there: 'Diablo Cody: Devil's Advocate', Hadley Freeman, *Guardian*, 20 January 2012.
But *Juno*'s star: 'Ellen Page: "Why are People so Reluctant to say They're Feminists?"', Hadley Freeman, *Guardian*, 3 July 2013.
The *LA Times*: 'The 80s: A Greenhouse for Teen Pregnancy', Laurie Buckland, *Los Angeles Times*, 14 March 1993.
This attitude shift is reflected: Planned Parenthood.
American movies have become: Interview with the author.
We're like lobsters: Interview with the author.
By 2008, the US government had spent: Guttmacher Institute.

Between 2006 and 2008: Planned Parenthood.

The Obama administration: Guttmacher Institute.

One big problem: Interview with the author.

Thus, the US ratings system: Interview with the author.

Occasionally a Conservative minister: Interview with the author.

The Princess Bride

The Princess Bride is a story about love: Interview with the author.

I was absolutely smitten: *As You Wish*, Cary Elwes.

It's safe to say: *As You Wish*, Cary Elwes.

four or five entrees: *As You Wish*, Cary Elwes.

I said to them both: 'The Princess Bride', *Which Lie Did I Tell?*, William Goldman.

Please understand that this: *As You Wish*, Cary Elwes.

Rob unfurled the poster: Interview with the author.

We were in dangerous terrain: 'The Princess Bride', *Which Lie Did I Tell?*, William Goldman.

Pretty in Pink

I was growing up: Interview with the author.

John was frozen in time: Interview with the author.

One of the great wonders: 'Teen Days that Shook the World: The Oral History of *The Breakfast Club*', Sean M. Smith, *Premiere* magazine, December 1999.

When we were filming: Interview with the author.

Teenage girl [audiences]: Interview with the author.

bubbly, shallow cinematic creature: 'The Bataan Death March of Whimsy Case File #1: Elizabethtown', Nathan Rabin, avclub.com, 25 January 2007.

Rabin is rightly uncomfortable: 'Why the Manic Pixie Dream Girl Must Never Return', Ben Beaumont-Thomas, *Guardian*, 16 July 2014.

I didn't want it to be a makeover scene: 'Teen Days that Shook the World', *Premiere* magazine, December 1999.

Clueless. That changed everything: Interview with the author.

Clueless was never meant to be: Interview with the author.

This is a very different kind of knight: *You Couldn't Ignore Me If You Tried*, Susannah Gora.

John could be very sullen: *You Couldn't Ignore Me If You Tried*, Susannah Gora.

When Harry Met Sally

RIP Romantic Comedies: 26 September 2013.

Why Are Romantic Comedies So Bad: 20 February 2013.

Death of the Rom: via Jezebel, 20 May 2013.

I was the first: Interview with the author.

Because I think I am an interesting woman: American Film Institute Archives, 17 December 2012.

not *Annie Hall* but a movie: 'When Harry Met Annie', Mark Harris, Grantland, 21 July 2014.

What *When Harry Met Sally . . .* is really about: Nora Ephron, *The Most of Nora Ephron*.

I realized that I had found a wonderful character: Nora Ephron, *The Most of Nora Ephron*.

I am over him: Nora Ephron, *The Most of Nora Ephron*.

Ephron 'struggled' with the screenplay: 'My Life as an Heiress', Nora Ephron, *New Yorker*, 11 October 2010.

I'm a guy: 'One Male to Bond Them All', Hadley Freeman, *Guardian*, 26 June 2014.

The reality is, I'm a dude: 'Funny like a Guy', Tad Friend, *New Yorker*, 11 April 2011.

Women's films, like weepies: Interview with the author.

There is also a creeping sexualisation: Interview with the author.

Ha ha! Poor Michael: Interview with the author.

To make a woman adorable: 'Funny Like a Guy', Tad Friend, *New Yorker*, 11 April 2011.

trickle-down equality: 'Women in the Seats, But Not Behind the Camera', Manohla Dargis, *New York Times*, 10 December 2009.

In 2013 women constituted: Source: Women Make Movies.

You're talking about a dozen: 'Funny Like a Guy', Tad Friend, *New Yorker*, 11 April 2011.

Studio executives think: 'Funny Like a Guy', Tad Friend, *New Yorker*, 11 April 2011.

Top Five Rick Moranis Moments

I took a break because: Interview with the author.

Ghostbusters

a series of soundtracks: *High Concept: Don Simpson and the Hollywood Culture of Excess*, Charles Fleming.

sank to the bottom: *High Concept*, Charles Fleming.

recruitment went up 400 per cent: *Back to Our Future: How the 1980s Explain the World We Live in Now – Our Culture, Our Politics, Our Everything*, David Sirota.

setting up manned tables: '*Top Gun* Boosting Service Sign-ups', Mark Evje, *LA Times*, 5 July 1986.

hyper-macho: 'Tales of the Military-Entertainment Complex: Why the US Navy Produced Battleship', Inkoo, Movieline, 6 February 2013.

When you know that you're going to need: *Operation Hollywood: How the Pentagon Shapes and Censors Movies*, David Robb.

ancient power struggles: 'Overthinking Ghostbusters', Adam Bertocci, runleirun.com.

totally sexist: 'Newsflash: the Original Ghostbusters Was Totally Sexist', Noah Berlatsky, ravishly.com, 3 February 2015.

Abbott and Costello: *Making Ghostbusters*, Dan Aykroyd and Harold Ramis, ed. Don Shay.

a well regarded history: 'The Making of *Ghostbusters*: How Dan Aykroyd, Harod Ramis and "the Murricaine" Built "The Perfect Comedy"', Lesley M.M. Blume, *Vanity Fair*, 4 June 2014.

Bill Murray, who revered: *Live From New York: An Uncensored History of Saturday Night Live*, Tom Shales and James Andrew Miller.

dead comedian's coffin: *Belushi: A Biography*, Judith Belushi Pisano and Tanner Colby.

Belushi's death was the soul: Interview with the author.

My first draft: *Making Ghostbusters*, Dan Aykroyd and Harold Ramis.

For actors, especially: *Making Ghostbusters*, Dan Aykroyd and Harold Ramis.

It was trust: *Making Ghostbusters*, Dan Aykroyd and Harold Ramis.

My career was completely: Interview with the author.

Sigourney insisted: *Making Ghostbusters*, Dan Aykroyd and Harold Ramis.

Katha Pollitt's Smurfette Principle: 'A group of male buddies accented by a lone female, stereotypically defined', Katha Pollitt, *New York Times*, 7 April 1991.

As soon as I read: Interview with the author.

Murphy was never: 'The Making of *Ghostbusters*', *Vanity Fair*.

but Aykroyd has said: 'An Oral History of Ghostbusters', Jason Matloff, *Premiere* magazine.

As writers, we'd never done: 'An Oral History of Ghostbusters', Jason Matloff, *Premiere* magazine.

I don't know anyone who wants: Interview with the author.

Tony [Soprano], Walter [White]: 'The Death of Adulthood in American Culture', A.O. Scott, *New York Times*, 11 September 2014.

the echt lesson: 'The Last Crusade', in *Gods and Monsters*, Peter Biskind.

It's emphasised in the screenplay: Interview with the author.

Ferris Bueller's Day Off

I remember how upset Crispin: Interview with the author.

The point was that self-confidence: Interview with the author.

Class has always been the central: Interview with the author.

the fidelity of observation: *The Biographical Dictionary of Film*, David Thompson.

John always meant: Interview with the author.

You know how Salieri: *You Couldn't Ignore Me if You Tried*, Susannah Gora.

Shermer High School: *Ferris Bueller's Day Off*, *The Breakfast Club*.

Hill Valley High School: *Back to the Future*.

Westerberg High School: *Heathers*.

a place of refuge: Director's commentary, *Ferris Bueller's Day Off* DVD.

I thought it was very relevant: Director's commentary, *Ferris Bueller's Day Off* DVD.

There is an avoidance of talk: Interview with the author.

Eighties films were willing to deal: Interview with the author.

Never underestimate Hollywood's eagerness: Interview with the author.

never had the emotional impact: Interview with the author.

Steel Magnolias

The status of women in movies: Backlash Book Club, medium. com, 8 August 2014.

Just look at 1983: Interview with the author.

People still talk to me about: Interview with the author.

It was very, very hard: Interview with the author.

I don't think that *Steel Magnolias*: Interview with the author.

the negative sisterhood movie: 'Poison Candy: The Other Woman and the Disastrous State of Female Comedies', Wesley Morris, Grantland, 25 April 2014.

Back in the 80s: Updated introduction to the 15th Anniversary Edition of *Backlash*, Susan Faludi.

In 2013 women made up only 21.8 per cent: *Gender Within Film Crews*, Stephen Follows.

I love directing women: Interview with the author.

The books website Goodreads: 'Readers Prefer Authors of their Own Sex, Survey Finds', Alison Flood, *Guardian*, 25 November 2014.

In fact, Silverstein's blog: 'Suck It Haters: Female-Led Films Make More Money', Inkoo Kang, Women and Hollywood.

We still don't know whether gender: 'Women Buy Half of All Movie Tickets. That Won't Mean More Female Characters', Amanda Hess, Slate, 27 March 2014.

Thelma & Louise [which came out in 1991]: Interview with the author.

In a study of the top 500: *Gender Inequality in 500 Popular Films*,

Dr Stacy L. Smith, Marc Choueiti, Elizabeth Scofield and Dr Katherine Pieper, Annenberg School for Communication and Journalism, University of Southern California.

In 2011 women accounted for: The Center for the Study of Women in Television and Film.

In 2013 one journalist: 'At the Movies, the Women are Gone', Linda Holmes, NPR.

That year, women made up: 'It's a Man's Celluloid World', Martha Lauzen, from the Center for the Study of Women in Television, Film and New Media.

And as *New York* magazine: 'Do They Ever Make Movies About Women?', Amanda Dobbins, *New York* magazine, 11 July 2013.

We can see that women are not: Interview with the author.

Women have advanced: 'Women in the Seats But Not Behind the Camera', Manohla Dargis, *New York Times*, 10 December 2009.

After all, according to the latest: *Gender Bias Without Borders: An Investigation of Female Characters in Popular Films Across 11 Countries*, Dr Stacy L. Smith, Marc Choueiti and Dr Katherine Pieper.

Some of the more profitable: Interview with the author.

Back to the Future

One afternoon, I was digging: Interview with the author.

Teen Wolf was a teen film: Interview with the author.

By the time I was cast: Interview with the author.

Bob Zemeckis pointed out: Interview with the author.

that reflect my psychological: 'Crispin Glover: Back to the Dissected Snails', Catherine Shoard, *Guardian*, 9 February 2011.

Gosh, we're in a high school: *Blockbuster*, Tom Shone.

The average teen films: *Back to the Future*, DVD extra.

It's in the eighties that: Interview with the author.

Batman

I could add: *Burton on Burton*, ed. Mark Salisbury.

I know people say: 'Dark Arts', an interview with Tim Burton, Hadley Freeman, *Guardian*, 22 July 2005.

I was very strange: *Burton on Burton*, ed. Mark Salisbury.

Certain images: 'Dark Arts', *Guardian*.

Burton has said: 'Dark Arts', *Guardian*.

gritty reality: Review of *Dark Knight*, Peter Travers, Rolling Stone, 9 July 2008.

Nearly half of Americans: 'More Say Iraq War Hurts Fight Against Terrorism', Pew Research Center, 21 July 2005.

We will destroy innocent: 'The Age of Conflict', David Brooks, *Weekly Standard*, 5 November 2001.

a conservative movie: 'What Bush and Batman Have in Common', Andrew Klavan, *Wall Street Journal*, 25 July 2008.

the cost of the war: 'How the US Public was Defrauded by the Cost of the Iraq War', Michael Boyle, the *Guardian*, 11 March 2013.

we need dark knights: 'The Dark Knight Turns Out to Be a Dick Cheney Fantasy', Party Ben, 23 July 2008.

certainly that wasn't: 'Dark Knight Star Aaron Eckhart Downplays Analogy Between Batman, George W Bush', Shawn Adler, MTV.com.

The president's vows: *The Terror Dream*, Susan Faludi.

to tear open his shirt: 'The Right Man', Peggy Noonan, *Wall Street Journal*, 30 January 2003.

Bush punctuates his rhetoric: Analysis: The Return of Evildoers', Peter Roff, upi.com, 15 October 2001.

Eddie Murphy's Eighties Movies

As Jimmy Early: 'It's a trip, it seems every five or six years you have to do something to remind [people] they like you,' 'Eddie Murphy Speaks', Brian Hiatt, *Rolling Stone*, 19 November 2011.

You know why it worked then: 'Eddie Murphy Speaks', Brian Hiatt, *Rolling Stone*, 19 November 2011.

That was very controversial: Interview with the author.

the black guy: Quote by Neil Levy in *Live from New York*, Tom Shales and James Andrew Miller.

If not for Eddie's talent and popularity: *Live from New York*, Tom Shales and James Andrew Miller.

The status of the black person: Interview with the author.

treated horribly: *Live from New York*, Tom Shales and James Andrew Miller.

Lorne Michaels cut it: *Saturday Night: A Backstage History of Saturday Night Live*, Doug Hill and Jeff Weingrad.

It's too white: *Live from New York*, Tom Shales and James Andrew Miller.

this weird, Waspy: *Live from New York*, Tom Shales and James Andrew Miller.

Eddie never catered: 'The Career Arc: Eddie Murphy', Bill Simmons, Grantland, 10 November 2011.

I never connected: *Pryor Convictions and Other Life Sentences*, Richard Pryor.

From the very beginning: 'Eddie Murphy Speaks', Brian Hiatt, *Rolling Stone*, 19 November 2011.

Trading Places, John Landis movies: 'Eddie Murphy Speaks',

Brian Hiatt, *Rolling Stone*, 19 November 2011.

There's this little box: 'Eddie Murphy Speaks', Brian Hiatt, *Rolling Stone*, 19 November 2011.

I know because of the level: 'Eddie', Spike Lee, *Spin* magazine, October 1990.

I don't think you can beat: 'Eddie', Spike Lee, *Spin* magazine, October 1990.

The scariest thing: 'Eddie', Spike Lee, *Spin* magazine, October 1990.

I am very black: 'Eddie', Spike Lee, *Spin* magazine, October 1990.

You get these black people: 'Eddie', Spike Lee, *Spin* magazine, October 1990.

If I was rubbing you: 'Eddie Murphy Speaks', Brian Hiatt, *Rolling Stone*, 19 November 2011.

I went back to the house: 'Eddie Murphy Speaks', Brian Hiatt, *Rolling Stone*, 19 November 2011.

Hollywood had to be convinced: Interview with the author.

His films introduced: Interview with the author.

Eddie's movies have grossed: Grantland, November 2011.

No matter what you do: 'Eddie Murphy Speaks', Brian Hiatt, *Rolling Stone*, 19 November 2011.

Epilogue

I was with all these other filmmakers: Interview with the author.

Actors are running: Interview with the author.

I remember going to see *Ghostbusters*: Interview with the author.

One of the great movie: 'The Career Arc: Eddie Murphy', Bill Simmons, Grantland, 10 November 2011.

There's that gag: Interview with the author.

Index

Acknowledgements

Enormous thanks to the following, for their love, support and advice. You guys can be my posse in an eighties teen film any time: Andy Bull, Carol Miller, Nell Freeman, India Knight, Catherine Shoard, Tim Robey, Julia Kingsford, Charlie Campbell, Ed Howker, Adam Curtis, Patrick Kennedy, Benedict Cumberbatch, Dixie Chassay, Kamila Shamsie, Michael Hogan, Peter Bradshaw and Arthur Ferdinand Freeman.

Huge thanks, too, to my editors at the *Guardian*, Catherine Shoard (again), Malik Meer, Tim Lusher and Nosheen Iqbal for commissioning me to interview various eighties legends for the newspaper during the writing of this book, thereby making it much easier for me to track them down. You guys are nothing like the evil bosses in eighties movies.

Endless gratitude to two people in particular: first, my agent, Georgia 'patience of Job' Garrett, who had faith in this book when no one else did, myself very much included (I know that's a terrible cliché for a writer to say about their agent, but it really is the truth here). Next, to my ceaselessly supportive editor, Louise Haines, who was the Johnny Castle to my Baby (in the sense of being a masterful instructor, mind. We didn't actually do any sexy high lifts, although, hey, there's still time, Louise). Thanks also to everyone at 4th Estate, especially Georgia Mason, Rebecca McEwan and Morag Lyall.

For professional insights and interviews, thank you so much to Celestia Fox, Steven Gaydos at *Variety*, Paul Feig, Judd Apatow, Col Needham at IMDB.com, Jill Soloway, Jeffrey Tambor, Peter Biskind, Mark Cousins, Tom Shone, Mark Kermode, Linda Ruth Williams, Lynda Obst and Melissa Silverstein. Rebecca Wind and Laura Lindberg at the Guttmacher Institute helped me with research on the history of US sex education while Natika Halal and Bekki Burbidge at the Family Planning Association, Harriet Gill at Brook Advisory and Lucy Emmerson at the Sex Education Forum provided me with the UK perspective. Joan Graves at the MPAA and David Cooke patiently talked me through the ratings systems in their two countries. Dr Helen Sharpe at the Institute of Psychiatry talked to me about the influence of celebrities' body shape on teenagers' self-image, a subject matter I didn't, in the end, write about in this book but may well return to in another. Eileen Jones at UC Berkeley and Dr James Russell at De Montfort University were fascinating about the depiction of social class in movies. Professor Mark Anthony Neal at Duke University and Professor Anna Everett at University of California Santa Barbara very kindly talked to me about African-American pop culture in the 1980s and helped me to place both Eddie Murphy and Spike Lee in context. All of the mistakes in the discussion of these subjects in this book are mine.

Finally, enormous thanks to all my eighties movie inter-
viewees for pretending not to notice that I was and am
utterly starstruck by them all: Molly Ringwald, John Landis,
Ivan Reitman, Jon Avnet, Matthew Broderick, Amy
Heckerling, Andrew McCarthy, Michael J. Fox, Cary Elwes,
Tom Hanks, Lea Thompson, Howard Deutch, Tim Burton,
Rick Moranis, Kathleen Turner, Geena Davis, Eleanor
Bergstein, Olympia Dukakis, Bob Harling, Bob Gale and
Ron Howard.